Hollywood at the Races

Hollywood at the Races

◄ ◆ ►

Film's Love Affair with the Turf

Alan Shuback

UNIVERSITY PRESS OF KENTUCKY

Copyright © 2019 by The University Press of Kentucky

Scholarly publisher for the Commonwealth,
serving Bellarmine University, Berea College, Centre
College of Kentucky, Eastern Kentucky University,
The Filson Historical Society, Georgetown College,
Kentucky Historical Society, Kentucky State University,
Morehead State University, Murray State University,
Northern Kentucky University, Transylvania University,
University of Kentucky, University of Louisville,
and Western Kentucky University.
All rights reserved.

Editorial and Sales Offices: The University Press of Kentucky
663 South Limestone Street, Lexington, Kentucky 40508-4008
www.kentuckypress.com

Unless otherwise noted, photographs are courtesy of the
Del Mar Thoroughbred Club.

Cataloging-in-Publication data is available from the
Library of Congress.

ISBN 978-0-8131-7829-5 (hardcover : alk. paper)
ISBN 978-0-8131-7830-1 (epub)
ISBN 978-0-8131-7831-8 (pdf)

This book is printed on acid-free paper meeting
the requirements of the American National Standard
for Permanence in Paper for Printed Library Materials.

Manufactured in the United States of America.

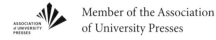

Member of the Association
of University Presses

To filmgoers and racegoers everywhere

Hollywood has gone nuts over horse racing, and by the same token horse racing has gone nuts over Hollywood.

Ed Sullivan, Silver Screen, September 1939

Contents

Illustrations follow page 142

Introduction

The invention of the wheel is frequently cited as a seminal turning point in the history of human development, but that grand event was surely predated by an equally important occurrence: the first time a man managed to climb onto a horse's back and ride the animal an appreciable distance without falling off. Since that long-ago day in the misty past, horses have become an integral part of human society, providing us with recreation, sport, companionship, a means of transportation, an ally in war, and an aid to labor, as well as supplying an object lesson in the appreciation of beauty. Simply looking at horses makes a person feel better.

With the horse sitting close to the center of human culture since the dawn of civilization, debates over the nature and worth of the beast were inevitable. First and foremost among the many questions to arise was, whose is the faster horse, yours or mine? Thus was horse racing born. Other questions would follow: Which horse can run the farthest or jump the highest? Which is the strongest horse? Which the most beautiful? Which can produce the best offspring? And with these questions there followed the inevitable, which is the most valuable? And so appeared the first horse trader, and the first horse thief.

The beginnings of officially organized Thoroughbred horse racing in late-seventeenth-century Restoration England gave rise to technical issues among horsemen, such as length of stride or the relative shortness thereof. One of the less pressing debates over the nature of a horse's action was whether the animal ever has all four of its hooves off the ground while in full gallop, but it was precisely this arcane question that ultimately led to the cornerstone of the so-called seventh art—the worldwide phenomenon popularly known as cinema, film, or the movies.

Artists of the period, sharp as they may have been, were in the dark about a horse's stride. Until the late nineteenth century, artistic observers of the increasingly popular sport of horse racing failed to come close to capturing a racehorse's stride in full gallop. Eighteenth- and nineteenth-century prints of races run at Newmarket, Epsom, and Ascot abound with clumsy-looking creatures, their forelegs splayed out before them, their hind legs splayed behind, their bellies mere inches off the ground, looking as if they would soon be sliding along the turf like otters down a mudslide.

The leading horse painter of the period, George Stubbs (1724–1806), was perceptive enough not to be taken in. He limited his essays into the world of racing to portrait studies such as *Turf, with Jockey up, at Newmarket,* in which the horse in question (named Turf) is shown standing calmly with all four feet on the ground in what has become the classic Thoroughbred portrait pose. Stubbs broke new ground in the realm of horse action with his 1762 masterpiece *Whistlejacket,* a portrait of the Thoroughbred that was the first to be acclaimed "the fastest horse in the world." It depicts in life size on a plain beige background the animal rearing on its hind legs. Stubbs seemed to understand that the action of a galloping horse was too fast for the human eye to perceive and, therefore, for the human hand to record.

Even the eagle-eyed Edgar Degas (1834–1917) never managed to "see" a galloping horse's action properly. Almost all his racing scenes depict horses walking in the parade ring, walking onto the racecourse, or walking in circles just prior to the start of a race. On the few occasions when he attempted to depict a horse in full gallop, he failed utterly. *The Fallen Jockey* (1866) gives us an impossible picture of a rider lying flat on his back while his mount flies past him, legs splayed out in front and back. Similar efforts such as *Horse Escaping* (1881) and *Horse Galloping* (1885) are equally wrongheaded.

Degas was either unaware of or had dismissed the pioneering work of Eadweard Muybridge (1830–1904), the photographer who first captured a horse's true galloping action on film. An eccentric Englishman who immigrated to America in 1850, Muybridge made a name for himself during the 1860s photographing the scenic American West, particularly the Yosemite Valley. In 1872 former California governor Leland Stanford employed Muybridge in a scientific effort to prove that a horse lifts all four feet off the ground while in full gallop. Stanford had bet a nonbeliever $25,000 that this was indeed the case. As Muybridge had made early use of time-lapse photography to record the erection of the San Francisco Mint, theirs seemed to be a partnership that would win Stanford a bundle.

The two men put their plan into action at Stanford's ranch in Palo Alto (now the site of Stanford University, which the former governor founded).

The owner of a string of racing trotters, Stanford supplied the money, and Muybridge provided the technical expertise. They set up a straight running track with a white canvas background. Muybridge deployed a dozen cameras with newly invented high-speed shutters and attached the shutters to trip wires on the track. A horse and rider were dispatched, running left to right on the course, and once the horse had attained a gallop, the trip wires were sprung and the photos were taken. Within twenty minutes, Muybridge had developed his pictures, providing proof of Stanford's claim that horses actually become airborne—however briefly—while in full gallop. Not that Stanford made any money on his bet. The experiment had cost him $50,000, twice what he won on the wager. Muybridge published this sequence of photographs in 1878 under the title "Sallie Gardner at a Gallop, or the Horse in Motion."

But not everyone was convinced. Painters everywhere, already highly sensitive to the challenge of this newfangled business called photography, were particularly loath to accept Muybridge's discovery at face value. Auguste Rodin railed that the sequence of photographs was a "fake" and that only the artist's eye, not a machine, could capture the truth of the matter. Since then, the world has come to accept the veracity of Muybridge's work. A year after the publication of his photographs, Muybridge added credence to his equine discovery with the invention of his zoopraxiscope. Widely regarded as the first motion picture projector, it consisted of a series of rotating glass disks, each disk holding a drawing or photograph. When the disks were spun in fast motion, the pictures of Sallie Gardiner galloping were projected onto a white screen, presenting what must be considered the earliest motion picture.

Today, thanks to Muybridge's pioneering efforts, everyone at a racetrack—even first-time racegoers—can plainly see that horses raise all four legs off the ground in full gallop. His contribution is a perfect example of how technology can improve human perception. It also kicked off a decades-long love affair between the cinematic and racing worlds, an affair that peaked during Hollywood's Golden Age (1930–1960) and lasted until more recent technologies—and social mores—undermined the customs of both filmgoing and racegoing.

1

Hollywood before Santa Anita
Down Mexico Way

Agua Caliente across the Mexican line became the fun spot of
Hollywood. Stars, producers, directors, gamblers and hangers-on
headed south for the luxury hotel where the wine ran freely and drinks
and hot tips were served in the racehorse clubhouse.

Raoul Walsh

All Dressed Up with Nowhere to Go

In December 1913, thirty-two-year-old Cecil B. DeMille stepped off a
train at Santa Fe Depot in Los Angeles, California. In tow was a film crew
hired by Samuel Goldfish (Samuel Goldwyn's first attempt at Americanizing
his name) to shoot a new western, *The Squaw Man,* for the Jesse L. Lasky
Feature Play Company. Arriving with no previous experience in the
infant film industry, DeMille hopped a cab to take him into the country-
side. Five miles west of downtown Los Angeles, he alighted in the bucolic
setting of Selma Avenue and Vine Street. There stood a former barn that
had recently been converted into a film studio at a junction that lies one
block south of what is now the corner of Hollywood and Vine.

Goldfish had ordered DeMille to shoot *The Squaw Man* in Flagstaff,
Arizona, but when the director arrived there, he found the town buried
under a blizzard, conditions hardly suitable for moviemaking. On his
own initiative, he packed cast and crew back onto the train and proceeded
to Los Angeles. Although other films had been made there and elsewhere
in Southern California (indeed, the first movie shot entirely in California
was the 1909 racing film *The Heart of a Race Tout*), *The Squaw Man*—
about a wrongly disgraced British aristocrat in the Wild West—became
the first big, commercially successful movie made in Los Angeles. DeMille
planted the seeds that would eventually blossom into the dreamscape
known universally as Hollywood.

DeMille, Goldfish, and Lasky followed two early studios, Biograph and Essanay, into the region. Biograph brought D. W. Griffith west in 1909, while Essanay lured Charlie Chaplin away from Keystone in 1914. By 1920, Hollywood was firmly established as the world's leading film-producing city. That was the year Griffith made *Way Down East* with Lillian Gish; Charlie Chaplin starred in *The Kid,* and Douglas Fairbanks played the lead in *The Mark of Zorro;* Lon Chaney had his first starring role in *The Penalty;* and Buster Keaton made four of his early shorts: *The Scarecrow, One Week, Neighbors,* and *Convict 13.*

Hollywood was booming. Movie moguls and their star performers were amassing fortunes that would have been unimaginable a few years earlier, the absence of a national income tax adding to their prosperity. But other than the mansions they were building in Beverly Hills, DeMille, Chaplin, Fairbanks, and up-and-coming stars like Mary Pickford and Rudolph Valentino had limited outlets to dispose of their excess cash.

Los Angeles was a far cry from New York when it came to entertainment and sporting venues. There was nothing comparable to Broadway, and professional sports teams were lacking. Until the early 1960s, there were only three major professional sports in America: baseball, boxing, and horse racing. All three were absent from Los Angeles. There would be no major league baseball in town until the Dodgers moved west from Brooklyn in 1958. If Hollywood's major league stars wanted to attend a baseball game, they had to travel to hardscrabble Wrigley Field to see the minor league Class AA Los Angeles Angels play. San Francisco was the site of California's important boxing matches, but the East Coast hosted most of the country's best bouts. Horse races were about as frequent in Los Angeles as major league baseball games—that is, they were nonexistent. Although the National Football League's Los Angeles Rams arrived from Cleveland in 1946, college football was much more popular than the professional sport until the 1960s. The two Los Angeles–based schools, USC and UCLA, played only nine or ten home games a year between them. The Rose Bowl, played in nearby Pasadena, was the region's premier sporting event, and although Hollywood celebrities flocked to the game, it was a once-a-year affair, played in the hangover haze of New Year's Day.

California businessman Lucky Baldwin had opened a racetrack on his private ranch in Arcadia, about twenty miles east of Los Angeles, on December 7, 1907. He called it Santa Anita, and business boomed for two winter seasons until April 17, 1909, when California's moralizing middle class put it out of business. Two months earlier, the state legislature had passed the odious Walker-Otis bill outlawing pari-mutuel wagering throughout California. In addition to Santa Anita, Tanforan Racetrack in San Bruno, south of San Francisco, was forced to close its doors. Tanforan experimented with nonwagering meetings in 1923 and 1924, but they proved unsuccessful. Who wants to go to the races if you can't get a bet down? It's like eating steak well-done, without salt and pepper.

The same puritanical forces that put an end to Thoroughbred racing in California sank their claws into the entire nation on January 17, 1920, when the Eighteenth Amendment outlawing the manufacture, transportation, import, and export of alcoholic beverages took effect. Suddenly, Californians were hit with a double whammy. It was now illegal to place a bet or have a drink anywhere in the Golden State.

Actors are a convivial, fun-loving group known for their capacity to spend money, especially on frivolous things like wild parties, roulette wheels, and racehorses. Sinfulness has its attractions, but when sin becomes illegal as well as immoral, incurring the wrath of the state as well as God, it becomes a bit too dangerous even for high-profile movie stars with big bankrolls and protectors in high places.

With opportunities for moral transgression in California dwindling to a precious few (like cheating on your husband or wife), Hollywood adopted the motto, "Go thou, and sin elsewhere." In this case, that place was Mexico—Tijuana, to be exact.

Highway to Hell

South of the border, there were no prohibitions against the sale or consumption of alcoholic beverages; nor were there many restrictions on gambling. The Mexican border lies just 130 miles south of Hollywood Boulevard, and the drinking and gaming establishments were located just a few yards further down a dusty Mexican road.

By the mid-1920s, just a few years after Prohibition went into effect up north, Tijuana's main drag, the infamous Avenida Revolucion, was lined with bars, hotels, and casinos, most of which catered exclusively to gringos who invaded the city in large numbers for a weekend walk on the wild side. Tijuana was the place to go to escape not just from the wife and kids or the restrictions of middle-class conventions but also from the long arm of the law. On December 30, 1912, one American desperado on the lam sent his spouse in Cambridge Springs, Colorado, a postcard from Tijuana. It read:

> Dear Wife,
> You see I have left the country but no doubt will return some time. Will write more fully in the near future.
> > As ever yours, Burnham[1]

With characters like this, along with banditos lurking in every alleyway (at least in the imaginations of some Americans) and the chance that revolution might break out in Baja California at any moment, Tijuana proved irresistible to Californians whose opportunities for illicit pleasure had been co-opted by the archconservative forces of the temperance movement. A smart marketing man might have reaped a pretty profit had he erected a sign on the Yankee side of the border reading: ABANDON BOURGEOIS RESPECTABILITY, ALL YE WHO ENTER HERE.

Hipodromo de Tijuana

On New Year's Day 1916, James "Sunny Jim" Coffroth, son of California state senator James Coffroth Sr., opened the Hipodromo de Tijuana. The new racetrack lay just 150 yards across the border and only 17 miles from San Diego. Coffroth, a former San Francisco boxing promoter who was forced to find other work when the gentlemanly art was outlawed in California two years earlier, partnered with John Spreckels, owner of the San Diego & Arizona Railroad. Spreckels immediately instituted plans to lay track from the Santa Fe Depot in downtown San Diego to the Hipodromo's main gate, thereby connecting Tijuana to Los Angeles's Union Station and establishing a direct link between Hollywood and his new racetrack. Before the burgeoning film community could take advantage, however, disaster struck. On January 15 torrential rains descended on Tijuana and surrounding areas both north and south of the border. Rivers overflowed, bridges and roads were washed away, and the racetrack, built in the riverbed of the Rio Las Palmas, incurred $100,000 worth of damage. Was this a wrathful God sending Coffroth and company a Noah-like warning?

Spreckels came to the rescue. Realizing that California was without gambling or major league sports of any kind, both he and Coffroth knew that it was only a matter of time until wealthy Californians would respond to the lure of their racetrack, which would become the foundation for the world's first Sin City. Spreckels threw $40,000 Coffroth's way, and by April 15, the Tijuana racetrack was back in business. But a year later, a worse disaster than the deluge befell the entrepreneurs: the United States entered World War I on April 6, 1917. Almost immediately there were reports that Germany and Japan were planning to build military bases in lower Baja California, just a few hundred miles south of Tijuana. The antigambling forces that had succeeded in outlawing pari-mutuel wagering in California had been demanding closure of the border even before America's entry into the war. Now they had patriotic ammunition to ensure that the border was sealed.

With Tijuana's lifeblood from the north cut off, Coffroth had no choice but to close his track for the duration of the war. The Hipodromo de Tijuana would not reopen until Thanksgiving Day 1920, by which time drinking had become illegal north of the border and the pocketbooks of a prosperous Hollywood clientele were bursting at the seams.

Among the films made between 1917 and 1920 were *Blind Husbands* by Erich von Stroheim and *The Mollycoddle* with Douglas Fairbanks. Hal Roach and King Vidor began their careers. Theda Bara, the original "vamp," starred in the risqué *Salome*. The Big Three of silent comedy—Charlie Chaplin, Buster Keaton, and Harold Lloyd—were averaging six shorts a year. D. W. Griffith contributed *Broken Blossoms* and *Way Down East* (not that the straitlaced Griffith would ever entertain the notion of traveling south of the border to bet on a horse race). Cecil B. DeMille and his longtime star Gloria Swanson made a series of sexy potboilers that reflected the pent-up emotions of the Hollywood set. But most prominent of all was Mary Pickford, the tiny star whose string of hits included *A Little Princess, Amarilly of Clothes-Line Alley, Stella Maris,* and *Daddy Long-Legs.*

After the war, almost everybody in the film industry was looking for some peacetime action, and Tijuana provided it. Before and after racing, visitors could cruise downtown bars such as El Baballito, the Black Cat, and the Klondike. An enterprising Japanese immigrant, Soo Yashuara, opened his Monte Carlo Casino to attract gamblers who might have felt intimidated by the upscale social ambience at the nearby Foreign Club, the town's premier casino (from which Mexicans were banned). And it was a short walk from the Monte Carlo to Yashuara's Moulin Rouge, a hot spot where the female employees served more than just drinks. In later years, Red Pollard, the more or less regular rider of Seabiscuit, would spend frequent nights at the Moulin Rouge when he was in town to ride.

The 1920 reopening of the Hipodromo de Tijuana was inauspicious from a sporting point of view. The first-day feature, the Spreckels Handicap, was named after the man who had bailed out the track in 1916, but the quality of the racing was poor. As there had been no Thoroughbred racing in Southern California since 1909, few American owners were stabling their horses in the region. Coffroth tried everything to get people into his new track. At one point, he hired a young man named Jim Crofton to dress up as a jockey and ride a horse through downtown San Diego announcing the post time for that day's races.

Despite the lack of equine quality, business was booming by the 1921 Independence Day weekend, when 65,000 Americans celebrated their national holiday by crossing the border into Mexico. The overflow crowd at the track surpassed 15,000. Among them were 100 revelers who had traveled from Los Angeles on two private Pullman cars rented for the day by Roscoe "Fatty" Arbuckle. The corpulent, fun-loving silent film comedian could afford the expense. Since 1913, he had made more than 100 short comedies, and since 1918, he had been taking down $1 million a year.

Coffroth may have had cowboy star Tom Mix promenading through the clubhouse, sans his ten-gallon hat, but the always smiling track owner was unhappy with the quality of the racing. That summer he made a recruiting trip to Kentucky, Maryland, New Jersey, and New York—four states with first-class racing—in search of better horses. His efforts were largely successful and were later aided by the 1926 closure of Juarez Racetrack, across the Rio Grande from El Paso, Texas. But what really attracted American horsemen to Tijuana was the prize money.

Good horses go where the good money is. The ban on gambling in California and on drinking in America created a vacuum in the Golden State that sucked cash into Tijuana. A new and improved Monte Carlo Casino, dubbed the "Devil's University," was opened just a stone's throw from the racetrack. A chic new restaurant, the Sunset Inn, was built next door, attracting the likes of Gloria Swanson, star of the Joe Schenck productions *Don't Change Your Husband* and *Why Change Your Wife?* Schenck, the president of United Artists (whose founding members were Douglas Fairbanks, his wife Mary Pickford, D. W. Griffith, and Charlie Chaplin), was a frequent weekend visitor at the track with his new wife, silent star Norma Talmadge. Wagering $20,000 or $30,000 on a single race was second nature to Schenck, whose pockets were seemingly bottomless.

With bettors like that stuffing cash through the pari-mutuel windows, prize money soared. The track's centerpiece, the Coffroth Handicap, was the biggest beneficiary. Run at a distance of 1¼ miles, it had been worth just $5,000 on February 22, 1917, when Sasin won it in the pedestrian time of 2:22 flat, albeit on heavy ground. After Coffroth's East Coast talent scouting for a better brand of Thoroughbred, the 1921 running—valued at $20,000—was won by the Bronx Stable's Be Frank in 2:05⅕, a much better time reflecting a great improvement in the quality of the winner.[2]

The 1923 Coffroth Handicap was worth $36,976, and with a prize of $51,300, the 1924 renewal attracted the great East Coast champion Exterminator. One of the great weight-carrying horses in history, he was assigned 130 pounds, spotting his seventeen opponents 5 to 33 pounds. Trainer Harry McDaniel had the foresight to bring Exterminator to Tijuana from his Maryland base for a prep race. On February 17, he was entered in a 1-mile, 70-yard conditions race worth just $700. It was his first start in ten months, but Exterminator won by a length, easily outclassing his four opponents. That bit of exercise set him up perfectly for the Coffroth on March 30.

Sent off as the 8–5 favorite, Exterminator was well placed in fifth by jockey Albert Johnson for most of the way. He made a menacing move at the top of the stretch but flattened out late. The weight proved too much for the 1918 Kentucky Derby winner. Affectionately known as "Old Bones," the gallant nine-year-old was past his prime and finished fourth, beaten by 1½ lengths. The winner was Runstar, bred and owned by John Spreckels's brother Alfred.

Annual increases of at least $10,000 brought the purse of the 1929 Coffroth Handicap up to $113,750. That renewal attracted a gigantic field of twenty-two runners from throughout America, and it was won by Golden Prince, who equaled the track record of 2:02⅗.[3]

The Coffroth Handicap had become the world's richest horse race, but the good money and frequent presence of Hollywood stars such as "It" girl Clara Bow, Chaplin, Keaton, and Lloyd, while providing a short-term boom for Tijuana, had given rival racetrack operators a new and better idea. Exit Jim Coffroth; enter Jim Crofton, the man Coffroth had once employed as a barker to drum up track business in San Diego.

Agua Caliente: City of Sin

On June 23, 1928, a quartet of sharp American businessmen whose scheming had earned them the collective title the "Border Barons" opened a gambling resort three miles east of the Tijuana racetrack. Agua Caliente (Spanish for "hot springs") was based on the Old World models of Deauville and Baden-Baden, as well as on the New World model of Saratoga. The Barons took advantage of the springs bubbling under their property, erecting a world-class casino next to their state-of-the-art bathhouse.

It was a tried-and-true formula for raking in the cash. Wherever there are hot springs—like at Germany's Baden-Baden, France's Vichy, New York's Saratoga, or Arkansas' Hot Springs, the site of Oaklawn Park—elderly rich people are sure to gather in search of a cure for what ails them. What better way of relieving the old fogies of their excess cash than to provide them with a casino right next door to the baths? Agua Caliente had the added advantage of being just across the border from a state where gambling and drinking were still illegal.

The plush grounds, ironically done up in the traditional Spanish Mission style, attracted more than just the elderly and included more than just the casino and the baths. There were private bungalows, a golf course, a dog racing track, and a bullfighting ring, making guests reluctant to leave the Agua Caliente premises once they had checked into the five-star hotel with nightclub and swimming pool. Four-course dinners priced at just $1.50 ($2 on weekends) ensured that guests wouldn't be tempted away by cheaper, déclassé eateries in town. By 1930, the casino was grossing $2 million per month, the equivalent of $40 million in today's money.[4]

Tijuana's Monte Carlo and Foreign Club Casinos paled in comparison. Billed as "America's Deauville in Old Mexico," Agua Caliente quickly became a magnet for Hollywood stars and moguls. The fast-living Raoul Walsh, fresh from filming *Sadie Thompson* with Gloria Swanson, was one of the first to take advantage of the amenities. On August 2, 1928, Walsh hopped into his car and drove down to Tijuana, ostensibly to see the local Derby at the Hipodromo. In reality, he was looking for an out-of-the-way place to get married on the Q.T. Along for the ride was his secret fiancée Lorraine Walker, a Hollywood hanger-on who was longing for a career as an actress. In the backseat were director Allan Dwan and his wife Marie

Shelton. Their first stop was the Hotel Agua Caliente, where Walsh had booked the luxurious Governor's Suite and where local judge Francis Miranda was waiting in the wings. As soon as they arrived, Judge Miranda was called into action, and Miss Walker became the lawfully wedded Mrs. Walsh, with Mr. and Mrs. Dwan serving as witnesses. With the ink barely dry on the marriage certificate, Walsh had more important things to attend to. No sooner had he kissed the happy bride than he was off to the casino downstairs, where, according to legend, he won $18,000 playing roulette, most of which he lost the next day at the track. The Walsh-Walker union lasted until 1946, although as Mrs. Walsh, Lorraine never fulfilled her dream of becoming an actress.[5]

This was racy stuff, but the one thing Agua Caliente lacked was a racetrack. The Hipodromo de Tijuana was still packing them in, but the old grandstand was a rickety wooden structure that visitors called the "outhouse." Despite deluge and war, Jim Coffroth had turned it into a gold mine, but faced with competition from the deep-pocketed Border Barons, its days were numbered.

Jim Crofton, chairman of the Foreign Club Casino, was the most visible of the four Border Barons. He had a keen interest in horse racing and owned a string of Thoroughbreds that competed with some success at Tijuana. With Crofton leading the way, the Barons were granted a license to build a racetrack on their sprawling Agua Caliente grounds, thus sealing the fate of the old Hipodromo. The Barons made personal trips to inspect the best racecourses in Europe and America. Architect Wayne McAllister, just nineteen years old, incorporated their findings into his design for the new grandstand, which cost $2 million—the amount the Agua Caliente Casino was taking in every month.

The new racetrack, located two miles east of the old one, opened on December 28, 1929. The stock market had crashed just two months earlier, initiating the Great Depression that would last until the eve of World War II, but no one at Agua Caliente seemed to notice. Hollywood would never feel the full effects of the Depression, as moviegoing provided the American public with an inexpensive and blessed distraction from their personal economic woes. With Tijuana denizens Raoul Walsh and Joe Schenck on the board of directors, Hollywood felt most welcome at the new track.

Hollywood stars flocked to Agua Caliente. Clark Gable and George Raft became regulars. Bing Crosby whet his appetite for racing (he would later found Del Mar Racecourse) with repeated trips to both the track and the casino, even serving as an honorary race-day steward on occasion. Howard Hughes wooed Warner Bros. starlet Marian Marsh, unsuccessfully, over $5 glasses of champagne. Douglas Fairbanks Sr. and Jr. compared handicapping tips while lunching at the trackside restaurant. Chico Marx dropped a small fortune on more than one occasion during days at the races and nights at the casino. William Powell thinned his considerable bank account as he patronized on-course bookies and roulette wheel croupiers. Wallace Beery founded an exclusive club at the casino limited to 100 of Hollywood's biggest names, every one of them ready, willing, and able to jump into the fun without a word of warning. Bandleader Xavier Cugat, a frequent performer at the casino nightclub and an amateur artist, captured the scene in a mural that depicted Will Rogers dancing with Eddie Cantor, Laurel and Hardy giggling together in the corner, and fellow bandleader Paul Whiteman flirting with Dolores del Rio.

The celebrity crowd wasn't limited to Hollywood, however. New York City's dapper mayor Jimmy Walker vacated City Hall for prolonged weekends at Agua Caliente. Perhaps His Profligate Honor was attracted by the presence of Bugsy Siegel, who would later use his Agua Caliente Casino experience to build the Flamingo, Las Vegas's first casino on the Strip. Al Capone was known for dropping $100 tips to waiters for delivering a pack of cigarettes. Watching over it all was "Gossip Girl" Hedda Hopper, who, when she wasn't in Tijuana herself, depended on the eyes and ears of her salacious spies to report on all the equally salacious scandals.

"Viva Agua Caliente! Care Free! Duty Free!" north-of-the-border billboards proclaimed. Newspaper and magazine advertisements read, "Agua Caliente in Old Mexico—Where Drinking Never Ceases!" These were thinly veiled invitations to smuggle booze back into bone-dry California. Otherwise upstanding citizens had secret "gas tanks" built into their roadsters, making it easier to sneak dozens of gallons of Beefeater, Hennessy, Canadian Club, and Chateau Laffitte across the border.

Years later, the *Los Angeles Times* would recall of Agua Caliente: "For the first time in their quixotic careers, the glamour girls and boys of Hollywood found a place where they could play in the manner of emperors and czars and in keeping with their large salaries. Their patronage naturally attracted other people with more dollars than sense."[6]

The San Diego & Arizona Railroad offered a $1 round-trip fare between San Diego and Tijuana. The train made one stop just beyond the casino's entrance and another opposite the racetrack's main gate. Anyone in a hurry could book a flight with Maddux Air Lines, which had planes leaving daily from San Francisco at 9:30 a.m. and from Los Angeles at 9:45. A special airstrip was built to allow passengers to be deposited a few hundred yards from the front door of the casino. It was barely a two-hour commute from the splendorous domesticity of Beverly Hills to the underworldly delights of Agua Caliente.

Sex and Violence

Between afternoons at the races and late nights at the casino, Agua Caliente's high-rolling denizens could relax for a few hours. Floor shows featuring some of Mexico's leading folkloric acts were nightly attractions at the Agua Caliente Casino Club. Among the performers were the Dancing Cansinos. Led by Eduardo Cansino, the last in a long family line of traditional Spanish dancers, the group included his wife, Volga Haworth, and their daughter, Margarita Carmen Cansino (the future Rita Hayworth).

Margarita's Mexican debut came in 1931 at the age of thirteen, but Tijuana would not hold her for long. The first appearance of the dark-haired beauty at the exclusive Foreign Club in downtown Tijuana and later at Agua Caliente's Casino Club caused a sensation. She performed hot numbers with her father, who did everything in his power to keep the public from discovering that she was his daughter.

A young, hot-to-trot American lad named James Hill uncovered the Cansinos' secret one night after their performance at the Casino Club. Hill (future producer of the Ben Hecht–Burt Lancaster collaborations *Sweet Smell of Success* and *Trapeze*) had accompanied his mother and father to Agua Caliente for a weekend walk on the wild side. He was just fifteen years old at the time but ready for some adult action. Hill had saved up $25 from his paper route and was looking to make an investment. Having heard that women were for sale in Tijuana, he was determined to hire a girl to relieve him of his virginity.

After the races one Friday evening, young Hill and his parents attended the Dancing Cansinos' performance. The young man was taken with thirteen-year-old Margarita's sultry stage presence as well as her precociousness. Disengaging himself from mom and pop, "Romeo" Hill prowled the grounds in search of his "Juliet." "Who should be turning the corner, and alone," he recalled, "but the very same girl we saw dancing earlier. I figured without the old guy (her father, but that fact unknown to him at the time) around, I was a cinch to make a deal, so I eased a ten off my roll. But I never got around to flashing it, because of the frightened look in her eyes, like you see when a faun is running from a fire."[7]

Margarita escaped the young lecher's clutches, only to run into the "old guy," who had seen their brief encounter. Daddy began to scold Margarita, who pleaded innocence. "No, Father," she stammered, "nothing happened." Her loving dad then warned her never to refer to him as "Father" in public. It was bad for business.

James Hill missed his chance that night but would succeed in 1958 when he became Rita Hayworth's fifth and final husband. At three years, their second liaison lasted a bit longer than their first.

By the time she was fifteen, Margarita had shown enough talent onstage to be offered a screen test by Warner Bros. But the poor girl, intimidated by a father who seemed to encourage an unnaturally close relationship, displayed such shyness that Warner lost interest. A year later, Fox Films talent scout Winfield Sheehan caught her Agua Caliente act. Impressed by her lithesome moves, he set up a screen test for her with ace Hungarian cinematographer Rudolph Maté, the man behind the camera in F. W. Murnau's *Nosferatu* and Fritz Lang's *Liliom*. Maté got Margarita to relax, and she sailed through the test with flying colors. Her first role was a brief dancing scene on an offshore gambling ship in the Spencer Tracy vehicle *Dante's Inferno,* a bit that was choreographed by her ever-present father. After a final gig with Eduardo at Agua Caliente in December 1934, she signed a contract with Columbia.

Margarita landed a number of small roles and was billed as Rita Cansino until 1937, when Columbia boss Harry Cohn took a cue from her mother's maiden name and she became Rita Hayworth. Up went her hairline, and down came her bustline; her dark brown hair was dyed red. Two years later, she was starring opposite Cary Grant in *Only Angels Have Wings,* her transformation into a Hollywood sex goddess complete. Twelve years later, her appetite for fame whetted by Agua Caliente's racy atmosphere, she would morph into La Princesse Aly Khan, wife of one of the world's most prominent Thoroughbred owners.

The suave sophistication of the young and lovely Rita found a rather crude masculine counterpart in Wallace Beery. Long established as one of Hollywood's leading heavies, Beery developed an offscreen reputation that made him one of Tinseltown's most notorious scoundrels. Like most thugs, Beery possessed an excess of charm, and he used it to good advantage both in Hollywood and in Tijuana.

Beery made a show of seeking out both the top and the bottom of Tijuana's casino society. In the late 1910s he was a frequent visitor at the Tijuana racetrack, but his prime reason for traveling south was the rough-and-tumble lifestyle on the Avenida Revolucion. After a day at the races, Beery would make his way into town for dinner and some gambling at Yashuara's Monte Carlo Casino, then take a step down in class—and up in danger—with a visit to the Main Event, one of two Tijuana nightclubs run by ex–heavyweight champ Jack Johnson.

The first black man to wear boxing's heavyweight crown, Johnson lost his title in 1915 in a controversial bout with Jess Willard in Havana, ending a seven-year reign at the top. In 1913 he was convicted of transporting an underaged white woman, prostitute Lucille Cameron, across state lines for reasons deemed immoral. Although that incident took place in 1912, before passage of the Mann Act outlawing such shenanigans, Johnson was convicted by an all-white jury in a trial presided over by future baseball commissioner Kenesaw Mountain Landis. The champ spent the next seven years on the lam, during which time he successfully defended his title three times, twice in Paris and once in Buenos Aires, before losing to Willard, who was accused of wearing leaded gloves in the bout. In 1920 Johnson grew weary of life as a fugitive and gave himself up to federal authorities. Transported to Fort Leavenworth, Kansas, he served a year in prison and never returned to Tijuana.

The Main Event was Johnson's club for white patrons, and across town was his all-black club, the Newport. Beery was one of the few white people Johnson allowed into the Newport. On at least one occasion, Beery escorted Gloria Swanson, his wife at the time, to the Newport, which showcased some of the best American jazz bands of the late 1910s.

Beery used his Tijuana experiences with Johnson to good advantage. In 1931 he starred in MGM's *The Champ*, the story of an alcoholic, gambling ex–heavyweight champion toughing it out in the border town, unable to land a fight. Anxious to impress his young son (played by Jackie Cooper), Beery's character buys the boy a racehorse that is entered in the fictional version of the Agua Caliente Handicap. And so Beery was able to parlay his love of booze, boxing, gambling, and racing into an Academy Award for best actor in *The Champ*, but his penchant for the excitement of the dark alley never deserted him. In 1937 his violent streak got him into hot water when he was accused of participating in the beating death of film comedian Ted Healy in a parking lot outside the Trocadero nightclub in Los Angeles, a nonscheduled bout in which Cubby Broccoli, future producer of the James Bond films, was also implicated. Beery was whisked out of the country by MGM's fixers, who managed to convince the police that the murder had been committed by a group of college students. Beery spent a four-month vacation sampling the delights of Paris, with frequent side trips to Longchamp Racecourse, until the studio was able to cool down the LA heat.[8]

Beery continued to patronize Tijuana, frequenting the upscale Agua Caliente. His Elite 100 Club provided the resort with a steady stream of high-rolling, deep-pocketed Hollywood stars, all of whom descended on the new racetrack there, which provided the best horse racing west of the Mississippi in the early 1930s.

Hollywood South of the Border

Jim Crofton's new track at Agua Caliente prospered for two reasons. It offered the best prize money in the world, and it attracted a star-studded clientele that made the place even more attractive to the general public.

The money persuaded some horsemen from Hialeah in Florida and the Fair Grounds in New Orleans to abandon their winter quarters in favor of the riches of Agua Caliente. As there was no wintertime racing in New York, Crofton persuaded some of that state's leading owners and trainers to eschew their winter base at Hialeah in favor of a season in sunny Tijuana, where they could drink to their hearts' content as well as spend their nights at the gaming tables.

On March 2, 1930, barely two months after the track's opening, Crofton carded a racing extravaganza that included three stakes races, attracting quality horses from throughout America. The feature was the $30,000 Agua Caliente Derby. The two cofeatures, the $2,000 Adolf Zukor Handicap (named for the head of Paramount) and the $1,200 Beverly Hills Handicap, provided clear evidence that Hollywood was playing a major role in the track's development.

Raoul Walsh, director of the silent classics *The Thief of Baghdad* and *What Price Glory?* knew the lay of the land and was a member of the Agua Caliente board of directors. After his quickie marriage in the Governor's

Suite, he had returned to filmmaking. Between stints directing Victor McLaglen in *Hot for Paris* and introducing John Wayne in *The Big Trail* for Fox Films, Walsh was in Tijuana on a gambling sabbatical when he ran into racing buddy William Shea at the casino. Shea owned a string of horses that raced in New York and Kentucky, but the stock market crash had hit him hard and he was looking to sell some of his Thoroughbreds. One of his horses, a three-year-old filly named Greyola, was stabled in Caliente and had been entered in the Agua Caliente Derby, just three days away. The asking price was $15,000. After examining Greyola in her stall, Walsh wrote Shea a check. That night, Walsh won $7,000 playing craps at the casino, recouping nearly half the purchase price.

Shea called Hialeah Racetrack in Florida looking for a jockey, and the next day, Frankie Catrone arrived to take the ride. A winner at prestigious Saratoga as a two-year-old, Greyola was the only filly in the 1⅛-mile Derby field of thirteen three-year-olds, yet she prevailed by a length, with Catrone busting her out of the gate on top and leading throughout. Among the vanquished was Jim Dandy, a horse with tender hooves who disliked the fast, hard going and finished a distant last. Less than six months later, Jim Dandy would get the muddy ground he loved at Saratoga, scoring one of the biggest upsets in racing history when he trounced Triple Crown winner Gallant Fox in the Travers Stakes.

Catrone, a capable jockey, never made it to the top of the rider ranks, but he became a prominent trainer on the Southern California circuit. His biggest victory as a conditioner came with Lucky Debonair in the 1965 Kentucky Derby.

Walsh earned $25,000 for Greyola's victory, plus half that amount in betting winnings. Shea convinced him to send Greyola to Kentucky, promising even bigger things. Walsh acceded but was shocked a few days later when he learned that his filly had died on the train carrying her to the Bluegrass State.[9]

With the Hipodromo de Tijuana closed, Crofton provided continuity for the region's racing by transferring many of the old track's big races to his sparkling new venue. The inaugural running of the Agua Caliente Handicap, which replaced the Coffroth Handicap, was worth $113,300, or $50 more than the 1929 Coffroth at old Tijuana. That total didn't include the $5,000 awarded to both the winning trainer and the winning jockey.

Tough-guy Walsh was not one to let something like the death of a horse get him down. Three weeks after the Derby, he was still in town touting the season's premier race, which attracted a large part of the film community from north of the border. "There won't be anyone in Hollywood on Sunday," he boasted of Agua Caliente's drawing power. "Everybody is here!"[10]

Among the fourteen runners in the 1¼-mile contest were 1928 Preakness winner Victorian and 1929 Kentucky Derby runner-up Naishapur. But these equine stars were outshone by the brilliance of the crowd. Among the 35,000 attendees were Charlie Chaplin, Buster Keaton, Bing Crosby, and the husband-and-wife team of Al Jolson and Ruby Keeler.

Victorian went off as the 2.10–1 favorite, and he duly obliged with a handy three-length victory, setting a track record time of 2:03⅕. Bred by one of America's racing scions, Harry Payne Whitney, Victorian was a son of 1913 Horse of the Year Whisk Broom II. There was no better race run west of the Mississippi in 1930. The new track had hit the sporting big time in its first season of operation.[11]

Agua Caliente offered an astonishing $1 million in purses at its 1930–1931 winter meeting. Of that amount, $117,500 was the prize for the second running of the Agua Caliente Handicap on March 22. Sun Beau, the two-time champion older horse in America, spotted nine rivals 13 to 37 pounds as the 3–5 favorite. The impost, however, proved to be too much for the six-year-old, who led briefly at the halfway point but weakened to finish fifth behind Mark Hall. Nevertheless, the message was clear: the quality of the racing was now equal to the quality of the clubhouse patrons.

Phar Lap

Agua Caliente was going great guns, but there were storm clouds on the horizon. The Depression was beginning to take its toll on Americans' leisure habits. In 1931 the Mexican government doubled Agua Caliente's tax rate on both racetrack and casino earnings. Business suffered, but the appearance of the great Australian champion Phar Lap in the 1932 Agua Caliente Handicap marked the high point of the track's brief but glorious history.

The six-year-old New Zealand–bred gelding had won thirty-six of his fifty starts Down Under, among them the Australian Derby and the Victoria Derby as a three-year-old and the prestigious Cox Plate twice at ages four and five. His greatest triumph, however, had come in the 1930 running of the two-mile Melbourne Cup Handicap, known as "the race that stops a nation" because it is a statewide holiday in Victoria.

That year, Aussie bookies lost so much money on Phar Lap's races that the horse became the target of an assassination attempt. On the morning of November 1, 1930, gangsters, apparently hired by fearful bookies, took a shot at him in the stable area at Flemington Racecourse. Fortunately, they missed, and Phar Lap lived to win the Melbourne Stakes later that afternoon. Three days later, he would win the Melbourne Cup, which had the bookies weeping all the way to the poorhouse, at least for one day. The following year, Phar Lap was assigned a backbreaking 150 pounds for the 1931 Melbourne Cup, where he finished eighth. By comparison, he had carried 138 pounds in his Melbourne Cup triumph a year earlier, while horses carry 126 pounds in all the world's classic races such as the Kentucky Derby and the Epsom Derby.

Having accomplished all he could in his homeland, Phar Lap was sent to California to prepare for a 1932 Stateside campaign. His American owner Dan Davis struck a deal with Jim Crofton, who agreed to pay to ship the horse from Sydney to San Francisco on the condition that Phar Lap run his first race at Agua Caliente. Phar Lap would also receive a $5,000 appearance fee for running in the Agua Caliente Handicap. The great gelding arrived at Agua Caliente on January 26, the subject of front-page stories throughout Mexico and the United States. Reports of a cracked hoof on his right forefoot were clouded in mystery, as the press was rarely allowed access to Phar Lap's royal presence. Davis and his new American trainer Tommy Woodcock were loath to let anyone near their charge, except for his most trusted handlers.

When Crofton cut the Agua Caliente purse from $100,000 to $50,000, skeptics claimed it was an anti-Australian move to prevent Phar Lap from surpassing the American horse Zev at the top of the all-time Thoroughbred earnings list. But Crofton was having financial problems. All the profits from the casino's first few years of operation had gone to pay off construction debts. So a cut in prize money might have been a financial necessity.

Phar Lap was assigned 129 pounds for the Agua Caliente Handicap, which meant that he would be giving his ten opponents from 9 to 39 pounds. That may sound like a lot of weight, but in reality, Phar Lap had his outclassed opposition over a barrel. Although he got away slowly and was in tight early, the 3–2 favorite was soon taken wide by his Australian rider Bill Elliott, who kept him out of trouble for the remainder of the race. Phar Lap circled the field, leading shortly before the halfway mark of the 1¼-mile race, and cruised to victory under a hand ride. At the finish line he was a comfortable two lengths ahead of the 7–1 runner-up Reveille Boy, setting a new track record of 2:02.80 (by comparison, 2015 Kentucky Derby winner American Pharoah traveled the same distance on a similar track at Churchill Downs in 2:03.02). Phar Lap's performance was all the more remarkable because it was his first start on dirt; all his previous races in Australia had been on grass.[12]

The 23,000 spectators could barely contain themselves. Starter Marshall Cassidy called Phar Lap "the greatest horse I've ever seen," and indeed, he is still considered the greatest horse in Australian racing history. He is certainly the best horse ever to run in Mexico.

Davis immediately began to entertain offers to run Phar Lap at tracks around America, but they never came to fruition. On April 5, at the Edward Perry Ranch near San Francisco, Phar Lap died under circumstances that have never been explained satisfactorily. The official cause of death was colic, but an autopsy revealed large traces of arsenic in his stomach. Could it be that disgruntled American bookies had succeeded where their Australian counterparts had failed? Phar Lap was all but unbeatable, so bookies stood to lose millions of dollars every time he raced, giving them good reason to want him eliminated. Less conspiratorial minds will tell you that small doses of arsenic were commonly used in the 1930s to treat any number of minor equine ailments. Did Woodcock inadvertently give the horse the wrong dosage? Or was Phar Lap killed on purpose? Sadly, we will never know.

Changing of the Guard

The purse for the 1933 Agua Caliente Handicap was reduced to $25,000 as Crofton ceded his position as track president to Hollywood producer Joe Schenck, the biggest of Agua Caliente's Hollywood investors. The head of Vitagraph Pictures, Schenck had been a regular at Tijuana since 1916. His production companies were responsible for most of Buster Keaton's silent comedy classics, including *The General, The Navigator,* and *Sherlock Jr.* In 1932 he produced his breakout talkie *Rain,* Somerset Maugham's Sadie Thompson story in which bad-girl Joan Crawford overcomes the tropical isle ministrations of self-righteous preacher Walter Huston.

Schenck's interest in racing was twofold. The highest of high rollers, he reportedly dropped $100,000 on a single race at the old Tijuana track (about $2 million in today's money), while his poker games with Chico and Harpo Marx are the stuff of backroom Hollywood legend. He also owned racehorses and provided many of the bill-topping acts at Agua Caliente's Casino Club.[13]

In a piece entitled "Where the Stars Lose Their Salaries," Doreen Podelty wrote, "In all of Tijuana—possibly a total of four square miles—there is nothing to do but eat, drink, gamble, dance and watch the horse racing."[14] But the writing was on the wall. The gringos north of the border couldn't help but notice that Agua Caliente was a gold mine. When the state legislature proposed a bill legalizing pari-mutuel wagering in California, Schenck vigorously campaigned against it. He hired Al Jolson to make singing radio commercials opposing the bill, but to no avail.

Pari-mutuel wagering and, by extrapolation, Thoroughbred horse racing were legalized in California in 1933. That autumn, the first race meeting was held at the Los Angeles County Fair (now Fairplex Park). In 1934 the Bay Area track that had closed in 1909, Tanforan, reopened. But the biggest blow to Agua Caliente was the reopening of Santa Anita on December 25, 1934. From that day on, Californians turned their backs on Agua Caliente in favor of the racetrack in Arcadia, just twenty miles east of Hollywood.

Agua Caliente had taken an equally heavy hit a year earlier with the repeal of Prohibition. Americans could now drink to their hearts' content as well as bet on races in California. Soon Agua Caliente was being battered on both sides of the border. In December 1934 Mexicans elected leftist Lazaro Cardenas as their new president. His hatred of gambling led him to close the entire Agua Caliente operation on July 30, 1935.

The track would reopen under new management for the spring-summer meeting in 1937, close again, and then reopen in 1938 in time to attract Seabiscuit to the Agua Caliente Handicap. The prize money had been reduced to a mere $12,500, a far cry from its $100,000-plus purses a few years earlier. Carrying 130 pounds and spotting seven inferior rivals 22 to 32 pounds, the gallant little five-year-old led virtually every step of the way and recorded an easy two-length victory as the 3–10 favorite.

Seabiscuit's appearance at Agua Caliente was a trip down memory lane for his owner. Charles Howard had been a regular at both the Hipodromo de Tijuana and Agua Caliente during their glory years, so he couldn't resist the opportunity to take one last look at his old stomping grounds. March 27 was declared Seabiscuit Day, and just like in the good old days, throngs of Americans swarmed across the border to see their favorite racehorse perform in what amounted to little more than a workout.[15] The crowd of 20,000 set a single-day record for betting handle. Bing Crosby was on hand to present Howard (his Del Mar partner) with the winner's trophy, but Seabiscuit's victory would prove to be Agua Caliente's swan song.

The Cinematic Legacy

Five million American tourists, an average of more than 13,000 per day, descended on Tijuana in 1932 in search of the illicit thrills the town had to offer. At the time, it was estimated that 500 prostitutes plied their trade along the Avenida Revolucion. If we assume that 10,000 of the 13,000 day-trippers were men, simple arithmetic reveals that there was one lady of the night for every twenty Yankee males, a ratio probably unsurpassed in the history of the world. On Labor Day 1934 alone, 42,000 Americans flooded the streets of Tijuana and the gaming halls of Agua Caliente. These numbers make Saratoga and Deauville seem like backwater book-making establishments by comparison.[16]

Today, Agua Caliente has been reduced to a sports book office with an occasional dog race thrown in for good measure. The grandstands of both Agua Caliente and the Hipodromo de Tijuana are long gone, but glimpses of the Agua Caliente track and casino can be seen in a handful of minor Hollywood films.

Universal's *Fast Companions* (1932) starred twelve-year-old Mickey Rooney (still being billed as Mickey McGuire) not as a jockey but as a troubled orphan who idolizes a crooked jockey. Rooney's admiration eventually helps the wayward rider mend his ways as he wins the fictional Caliente Sweepstakes. The race scenes were filmed at Agua Caliente a couple of months after Phar Lap's victory in the most famous Agua Caliente Handicap of all.

A year later, Mexican character actor Leo Carrillo starred in *Racetrack,* a film with a similar Runyonesque plot. He plays a race-fixing bookie at Caliente who reforms his ways after meeting a cute little homeless kid and his lovable, widowed mother.

The racing scenes in the 1935 production of *Unwelcome Stranger* were filmed at Agua Caliente. This is yet another variation on the same theme: a racehorse owner adopts a lame orphan who eventually rides his horse to victory in the big race while overcoming the underhanded tactics of a rider played by Frankie Darro, Hollywood's go-to guy for the crooked jockey role.

But for an idea of what Agua Caliente must have been like in its heyday, nothing beats the 1935 Warner Bros./First National production of *In Caliente*. Filmed largely at the resort itself shortly before its initial closing, this musical comedy stars the everlastingly beautiful Dolores del Rio as a nightclub singer; Del Mar cofounder Pat O'Brien plays her love interest. Taking full advantage of the casino's opulence, it features two Busby Berkeley dance numbers, most memorably "The Lady in Red."

After *In Caliente,* however, Hollywood lost interest in Tijuana. Already in operation, Santa Anita was much closer to home, while plans for Del Mar and Hollywood Park were on the drawing board.

2

Santa Anita
Hollywood Cashes In

Our plan is to build a track that will rank second to none in the country.

Hal Roach

The Race to Pari-mutuel Paradise

By 1932, it didn't take a genius to see that Agua Caliente was a gold mine, that the gold being extracted was coming largely from American pockets, and that much of that gold was coming from the rich vein supplied by the seemingly limitless resources of the Hollywood film community. The state of California was being pressured by open-minded entrepreneurs from San Francisco to San Diego to reinstitute the pari-mutuel wagering laws it had abolished in 1909. This would allow Thoroughbred horse racing to reestablish itself in the Golden State and thus redirect the rich proceeds of the sport not only to racetrack operators but also to state coffers in Sacramento. For it is a truism that wherever horse racing prospers, the state in which it prospers shares the wealth.

"In all Tijuana—possibly a total of four square miles—there is nothing to do but eat, drink, gamble, dance and watch the horse racing."[1] And bet on the horse racing as well. The question was how to lure all those American eaters, drinkers, and horse racing fans back to California. The answer lay in getting the state to legalize pari-mutuel wagering, the lifeblood of racing that drives racetrack profits as well as tax revenue. California had never passed a law banning horse racing—far from it. Anyone who could afford to build a racetrack could run race meetings in the state. The problem was financing the races because, without betting, funding in the 1930s was limited to admission and parking fees paid by spectators and entry fees paid by owners to get their horses into stakes races—a mere pittance compared to the amounts that could be generated by betting. Such nonbetting meetings were tried at Tanforan after pari-mutuel wagering was banned in California in 1909, but they quickly fizzled out. If people can't bet on a race, it is very difficult to get them interested in racing at all.[2]

An early skirmish to revive pari-mutuel betting in California came to nothing in 1926 when a badly promoted bill was slaughtered in the state legislature. But with hundreds of millions of Yankee dollars flowing across the border every year, a more professional tack was taken in 1932 in the form of a statewide referendum. It looked like it was going to pass but then ran out of steam near the finish line when a number of horsemen backed off the proposition, claiming that the takeout—the percentage of money wagered that would go toward funding prize money—was too low. On November 8, the referendum was rejected by a vote of 956,028 to 904,840.

If at first you don't succeed, try, try again. On April 13, 1933, the state senate passed the Woolwine-Maloney pari-mutuel bill by a vote of 22–16. Whisked over to the state house the same day, it passed 58–8 and was then sent to the office of Governor James Rolph Jr., where it hit a snag. Rolph had quietly supported the bill in its early stages, but when it arrived on his desk, he dillydallied. There it sat for two weeks, or as long as the law allowed, until he finally nixed it. Apparently, he had been influenced by none other than William Randolph Hearst (the tycoon on whom Orson Welles based his title character in *Citizen Kane*). The Hearst chain of newspapers, among them the *Los Angeles Examiner,* was vehemently anti-gambling. Hearst invited the rather gullible Rolph to his magnificent San Simeon estate for a weekend of wining and dining, and a few days later, the governor vetoed the Woolwine-Maloney bill.[3]

Two months later, voters were presented with another referendum. By this time, they had had enough of the political intrigue that was depriving them of the pleasurable pastime of throwing their money away on the ponies. The referendum passed by a margin of 300,000, the equivalent of winning a horse race by the length of the stretch.

Now the race was on to see who would be the first to open a racetrack in California and begin reaping the rich rewards that beckoned.

Roach's Gang

Hal Roach, producer, director, writer, and all-around entrepreneur, won an early reputation in Hollywood as a money-spinner with a knack for finding and developing comedic talent. In 1914 he founded the Hal Roach Studios and devoted himself to making films that would make people around the world laugh out loud. One of his early stars, Harold Lloyd, was going nowhere after appearing in seventy-five shorts as a character called Lonesome Luke. Then, one day, Roach noticed that a stagehand had everyone in stitches simply by donning a pair of horn-rimmed eyeglasses. Roach figured that if it could work for that guy, it could work for Lloyd, so he stuck a pair of round, horn-rimmed specs onto Lloyd's otherwise bland mug, transforming him into the shy, bumbling, lovable everyman who, along with Charlie Chaplin and Buster Keaton, became one of the royal triumvirate that ruled silent comedy. Roach produced and sometimes wrote or directed nearly a hundred shorts starring Lloyd from late 1917 to late 1921, when the duo switched to feature films. They made five features—most notably, *Grandma's Boy, Safety Last,* and *Why Worry*—through 1923, when Lloyd left Roach to strike out on his own.

The producer didn't skip a beat. It so happened that Roach had a rotating cast of about a dozen charming little brats at the studio who went by the name Our Gang. From 1922 through 1944, Joe (the fat kid), Farina, Wheezer, Mary Ann, Chubby, Stymie, Scotty, Porky, Buckwheat, Darla, Spanky, and Alfalfa, as well as Pete the Pup, kept audiences around the globe in stitches. Roach even managed to get Our Gang into a racing film. At twenty-seven minutes, 1923's *Derby Day* is one of the lengthier entries in the Our Gang repertoire. The kids set up a hotdog stand across the street from a racetrack, and a pretty little girl, the daughter of one of the owners with a horse in the big race, sneaks them into the track. The gang is so impressed by what they see that they decide to put on a horse race of their own, but it winds up looking more like cow versus mule versus goat versus dog.

But what really put Roach on the road to riches and glory was his idea to pair Englishman Stan Laurel and Georgian Oliver Hardy as a comedy duo. Stan and Ollie proved so popular that Roach was able to charge distributors feature film rates for their short films. By 1933, when the California Horse Racing Board (CHRB) began to entertain requests for licenses to run racetracks, Laurel and Hardy were fresh off their Oscar-winning short *The Music Box* and were working on what many consider their feature masterpiece, *Sons of the Desert*. Roach parlayed his Our Gang–Laurel and Hardy daily double into a gold mine. "Our Gang behaved like adults," he recalled late in life, and "Laurel and Hardy behaved like children."[4] That comic combination had Roach thinking about new ways to spend his money in 1933, when horse racing was about to become Hollywood's siren song.

The first person to be granted a license to build a new racetrack in California was Anita Baldwin, the daughter of Lucky Baldwin, the man who had had a brief but glorious fling with the original Santa Anita (1907–1909) before pari-mutuel wagering was outlawed in California. Anita teamed with Joseph Smoot, builder of that most beautiful of Florida racetracks, Hialeah Park, to form the Los Angeles Jockey Club and open a track on her own property not far from the site of her father's Santa Anita (named for his daughter). It would be a fitting tribute to and continuation of the Southern California legacy, even from a Hollywood perspective. The last race on the final card at Lucky Baldwin's original Santa Anita, run on April 17, 1909, had been filmed by Francis Boggs and worked into the climax of his eleven-minute short *The Heart of a Race Tout,* widely regarded as the first film shot entirely in California. But the new venture came to naught. Eight months into construction, with the grandstand half built, the money ran out, leaving a pile of unpaid bills. Smoot disappeared into the night and left poor Anita holding the bag.

Meanwhile, Roach had formed the Los Angeles Turf Club and planned to build a new track in Culver City, right around the corner from his movie studio. Roach believed that the closer the track was to Los Angeles, the better positioned it would be to take advantage of the city's burgeoning population and serve the film community. Culver City is just six miles from the corner of Hollywood and Vine and four miles from the heart of Beverly Hills. But Roach's neighbors in Culver City didn't care for the idea, expressing their disapproval by refusing to waive local zoning laws that would have allowed construction to begin. As a result, Roach never received a permit from the CHRB to build a track.

Carleton Burke, chairman of the state racing commission, tried to open a track on the site of Lucky Baldwin's old park, but nothing came of that attempt either. While all this was going on, Dr. Charles H. Strub, a dentist turned investment broker and minor league baseball team owner, was busy making his own racing plans in San Francisco. An adept businessman, Strub had bounced back twice from devastating losses that would have sobered a lesser man—the first time when he lost his dental practice in the aftermath of the San Francisco earthquake in 1906, and the second time when he lost much of his money in the 1929 stock market crash. Ever resourceful, Strub stayed afloat through some shrewd real estate deals and the novel management of his baseball team, the San Francisco Seals. Under Strub, the Seals developed a homegrown scouting system that signed up the best local talent far from the eyes of the big league. At the time, the West Coast had no major league baseball, St. Louis being the westernmost city with a team. Among the Seals' best players were future Hall of Famers Lefty Gomez and Joe DiMaggio, as well as Oklahoman brothers Paul and Lloyd Waner, known as "Big Poison" and "Little Poison." From the mid-1920s to the mid-1930s, Strub sold his players to major league teams for a $1 million profit. Gomez, DiMaggio, and Frank Crosetti all went to the cash-rich juggernaut that was the New York Yankees.

Armed with the cash, Strub formed the St. Francis Jockey Club, named for San Francisco's swankiest hotel. The club included many of the city's most prominent citizens, a lure the CHRB couldn't fail to notice in granting Strub a license to build a new racetrack. But even with all his Northern California connections, Strub couldn't overcome local opposition to the project. The puritanical influence in San Francisco on both the political Right and Left proved insurmountable.

Strub withdrew his application for a permit in San Francisco and looked south to Los Angeles. He had heard of Roach's difficulties in Culver City, and Roach knew of Strub's problems up north. So they put their heads together, reenergized Roach's Los Angeles Turf Club, and offered shares at $5,000 apiece in an effort to attain the $1 million necessary to get the project under way. Roach was instrumental in bringing in Hollywood shareholders, but 20th Century Fox boss Darryl Zanuck was not among them. He pooh-poohed the idea and apparently convinced a number of other producers that the project would be a bust. Zanuck wasn't alone in his feelings. One newspaperman belittled the idea of horse racing in the Los Angeles area because "98 percent of the people around here are longhairs, the other 2 percent are tightwads."[5]

But Roach soldiered on, eventually obtaining more than half the amount needed to get started. He assured prospective investors that their money would be well spent and told the *Los Angeles Examiner* that all profits would be plowed back into the track. "Promotion is the farthest thing from our mind. It is a sporting proposition for sportsmen only, and if the commercial angle enters into it, we will drop the entire venture." As a sweetener, the Los Angeles Turf Club announced plans for a race worth

$100,000, the Santa Anita Handicap, at a time when the Kentucky Derby was worth a mere $30,000.[6]

"I got letters from all the people who had tracks all over the country," Roach said. "They said if you build a $250,000 track and have a $25,000 race, maybe you can make some money. But with a million-dollar track and a $100,000 race, you're going to lose your shirt." Roach, who was always his own man, shrugged off the criticism. His pitch worked. Among the early shareholders in Santa Anita were Bing Crosby, Will Rogers, Joe E. Brown, and Al Jolson from the Hollywood side and C. V. Whitney Jr., Jock Whitney, Colonel Matt Winn, and E. R. Bradley from the racing side.[7]

There was a difference of opinion about where the new racecourse should be built. Roach still firmly believed in the advantages of Culver City and its proximity to Los Angeles (plus it was just a short ride from his office), but Strub and his location scout Gwynne Wilson (a key figure in the mounting of the 1932 Los Angeles Olympic Games) carried the day. The new Santa Anita would be built in Arcadia at the foot of the glorious San Gabriel Mountains, just a few miles west of Lucky Baldwin's old track.

The CHRB granted Roach and Strub a license on January 9, 1934. In the wake of Anita Baldwin's failure, the Los Angeles Turf Club bought 214 acres from her for $236,300, enabling her to recoup most of her earlier losses. Roach was named president of the Los Angeles Turf Club, and Strub was its vice president. Construction of the track began in March, leaving little time to get racing started by the CHRB-mandated opening day of January 1935.

Wilson hired architect Gordon Kaufman, who was known for the Art Deco style that was all the rage in the 1930s, especially in Hollywood. Kaufman had presided over the building of the Hoover Dam, the *Los Angeles Times* building, and the California Institute of Technology. Unfortunately, neither he nor Wilson had ever set foot on a racetrack. So the two of them embarked on a reconnaissance trip, visiting twenty tracks around the country. Hialeah in Miami and Arlington Park near Chicago proved to be the most influential, and Kaufman was soon at work designing the plans for Santa Anita, with a clubhouse and grandstand in one building and an adjacent Turf Club just beyond the finish line. Unbeknownst at the time, the Turf Club would prove to be a sticking point with the most powerful Hollywood producers and would eventually lead to the development of Santa Anita's hated rival, Hollywood Park.[8]

Green Christmas

If there was pressure on Roach, Strub, Wilson, and Kaufman to open by January, they handled it with aplomb. Opening day was set for Christmas Day 1934, when no one in Hollywood would be at work. As president of the club and the most visible member of the track's board of directors, Hal Roach was assigned the role of official greeter, and on Christmas Eve he wrote an opening-day speech and stuffed it into his suit pocket.

Christmas Day in Los Angeles dawned just like Irving Berlin described it in the prelude to his classic "White Christmas": "The sun is shining, the grass is green, / The orange and palm trees sway." The weather was magnificent, and when Roach arrived at his equally magnificent new horse park, he was greeted by smiling faces all around. Bing Crosby was in his box on the finish line. Al Jolson and his tap-dancing wife Ruby Keeler were there, as well as America's premier humorist, Will Rogers. With visions of sugar plums dancing in his head, Roach stepped up to the podium, reached into his jacket pocket for his speech, and found nothing! He rummaged through his pants pockets, both front and back, but found that they were as empty as a horseplayer's after the last race. So Roach was forced to improvise. After welcoming everyone to the track and wishing them a Merry Christmas, he came up with a one-liner that inadvertently made him look as foolish as Stan Laurel in one of his sillier moments. "Bet only what you can afford to lose," he cautioned the gathered throng of 30,777, "not what you expect to win."[9] By the time that line had passed through the track's publicity department to the news services and various sports desks around the country, it had morphed into headlines like "Santa Anita Advises Patrons Not to Bet!"

Roach needn't have worried. The holiday crowd was in a spending mood, and they had some good horses to bet on. Strub had spent the month of August at Saratoga, the racetrack in upstate New York where racing families such as the Whitneys, the Vanderbilts, the Phippses, and the Wrights of Calumet Farm fame retreated for the summer. His promise of a $100,000 race—the "hundred grander"—got the attention of racing's elite. Getting the eastern establishment to recognize far-off Santa Anita was paramount to its success. Strub sweetened the pot by offering a minimum purse of $800 per race, at a time when most tracks outside of New York had minimums of $400 to $600. The timing of the inaugural meeting was also crucial. By securing forty-three wintertime days from

December 25 to March 9, Santa Anita would be running when all the eastern and midwestern tracks were closed, making it that much more attractive to the big barns in New York and Kentucky.

The opening-day feature, the $5,000 Christmas Stakes, was won by High Glee, a filly owned by Cornelius Vanderbilt (C. V.) Whitney, the cream of eastern racing's elite. She defeated Head Play, winner of the previous year's Preakness Stakes, the second jewel of the Triple Crown. Strub and Roach graciously arranged for Anita Baldwin to make the trophy presentation, providing a sense of continuity between the old track and the new.[10]

Reviews of Santa Anita's opening day were mixed. No one could argue with the quality of the racing, but the total handle for the day amounted to $264,000—an average of $8.50 per person, or a little more than $1 per person per race. That was a little less than Roach and Strub had hoped for. Still, $264,000 in 1934 was the equivalent of $5.5 million in today's money, and many of the racegoers in the stands that day were brand new to the game and were likely betting very conservatively. They would prove to be quick learners.

Variety's day-after headline blared "Santa Anita Opening O.K.," but it reported that fans in the grandstand were boiling about the $1.10 admission fee and the 25-cent charge for parking, and no one was happy about paying half a dollar for a mixed drink. The show business bible predicted that Santa Anita would be successful only if it started handing out free passes, but Strub was adamantly opposed to that idea.

The Hundred Grander

Santa Anita had been quick out of the gate, and the remainder of the inaugural meeting would prove to be just as successful—and just as lucrative. During the week, the new track received a belated Christmas present from Mexico when recently elected president Lazaro Cardenas outlawed gambling throughout the country. Initially, this didn't affect American-owned and -operated Agua Caliente, but a few months later, Cardenas closed down Agua Caliente as well, eliminating all of Santa Anita's competition. The Mexican track would reopen a year later, but by then, it had become a spent force.

Eastern elites continued to dominate the best races during that first season. Greentree Stables, owned by Mrs. Payne Whitney but operated largely by her son Jock Whitney, prevailed in the first Santa Anita Derby with Gillie, while C. V. Whitney doubled his pleasure when his filly Jabot beat the boys, including 1931 Preakness winner Mate, in the San Carlos Handicap.

But there were bigger names waiting in the wings. The Hundred Grander, better known as the Santa Anita Handicap, was scheduled for February 23. Ensconced on the backstretch since November, preparing for the big day, was the great Equipoise. The champion two-year-old of 1930 had missed his three-year-old campaign because of a bad foot but had bounced back in glorious fashion to be named Horse of the Year in both 1932 and 1933. He had been slated to begin stud duties in Kentucky in 1935, but when owner C. V. Whitney heard about the Hundred Grander, he delayed Equipoise's retirement and sent him west.

Also on the grounds was Twenty Grand, owned by Mrs. Payne Whitney (C. V.'s aunt). After winning the Kentucky Derby and the Belmont Stakes in 1931, Twenty Grand missed landing the Triple Crown when Mate beat him by half a length in the Preakness Stakes. Twenty Grand had been retired for two years but, having proved infertile, was sent to Santa Anita for a last hurrah. Also running in the Santa Anita Handicap would be Mate, Twenty Grand's Triple Crown spoiler; Cavalcade, the previous year's Kentucky Derby winner and Horse of the Year; and 1932 Belmont Stakes winner Faireno. High Glee and Head Play, the first- and second-place finishers in the Christmas Stakes, were also entered, as was speedy track specialist Ted Clark, winner of the San Felipe and Santa Margarita Handicaps earlier in the meeting.

All told, twenty horses lined up for what was already being called the "Big 'Cap," the nickname of the Santa Anita Handicap to this day. Roach was calling it "the best field in the history of racing," and the Hollywood contingent was out in force. Leading the field was Bing Crosby, who never missed a big race day in his life. Fred Astaire, catching his breath just two weeks before the release of *Roberta*, his first film with Ginger Rogers, had placed a bet on Twenty Grand. Perhaps he was employing the infallible system of betting on that horse because there were a total of twenty grand horses in the race, or maybe he was just playing a hunch; it's also possible that he was showing loyalty to his backstage buddy Jock Whitney, whose mother owned the horse.

The 1¼-mile race was actually worth $108,400, after entry and starting fees were added. Ted Clark, who had led throughout in his two previous triumphs over the track, broke on top and quickly opened a four-length lead as the field passed the stands for the first time. It was something of a rodeo behind him, as twenty horses were probably four or five more than the track could handle. Any number of them lost their chance in the scrimmages that developed on both turns. Ted Clark led into the stretch but couldn't stay the ten furlongs. Out of nowhere came the Irish-bred steeplechaser Azucar to win by two lengths over another unheralded entry, Ladysman. In spite of his reputation as a plodding stayer over the jumps, Azucar (Spanish for "sugar") had caught oddsmakers' eye when he won the 1⅛-mile New Year Stakes on January 1. The wise guys were on to him, and he went off at a rather pinched 11.40–1.

Although it looked like a great race on paper, the inaugural Santa Anita Handicap had the feel of an old-timers' event. Seven-year-old Equipoise finished seventh. Mate was also a seven-year-old, and Faireno was six. Poor Twenty Grand, another seven-year-old who finished far behind, had not seen a racetrack for more than two years until his Big 'Cap prep a few weeks earlier.

Not that Hal Roach and Charles Strub were complaining. A total of 34,269 people had paid their way into the track, and they had wagered a colossal $802,553—three times as much as on opening day, and the equivalent of more than $16 million in today's money. And this was in the middle of the Depression![11]

Roach was as good as his word and plowed the profits from the track's first season back into improvements: $330,000 for 1935–1936 and $1 million for 1936–1937. In 1936 Santa Anita became the first track to employ the Teletimer clocking device, enabling horsemen and bettors to use fractional race times as a handicapping tool. But it was the great Seabiscuit who put Santa Anita on the national sporting map with his three runs in the Hundred Grander. He finished a heartbreaking second by a nose in both 1937 and 1938 before winning in 1940, giving away as much as 30 pounds to some of his thirteen rivals and setting a track record of 2:01⅖ for 1¼ miles. His victory made him the all-time Thoroughbred earner at $437,730, and he did it in front of a crowd officially numbering 68,526 (that's about how many people visit Santa Anita these days during the course of a month). Things looked rosy in Arcadia, but there were dark days on the horizon.

Camp Santa Anita

The early days of Santa Anita were equally prosperous for Hal Roach on the cinematic side of business. Between 1935 and 1940 he produced the classic Laurel and Hardy short *Tit for Tat* and the team's sterling features *Way Out West* and *Swiss Miss.* He won an Oscar for the Our Gang short *Bored of Education* with Spanky and Alfalfa. More importantly, he made a successful leap into more serious subject matter with the Cary Grant–Carole Lombard fantasy *Topper* and a first-rate production of John Steinbeck's novel *Of Mice and Men,* which he dubbed "Laurel and Hardy without the laughs."[12]

A statue of Seabiscuit was erected in the paddock at Santa Anita in January 1941, and everything seemed to be in place for a prosperous decade when, without warning, the Japanese bombed Pearl Harbor on December 7, 1941. Panic gripped the nation, especially on the West Coast, where the government feared submarine attacks. Bunkers were built along the coast. The New Year's Day Rose Bowl game in Pasadena between Oregon State and Duke was transferred to Duke's home stadium in Durham, North Carolina. And on December 15, Santa Anita's winter meeting, due to start on the day after Christmas, was canceled.

Charles Strub tried to save the meeting. He offered to start racing in midmorning so that racegoers could get home before the statewide blackout went into effect. He also pointed out that racing in Britain, Canada, and Australia, three nations that had been at war since September 1939, had continued without interruption. He cited this as proof that Thoroughbred racing is a form of entertainment that bolsters public morale in wartime. But Strub's arguments fell on deaf ears. The sticking point was the large crowds, which the federal government had banned up and down the West Coast. The same fate befell Del Mar and Hollywood Park. Only Bay Meadows in San Mateo, twenty miles south of San Francisco, escaped the ban. There, track director Bill Kyne, an astute politician, managed to convince the War Department to allow his track to remain open, but at a price. Bay Meadows had to fork over 92 percent of its profits to the war effort for the duration of the conflict.

Kyne's efforts ensured that at least some Los Angeles–based horses would remain in California, but the big stables owned by the likes of the Vanderbilts and the Whitneys immediately sent their Southern California contingents back to the East Coast, a move that didn't bode well for post-war racing in the state. In the meantime, Santa Anita was turned into a clearinghouse for Japanese Americans on their way to more permanent detention camps throughout the West. As many as 20,000 Americans of Japanese descent passed through the racetrack grounds—euphemistically renamed the Santa Anita Assembly Center—from March 30 to October 27, 1942. At that time, the track became Camp Santa Anita and was used as a training ground by the US Army. Among the grunts was Strub's son, Robert.

With thousands of people camped out at Santa Anita—first the Japanese and then the soldiers—one might wonder about the government's edict banning large crowds on the West Coast, but hindsight is largely a game of political one-upmanship that results in nothing but Pyrrhic victories. Track officials didn't complain—at least not publicly. Strub promised complete cooperation with the US Army, and Hollywood chimed in. Bing Crosby led a steady stream of entertainers to Camp Santa Anita. He appeared with his new "Road" partner Bob Hope, who brought along Kate Smith, Red Skelton, Phil Silvers, and a bevy of long-legged beauties possessed of a certain talent sure to impress the homesick soldiers. Strub's former San Francisco Seals star and current Yankee Clipper Joe DiMaggio even showed up to play in an exhibition game against a team of camp all-stars.

Early in 1942 Hal Roach joined the army. On July 14 he was named a major in the US Signal Corps, but at age fifty, he never left his studio; he merely changed his perspective. The Signal Corps was in charge of all official armed services films and communications. Fort Roach, as it was known during the war, was leased to the US Army Air Corps and, as the First Motion Picture Unit, churned out more than 400 morale, propaganda, and training films, many of the latter filmed at Camp Santa Anita. When the war ended, so did Roach's involvement with racing. Charles Strub became president of the track, a position he held until his death in 1959.

After the war, Santa Anita entered the most prosperous period of its colorful history. Once the threat of a Japanese invasion had evaporated, the track was returned to Strub and company on September 9, 1944, and they got the go-ahead for a winter meeting set to begin on December 30, 1944. The last recruits had left Camp Santa Anita, and the government had granted the racetrack $1.5 million for improvements in thanks for its wartime use of the facility. But then came the Battle of the Bulge. With American forces on the run in Belgium, a siege mentality briefly held sway in Washington, and the winter meeting was canceled. A nervous James Byrnes, the director of war mobilization and reconversion, urged that all horse racing in the country should cease by January 3, but cooler heads ultimately prevailed.

After V-E Day on May 9, Santa Anita got the green light for a thirty-five-day spring meeting, a move the shrewd Strub had anticipated. A week later, on May 15, the track reopened. Californians flocked to the renovated facility in celebration of the war's end. On Memorial Day, a record 76,649 spilled out of the grandstand and onto the track apron, the backstretch, and the infield. By closing day on the Fourth of July, when 60,127 fans showed up, the spring meeting had established an astonishing average daily attendance of 35,247. Victory is sweet, indeed. In 1946 the Treasury Department listed Strub as the fourth highest paid executive in the nation, with an income of $396,901.[13]

And stock in Santa Anita was booming. An original share purchased in 1933 for $5,000 was valued at $75,000 in 1946. Darryl F. Zanuck, who had declined to invest in the racetrack, was probably kicking himself. But at least he still had his day job.

Hollywood at Santa Anita

More motion pictures have been made at Santa Anita than at any other racetrack in the world, and it is easy to see why. The beauty of the Art Deco facility with the San Gabriel Mountains as a backdrop, the track's proximity to Hollywood, and Hollywood's passion for racing combined to make Santa Anita the go-to spot for filmmaking. In the 1930s alone, Hollywood made nearly sixty horse racing movies, many of them with key scenes filmed at Santa Anita.

The paint was hardly dry on the backstretch barns when Will Rogers sidled out to Arcadia to shoot scenes for *In Old Kentucky* in 1935. In 1936 Warner Oland, the first onscreen Charlie Chan, was on hand for *Charlie Chan at the Race Track,* a movie that includes a detailed analysis of the track's new Teletimer system. That same year, sophisticates William Powell and Jean Arthur solved the murder of a jockey in the shadow of the finish line in *The Ex–Mrs. Bradford.* MGM headman Louis B. Mayer, then in the process of assembling one of the most powerful racing stables in the country, sent the Marx Brothers to Santa Anita to film scenes for *A Day at the Races* in 1937, the same year Mickey Rooney, Hollywood's favorite cinematic jockey, could be seen larking about in *Thoroughbreds Don't Cry.* A year later, Rooney teamed with Wallace Beery in *Stablemates,* shooting key scenes at Santa Anita. And the track served as the set for portions of *Straight, Place, and Show,* with the whacky teaming of Ethel Merman and the Ritz Brothers.

Horse racing became such an integral part of Hollywood culture that directors began to use racetracks in pictures that weren't about

Table 1. Selected Racing Films from the 1930s

Film	Year	Studio
Broadway Bill	1934	Columbia
Unwelcome Stranger	1935	Columbia
Sporting Blood	1931	MGM
Broadway Melody of 1938	1937	MGM
A Day at the Races	1937	MGM
Saratoga	1937	MGM
Thoroughbreds Don't Cry	1937	MGM
Stablemates	1938	MGM
From Hell to Heaven	1933	Paramount
The Lemon Drop Kid	1934	Paramount
Sing You Sinners	1938	Paramount
The Lady's from Kentucky	1939	Paramount
Million Dollar Legs	1939	Paramount
Racing Luck	1935	Republic
The Gentleman from Louisiana	1936	Republic
Fighting Thoroughbreds	1939	Republic
Men of Chance	1931	RKO Radio
Sweepstakes	1931	RKO Pathé
Hot Tip	1935	RKO Radio
The Ex–Mrs. Bradford	1936	RKO Radio
Racing Lady	1937	RKO Radio
You Can't Buy Luck	1937	RKO Radio
The Day the Bookies Wept	1939	RKO Radio
Two Thoroughbreds	1939	RKO Radio
Call It Luck	1934	Fox Films
In Old Kentucky	1935	Fox Films
Charlie Chan at the Race Track	1936	20th Century Fox
Kentucky	1938	20th Century Fox
Speed to Burn	1938	20th Century Fox
Straight, Place, and Show	1938	20th Century Fox
Big Boy	1930	Warner Bros.
Down the Stretch	1936	Warner Bros.
Three Men on a Horse	1936	Warner Bros.
Wine, Women and Horses	1937	Warner Bros.
Going Places	1938	Warner Bros.
Little Miss Thoroughbred	1938	Warner Bros.
Torchy Gets Her Man	1938	Warner Bros.

Pride of the Bluegrass	1939	Warner Bros.
Sweepstakes Winner	1939	Warner Bros.
King of the Turf	1939	United Artists
Fast Companions	1932	Universal
Don't Bet on Love	1933	Universal
The Big Race	1934	Universal
Breezing Home	1937	Universal

racing per se. Ernst Lubitsch, that most European of Hollywood directors, used Santa Anita as a stand-in for Paris's elegant Longchamp in his 1937 Marlene Dietrich romance *Angel,* even though Longchamp is a turf course and Santa Anita had only dirt racing at the time. William Wellman filmed Janet Gaynor and Frederic March at the track in the first screen version of *A Star Is Born.*

Racing and Hollywood had formed a mutual admiration society that would last throughout Hollywood's Golden Age. The input of people like Hal Roach and Bing Crosby had been integral in making Santa Anita the brightest new star in the racing galaxy. It was becoming evident that a single wintertime meeting at Santa Anita had merely whet the region's craving for Thoroughbred action. So when state racing officials wanted to provide California horseplayers with year-round opportunities to deposit their money at pari-mutuel windows, Hollywood stepped up to the plate with plans for two new racetracks: Del Mar and Hollywood Park.

3

Del Mar

Bing Crosby and Where the Turf Meets the Surf

> I don't see how I can tell my story without bringing in my passion for horseflesh.
>
> *Bing Crosby*

The Road to Del Mar

The creation of Santa Anita Park in 1934 fulfilled a long-standing need for a professional sport in Los Angeles, but it left new racing fans hungry for more. A mere two months of wintertime racing per year at the new track wasn't enough. Hollywood played an integral role in the development of Santa Anita, but Tinseltown's main contribution was the presence of movie stars and moguls in the clubhouse boxes.

Santa Anita's potential had not gone unnoticed in the film community; nor had it been ignored in Kentucky and New York. But for racing to be genuinely successful in Southern California and challenge the eastern racing elite, it would have to run on a year-round basis; otherwise, it risked becoming a seasonal, provincial pastime. Bing Crosby would step up and fill the gap opened by the founders of Santa Anita out in the San Gabriel Valley.

Crosby did not enter this world with horse racing in his veins. He was born in 1903 into a devoutly Catholic family in Tacoma, Washington, far removed from the hardboot life on the Churchill Downs backstretch or the exclusive box seats at Belmont and Saratoga. But the son of Harry and Catherine Crosby possessed a predilection for sports that would ultimately lead him to the track, where he would become one of America's leading horse racing personalities.

Long before he ever crooned lazily and lovingly into a microphone, and even longer before he became the founding father of Del Mar Racecourse, Bing Crosby had shown a facility for almost any sport he tried. Baseball, football, and basketball came naturally to him, and he played all three at Gonzaga High School in Spokane. At Gonzaga University he played second base for the baseball team but soon realized that he was just too small and too slow for football and basketball, so he gravitated toward tennis, where the long breaks between sets enabled him to enhance his considerable social skills.

After leaving Gonzaga during his senior year to pursue a singing career, Crosby discovered the pleasures of golf. He developed a lifelong love affair with the game after playing a few rounds with fellow cast members from his first film, *The King of Jazz,* at Hollywood's Lakeside Golf Club in 1930. Perhaps it was the dual nature of golf that appealed to him. Though a highly competitive sport, it can also serve as a social outing where friends can be made and business conducted before, during, and after a round of eighteen holes played at a leisurely pace, especially for those with a laid-back nature like Crosby's.

Bing took it easy in almost all aspects of his storied career, so horse racing—one part equine sport, one part gambling opportunity, and one part social occasion—was right up his alley. He took to it just as he took to hunting and fishing, sports where patience and good conversation fill in the time between sporadic bouts of excitement, traits for which horse racing is justly renowned.

During the time Crosby was fronting for the Paul Whiteman Orchestra, his buddies in the band got him interested in making the occasional excursion to Tijuana for the races at Agua Caliente. The 260-mile round-trip from Los Angeles was necessary for any lover of horseflesh or any gambler who wanted to make a legal bet while experiencing the ambience of a racetrack. "With the coming of fame, we became regular callers at Agua Caliente," Bing recalled. "Since we had Sunday and Monday off, we'd go there occasionally for the weekend. What with driving and playing roulette, golf, and the races and belting a little tequila around, come Tuesday, when I stood or swayed in front of the microphone, my pipes were shot."[1]

Even for those who are only $2 bettors, racing is a game that requires a little extra cash, and by the early 1930s, Crosby was making plenty of money as a recording artist, a radio and nightclub performer, and a movie star. Weekend jaunts to Agua Caliente thus became more frequent, climaxing in a big bash on March 20, 1932. That was the day the great Australian champion Phar Lap made his North American debut in the

Agua Caliente Handicap. Bing was one of the 23,000 at the track for what promised to be the racing event of the year. They were not disappointed. Running on a dirt track for the first time and carrying a high weight of 129 pounds, Phar Lap won by a handy two lengths while setting a new track record for 1¼ miles.

With his appetite for horse racing properly honed, Crosby invested $10,000 in Santa Anita to guarantee himself a lifetime box on the finish line. He was there when the new track opened on Christmas Day 1934. After enjoying the very secular Yuletide pleasures of the track, Bing switched to sacred mode that evening and performed "Silent Night" and "Adeste Fideles" on his Kraft Music Hall radio program. He would attend virtually every day of the winter meeting at Santa Anita, playing the horses and entertaining everyone who stopped by his box to say hello.

By 1935, Bing Crosby had become a household name. His number-one songs included "My Blue Heaven," "Ol' Man River," "Dinah," "It's Easy to Remember (but oh so Hard to Forget)," and the Depression anthem "Brother, Can You Spare a Dime?" He had already made fifteen films, among them *We're Not Dressing,* with Carole Lombard and Burns and Allen, and *Mississippi,* in which he had the unenviable task of trying to steal scenes from his racing and golfing pal W. C. Fields. As a result of all this success, he had money to burn.

Racing aficionados with large cash reserves frequently aspire to bigger things. Some, rather than plunking down $100 on a nag they have no emotional involvement with, decide to buy a horse or two (or three or four). Bing was no different. Spending as much time as he did in the Santa Anita clubhouse, he was bound to meet an array of professional horse people. One of them was Jock Whitney, the proprietor of Greentree Stables, one of the leading racing operations in the country.

Whitney sold Crosby his first horse. Saddled with the discouraging name of Zombie, he was, according to his greenhorn owner, "a steed of peerless lineage and dubious ability." Unfazed, Crosby registered his racing silks (blue with gold polka dots, blue sleeves with gold chevron, blue and gold quartered cap) with the Jockey Club, taking his color cues from his first radio theme song, "Where the Blue of the Night Meets the Gold of the Day." He then sent Zombie to be trained by fellow Washingtonian Albert Johnson, but the poor creature never broke his maiden. After two years of trying, he managed nothing better than a pair of third-place finishes.[2]

Crosby knew what he was doing when he hired Johnson as trainer. He had been one of America's preeminent jockeys during the Roaring Twenties, when horses like Man o' War, Black Gold, Zev, and Reigh Count roamed the range. He competed against legendary riders Earl Sande, Charlie Kurtsinger, and Laverne Fator. Johnson won four Triple Crown races himself: two Kentucky Derbies, in 1922 aboard Morvich and in 1926 on Bubbling Over, and two Belmont Stakes, on American Flag in 1924 and the following year aboard Crusader. He was also the regular rider of the multiple champion Exterminator in the latter stages of the great handicapper's career. Difficulty making weight sent Johnson to France in 1930, where he had a brief, unsuccessful stint as a jump-race rider. Back in America, he attempted to establish himself as a trainer. But like many ex-jockeys seeking to renew their racing fortunes, Johnson had little luck attracting clients, until Crosby sent him Zombie.

Through Johnson's racing's connections, Crosby's stable soon numbered twenty-one Thoroughbreds of varying degrees of ability, most of them gravitating toward the bottom of the talent pool. Then, as now, buying a racehorse involved considerable expense. "It was a pure gamble," Bing said of his first foray into the high-stakes world of Thoroughbred speculation. "Heavy financial outlay doesn't necessarily produce winners."[3] But Crosby persisted. In fact, he would soon expand his budding Thoroughbred empire into Argentina, even as he began to draw up plans for Del Mar.

The year 1934 was pivotal for Crosby as a recording artist. He parted company with Brunswick Records, for which he had recorded a dozen number-one hits, and signed with Decca. At the same time, Bing and his wife, ex–chorus girl Dixie Lee, had fallen in love with a piece of property north of San Diego called Rancho Santa Fe, a 97-acre tract that the couple would develop into a Thoroughbred breeding farm complete with a 200-year-old hacienda large enough to accommodate their fast-growing, all-boy brood. "I was genuinely trying to improve the breed of California racing," Crosby said of his budding Thoroughbred operation. That was a tall order, given the lack of racing opportunities in the state and the overpowering dominance of the Kentucky breeding industry.[4]

Rancho Santa Fe became the first of two farms associated with Binglin Stable, which Bing formed in partnership with Lindsay "Lin" Howard. Son of prominent California horseman Charles Howard (who would rise to national fame as the owner of Seabiscuit), Lin was an ace polo player on the California circuit. His accomplishments in that elegant but rough-and-tumble sport brought him to the attention of the Argentines, long regarded as polo's international masters. Lin invited Bing to accompany him on a trip to Buenos Aires, where the polo-playing community sits at the right hand of the racing and breeding communities under the auspices of the all-powerful Argentine Jockey Club. On an excursion through Thoroughbred country north of the city, they took advantage of an opportunity to buy a fallow piece of ranchland that they named Caballeriza Binglin Stock Farm. From there, they began to buy Argentine-bred Thoroughbreds, which are known throughout the world for their stamina and toughness, as well as their ability to run on any kind of track, be it turf or dirt, firm or soft, fast or muddy. If racetrack surfaces were made of broken glass, Argentine-breds would rule the roost.

A second American farm—this one officially named Binglin Stable—was established in Moorpark in Ventura County, about fifty miles up the coast from Los Angeles. Rancho Santa Fe would be Binglin's breeding center, where stallions and mares were mated and foals were born, while the Moorpark operation would be the place where yearlings were broken, as well as providing an off-season respite for horses-in-training. Crosby was following the formula established in Kentucky by the nation's most powerful racing and breeding families, the Whitneys and the Vanderbilts.

Starting a breeding and racing operation on a scale like Binglin might be a full-time task for lesser mortals, but Bing Crosby had even bigger ideas. Even as his new stables were being built, he was taking the first steps in the development of a new racetrack in Del Mar, not far from his home at Rancho Santa Fe.

As early as 1880, horse races had been held on the beach near Del Mar as part of the San Diego County Fair, in imitation of the strand meetings that were so popular in England and Ireland. In 1882, with the Southern California real estate market on the cusp of a boom, a New York land speculator named Jacob Shell Taylor bought a 338-acre strip of California coastline. It was a smart move, as the California Southern Railroad was about to build a rail line between Los Angeles and San Diego. Taylor was particularly excited about a bit of property tucked away behind a natural cove on the oceanfront. He called it Del Mar, Spanish for "by the sea," and began hawking 7,000-square-foot plots of land. The housing development would eventually flounder, a victim of Taylor's speculative scheming. The town of Del Mar as we know it today actually came into being in 1905, when Harry Huntingdon (of Huntingdon Art Gallery fame) turned the place into a seaside winter resort for the well-heeled.

By 1933, the town fathers had developed a keen desire to attract the San Diego County Fair to Del Mar. They revived the long-defunct 22nd District Agricultural Association, an organization meant to promote all things related to farming in the region, including horse racing, but a startling lack of funds stopped their efforts cold. The project seemed doomed, when suddenly the good fortunes provided by the horse racing industry intervened.

The legalization of pari-mutuel wagering in California in 1933 paved the way for the opening of Santa Anita and the Bay Meadows Racetrack, as well as the reopening of Tanforan near San Francisco. With a steady source of revenue provided by betting, the state of California found itself in a position to be generous. In 1935 it granted the 22nd District the money it needed to buy land in Del Mar for its fair. A year later, Franklin Roosevelt's New Deal got into the act. The Works Progress Administration (WPA) granted the 22nd District $500,666 for the construction of fairground facilities.

With that, the new Del Mar Fairgrounds was off to the races. The problem was, there were no races to bet on. The first fair in October 1936 conducted some nonbetting harness and quarter horse contests, but without the vigorish provided by wagering, they proved unpopular. What was needed was the frisson produced by the clash of top-class Thoroughbreds trained by seasoned professionals and ridden by first-rate jockeys.

Enter Bill Quigley, a local businessman and former all-American fullback at the University of Pennsylvania. Quigley had become so enamored of the climate and culture of Southern California when playing in the 1917 Rose Bowl that he eventually moved to La Jolla. His interest in racing led to a position as a part-time steward at Santa Anita. Quigley liked the idea of racing at the Del Mar Fair. The property was just a stone's throw from the Pacific Ocean, where the cool sea breezes would provide a unique atmosphere in American racing. He also knew that his new neighbor at Rancho Santa Fe, Bing Crosby, was a regular customer at Santa Anita and that Bing was in the process of building a racing stable. Quigley found an attentive listener in Crosby, who was gung-ho about all things equine. Bing collected promises of cooperation from a number of his Hollywood friends and associates, and on May 6, 1936, the first board meeting of the newly formed Del Mar Turf Club was called to order at Warner Bros. studios in Burbank. Crosby was unanimously elected president. His good friend Pat O'Brien, star of *American Madness, Laughter in Hell, Bombshell,* and *Angels with Dirty Faces,* was one of Warner's top actors and became vice president. Bing's older brother Everett was appointed secretary-treasurer, while inveterate horseplayer Oliver Hardy and Lloyd Bacon, who had just directed O'Brien in the musical comedy *In Caliente,* were named to the board of directors.

Santa Anita had become a going concern by 1936, so Hollywood types were eager to board the Del Mar express for a piece of the action, especially with the charismatic Crosby at the helm. In short order, the Del Mar Turf Club's executive committee attracted the close-mouthed Gary Cooper as well as the big-mouthed Joe E. Brown. Hardy enticed Leo McCarey, his director in the classic Laurel and Hardy silent *Big Business* and the horsey comedy *Wrong Again,* onto the committee, but McCarey, a bit skittish about the short-term viability of the project, soon dropped out. He was quickly replaced by even bigger names: Clark Gable and George Raft. Major league horseman Charles Howard added racing gravitas to the committee, as did his son Lin, Crosby's Binglin partner. Quigley, the instigator of it all, was named general manager.

As handshakes and smiles were bandied about, it all sounded too good to be true—and in fact, it was. The Depression was still raging, and even though Hollywood wasn't hit nearly as hard as America's manufacturing and financial sectors, seed money for something as seemingly frivolous as a racetrack wasn't easy to come by. And then the WPA withdrew its support. Even the businessmen and politicians who were backing the Del Mar Turf Club were having a tough time raising cash. A stock venture starting at $100 per share failed to take off. The idea of a new racetrack sounded good to prospective investors, but many, like McCarey, were scared off because Southern California had yet to prove itself as a summer resort, and Del Mar planned to race in July and August, augmenting Santa Anita's winter season. There was also concern about the distance— seventy-five miles—between the new track and Los Angeles, the region's most highly populated area and the place where all of Hollywood's high rollers and most of Santa Anita's patrons resided.

Crosby, however, never flinched. He worked ceaselessly throughout 1936 to promote the financing of Del Mar, even as he was busy recording yet another number-one hit, "Pennies from Heaven," which was featured in the film of the same name. That year, he also starred in *Anything Goes* and *Rhythm on the Range*. On December 8 his efforts began to pay off when the Del Mar Turf Club signed a ten-year lease with the 22nd District for $100,000. Work on the grandstand began. And then everything ground to a halt again. There was simply no more money to be had. And once again, Crosby—with considerable help from O'Brien—came to the rescue. The two of them did what men in their position are supposed to do. They took the bull by the horns and came up with the money— virtually out of their own pockets—by obtaining a combined $600,000 in interest-free loans against their life insurance policies.[5]

Del Mar Racecourse would see the light of day after all. The California Horse Racing Board (CHRB) awarded the new track twenty-two days of racing to be conducted from July 3 to July 31. San Diego architects Sam Hamill and Herbert Louis Jackson reignited plans for their Spanish Mission grandstand. The work proceeded at a frantic pace as opening day loomed on the horizon. Hamill's idea was to replicate the spirit of the Spaniards who had colonized California, the rancheros and the Franciscan monks who had built a string of missions from San Diego to San Francisco. To that end, he and Jackson succeeded admirably, even though they barely crossed the finish line in time.

The paint was hardly dry on some of the walls when Del Mar opened for its first day of racing. Many of the smaller outer buildings at the facility weren't finished yet, but as everyone in the entertainment business knows, the show must go on.

The Curtain Rises

Del Mar Racecourse opened for business on Saturday, July 3, 1937, with Crosby himself manning the main gate. The first lucky patron through the turnstiles was a wide-eyed Mrs. W. R. Richardson. Newsreel cameras whirred like crazy as Bing handed her a ticket and she promenaded toward the grandstand, the first of about 15,000 people who came to Del Mar to see what all the excitement was about.

Opening day turned out to be memorable in more ways than one. The first race had been scheduled to go off at 2:00 p.m. but was delayed for twenty-four minutes because a special "express" train from Los Angeles carrying racegoers and some of the horses that were scheduled to run in later races got bogged down en route. The crowd, already gathered in the grandstand and growing more impatient by the minute, roared with relief when the train finally arrived. As the last of the revelers emerged from the train's bar car, the final obstacle to Del Mar Racecourse had been cleared.

Crosby stepped to the microphone and announced: "We hope you all enjoy the meeting and have a measure of success at the payoff windows." Meanwhile, he had exchanged his ticket seller's uniform for more traditional summertime garb: a dapper blue blazer, white slacks, bow tie, wingtip shoes, and boater. He wanted to look his best because he had a horse with a very good chance in the first race.[6]

High Strike, a two-year-old gelding fully equipped with blinkers and bandages on both front ankles, hardly looked the part of a winner, but he was being touted by clock-watchers at morning workouts as one of the more promising horses in the Binglin corner of Albert Johnson's stable. Word was out that he might be a good one, so the smart guys were getting down on him. The novices chimed in as well, figuring that a Crosby-owned winner in the first race run at the Crosby-financed track might be worth a stab. High Strike went off as the 3.10–1 second choice. Jockey Jackie Burrill busted him out of the gate on top in his five-furlong maiden contest and never looked back. At the finish line, High Strike had a comfortable two lengths on the runner-up. Naturally, Crosby and Johnson were all smiles. Bing, a betting man, had almost certainly put a few dollars on his horse to win, but there were the usual cynics who carped that the fix was in. They probably hadn't bet on High Strike.

High Strike would ultimately prove that his performance that day was an honest one, and it set him on the road to bigger things. Later in the inaugural Del Mar meeting, he would win the Chula Vista Handicap. As a three-year-old he would confirm his high standing by taking the Oceanside Handicap and the Laguna Beach Handicap, both at Del Mar. A year later, he would find the Del Mar winner's circle one last time in the Long Beach Handicap.[7]

With a zephyr blowing sweetly off the Pacific on a cloudless afternoon, Crosby and associates struck it first-time lucky. The atmosphere at the new track was electric. Bing had persuaded some of Hollywood's brightest stars to make the trek south. Adding to the racy atmosphere were Barbara Stanwyck and Robert Taylor. The couple had fallen in love earlier in the year while costarring in W. S. Van Dyke's *His Brother's Wife* and would be married in 1939. Oliver Hardy served as the day's honorary steward, a nominal position that left him plenty of time to study the racing form. Bette Davis and perennial cinematic sidekick Una Merkel shared a table in the clubhouse restaurant, and Bing himself mingled with the crowd before heading up to the radio booth high atop the grandstand.

Radio was always dear to Crosby's heart. He is one of the few people to have three stars on Hollywood Boulevard's Walk of Fame: one for film, one for recording, and one for radio. So it was only natural that at the height of the Radio Age he should employ the medium to bring Del Mar to the public's attention. Bing called the fourth race as it was broadcast over the NBC radio network, and he and O'Brien engaged in some good-natured patter over the loudspeaker. They had reason to be in a chipper mood. The crowd of 15,000 would wager $183,015 on the eight races run on opening day. An average of barely $12 per person might not sound like much, but $12 in 1937 was the equivalent of at least $200 in today's money—a per capita average that any racetrack in the country would die for.

After Grey Count prevailed in the Inaugural Handicap, Barbara Stanwyck presented the winning trophy to Texas oilman and cattle rancher Buddy Fogelson, who would later wed Greer Garson of *Mrs. Miniver* fame. Following the victory of Clean Out in the featured San Diego Handicap, many in the throng who had been cleaned out at the pari-mutuel windows headed for the exit, but a substantial number stayed behind for an evening program of entertainment that promised to be every bit as exciting as the races themselves—and a good deal less expensive.

After a brief respite to allow the performers and the audience to refresh themselves at the bar, Crosby again took to the microphone as host of the evening's revelries, which continued until the early-morning hours of the Fourth of July. Bing's crooning and the antics of guest stars that included vaudeville legends Joe Frisco and Jimmy Durante proved so captivating that the show became a regular Saturday feature. Red Skelton told jokes. Durante climaxed his manic routine by smashing his piano to pieces (providing rock stars Jimi Hendrix and the Who with a precedent for their own destructive antics). And Bob Hope, who was not really enamored of horse racing, showed up to trade good-humored barbs with Bing. "The reason I came to Del Mar was because Bing asked me to," Hope recalled years later, "and when Bing asks, you do it."[8]

Bing's charismatic nature had something to do with it, for sure. The opening-day crowd had so enjoyed themselves that attendance on Del Mar's second day of racing totaled 18,000. But even with the good sport and the weekly Saturday night festival of stars, Del Mar's bubble soon burst.

After the opening weekend glitter had worn off, attendance declined steadily throughout the remainder of the meeting. The average—16,500 after the first two days—dropped to 4,654 by the end of the month. And the average daily handle fell to just $101,104. Del Mar was bleeding money.

See the Sea and the Stars

Fresh ideas were needed to boost the status of the 1938 meeting, which had been moved to August. Charles Howard and the track's marketing team began to tout Del Mar as the "Saratoga of the West," a reference to the historic, highly successful August home of racing in New York. They had a point, even though the quality of racing at Del Mar was not in the same league as that of Saratoga. Since its inception in 1864, Saratoga showcased some of the finest Thoroughbred talent in the world in a bucolic spa town set in the foothills of the beautiful Adirondacks. Just as the New York racing community picked up stakes from Belmont Park for the 150-mile trek to Saratoga in August, it was hoped that the public would see Del Mar as the summer home to which Santa Anita horsemen and horseplayers repaired. Newspapers ads and radio commercials stressed Del Mar's pristine Pacific beaches and the opportunity to rub elbows with some of Hollywood's most glamorous stars.

Crosby got the ball rolling by introducing a theme song summing up the pleasures of a day at Del Mar. Entitled "Where the Turf Meets the Surf," it was written by Bing with a little help from the songwriting team of Jimmy Monaco and Johnny Burke. Monaco had composed "You Made Me Love You (I Didn't Want to Do It)," while Burke had penned the lyrics for the Crosby hits "Pennies from Heaven" and "Swingin' on a Star." Crosby lent his talents to both the music and lyrics:

> There's a smile on every face
> And a winner in each race
> Where the turf meets the surf
> At Del Mar.

Musical tastes have undergone many changes since this little ditty made its debut in 1938, but "Where the Turf Meets the Surf" has remained part of the Del Mar soundscape. To this day, Bing's 1941 recording of the song is played before the first race and after the last race at every Del Mar meeting.

But it takes more than a song and a prayer to make a successful race-track. Crosby and O'Brien worked overtime to attract a glittering lineup of Hollywood personalities. Friday, August 5, 1938, was billed as Motion Picture Day, and every race on the card was named for some aspect of the film industry. The first race was called the Exhibitors Allowance, in honor of the industry's worldwide distribution system. The second race was dubbed, with clear ironic intent, the Actors Maiden, and the third was the Producers Stakes; this was followed by the Screen Writers, the Cameramen, the Stars, and the Directors Stakes. The concluding feature was dubbed the Motion Picture Handicap; its first running at the 1937 meeting had been won by Best Bid, a mare owned by the head of Columbia studios, Harry Cohn.

The inaugural Motion Picture Handicap had been worth a mere $1,000, so Quigley, doing yeoman's work as Del Mar's general manager, tripled the purse to $3,000 in an effort to attract a better class of horse. What set the second Motion Picture Handicap apart were the race's novel conditions. Instead of being limited to horses that had never won a stakes race or three-year-old fillies that had never won two races other than a maiden or a claiming race, the Motion Picture Handicap was restricted to three-year-olds and upward whose owners were directly connected with the motion picture industry.

The prerace paddock resembled the lounge at the Biltmore Hotel on Academy Awards night, with Bing as master of ceremonies. The race was won by a colt named Dogaway who was owned by Robert Riskin, screen-writer for the Frank Capra–directed films *Mr. Deeds Goes to Town, You Can't Take It with You, Meet John Doe,* and *It Happened One Night,* as well as Capra's 1934 racing flick *Broadway Bill.* Second was Claracole, named for owners Clark Gable and Carole Lombard. Third was Joe E. Brown's Murph. Crosby, playing the perfect host, tried to look pleased even though his entry trailed home dead last.[9]

But horses with fancy connections weren't the only attractions Crosby employed to ensure a big crowd at Del Mar that day. Weeks earlier, Bing had convinced his studio, Paramount, to present the premiere of his new movie, *Sing You Sinners,* at Del Mar. Costarring Fred MacMurray and introducing twelve-year-old Donald O'Connor, it featured the three of them soft-shoeing their way through the Hoagy Carmichael–Frank Loesser number "Small Fry" and "I've Got a Pocketful of Dreams" by the team of Monaco and Burke (Bing's collaborators on "Where the Turf

Meets the Surf"). A large screen was set up just past the finish line in front of the clubhouse, where most of the film community had gathered. Though not in the same class as Crosby's more notable films *Going My Way* and *The Country Girl, Sing You Sinners* is a serviceable product in which Bing plays Joe Beebe, a young singer who stakes his career on a cheap horse's ability to win the big race, a theme that would be repeated again and again in racing pictures of the era.

The marketing innovations he introduced at Del Mar were nothing new to Crosby. His show business career was studded with similar capers. In 1938 he became the first major artist to prerecord his radio shows, and he was a pioneer in the development of videotape, working with engineering whiz Jack Mullin on both tape and video players. In 1952 he sold his interest in these products to the 3M Company for a considerable profit.

But Crosby was equally innovative in the racetrack business. By 1936, most American tracks were employing photo-finish cameras to determine the winner when horses crossed the finish line too close together for the stewards to call. These early models, which used a series of trip shutters, proved inaccurate, however. In 1937 Lorenzo del Riccio, a former optical engineer at the New York offices of Paramount Pictures, developed what he called a Photo-Chart camera. Used for the first time at Del Mar's grand opener in 1937, the Photo-Chart became the prototype on which all modern photo-finish equipment is based.

Motion Picture Day created loads of good publicity for Del Mar, but in the end, a racetrack lives and dies by the quality of its horses. Track officials were not neglecting that end of the stick either.

The Great Match

Weeks before Motion Picture Day, Charles Howard, Lin Howard, and Crosby had begun negotiating for a match race between America's darling Seabiscuit and a little-known Argentine-bred horse named Ligaroti. The race was intended to bring Del Mar to the attention of the racing world at large.

The elder Howard owned Seabiscuit, the diminutive, crooked-legged colt who had captured the public's imagination in 1937 by winning eleven stakes races at ten different tracks in five states: Massachusetts, Rhode Island, New York, Maryland, and California. Trained by Tom

Smith, Seabiscuit earned honors as the nation's best handicap horse as a four-year-old. Then, in a five-month stretch spanning his four- and five-year-old seasons, he endured a frustrating three-race losing streak, being defeated by a nose each time. The last loss was in the Santa Anita Handicap, when he spotted the winner 30 pounds. Seabiscuit returned to his winning ways in the Agua Caliente Handicap, this time overcoming the same 30-pound disadvantage. Crosby was at Agua Caliente that day to present the winner's trophy to Del Mar board member Howard. Subsequent victories in the Bay Meadows Handicap and in the prestigious Hollywood Gold Cup established Seabiscuit as the best horse in the country, if not the world. Seabiscuit could write his own ticket, and owner Howard knew it. A savvy businessman who had made his fortune selling cars, Howard was entertaining offers from every major track in the country for Biscuit's coveted presence.

But who was Ligaroti? According to Crosby, Ligaroti's owner, "He just might beat anybody over a distance of ground." Many people took this statement with a grain of salt. Bing was, after all, one of the best self-promoters in show business. He had even cast Ligaroti in the role of the horse that saves the day in *Sing You Sinners*. No-nonsense handicappers, however, understood that Ligaroti was a serious racehorse. Binglin Stable had purchased the horse through Crosby and Lin Howard's Argentine connections. Binglin had already achieved modest success with the Argentine import Sabueso, but Ligaroti promised to be something special. He had won thirteen of his twenty-one starts in South America, including five stakes races in a row in Argentina and Brazil. His biggest victory Stateside had come earlier in the summer at the recently opened Hollywood Park, where he won the American Handicap and broke the fledgling track record for 1⅛ miles by 3⅕ seconds.

But Seabiscuit had already beaten Ligaroti in his most recent outing, when he finished an unlucky fourth in the Hollywood Gold Cup. Bumped while making a move on the backstretch, the Argentine-bred horse fell behind and lost any chance of winning. Gamely, he rallied late in the race and managed to get up to fourth, but he was six and a half lengths behind Seabiscuit at the finish line, despite carrying 15 pounds less than the winner.

So when Lin Howard proposed a match between Ligaroti and Seabiscuit, his father was incredulous at first. Crosby, however, immediately saw the value of bringing the best and most popular horse in America to Del Mar to run against a horse owned by himself and the son of Seabiscuit's owner. It was a pure La-La Land story line that not even the most quixotic Hollywood screenwriter could have dreamed up. Himself a member of Del Mar's board of directors, the elder Howard didn't need too much convincing to see the benefits of a Seabiscuit-Ligaroti match. The father-son and North America–South America angles were played up. In addition, there was the trainer matchup: Seabiscuit was conditioned by Tom Smith, while Ligaroti was under the care of Tom's son, Jimmy, who had joined Albert Johnson as one of Binglin's trainers.

The race was scheduled for Friday, August 12, exactly a week after Del Mar's successful Motion Picture Day. The distance was set at 1⅛ miles, and the race would be worth a winner-take-all $25,000, or fully one-quarter of every dollar Del Mar had allotted for purse money for the entire 1938 season. Seabiscuit would carry 130 pounds, and Ligaroti would tote 115, thus getting the same 15-pound break in the weights he had enjoyed in the Hollywood Gold Cup four weeks earlier.

Post positions were determined by a coin toss. Trainer Tom won and took the rail for Seabiscuit. This was a wise choice, as the inside is generally considered advantageous in a match race, where speed and an early lead often prove decisive. But instead of wearing the customary saddle-cloths bearing the numbers 1 and 2, Seabiscuit and Ligaroti carried the letters A and B, respectively. This was because the CHRB had refused to allow pari-mutuel wagering on the race, citing the Howards' familial relationship. As events unfolded, that ruling had a major impact on the running of the race. Charles and Lin had a side bet of their own, however. Charles wagered $15,000 on Seabiscuit to Lin's $5,000 on Ligaroti. Odds of 3–1 on Ligaroti seemed about right, even considering his weight advantage. Seabiscuit would be ridden by George Woolf, one of the country's leading jockeys, while Ligaroti would have the talented journeyman Spec Richardson in the irons.

The entire nation directed its eyes westward in anticipation of the great match, for in the 1930s, the nation's top racehorses were as popular as its best baseball players and champion boxers. A record crowd of about 22,000 gathered at Del Mar on race day, and every one of them had an opinion. Pat O'Brien had put together a makeshift Ligaroti fan club, and an entire section of the clubhouse was reserved for Ligaroti backers. Banners with the Argentine champion's name bedecked the grandstand, where Gable and Lombard, Spencer Tracy, and Ray Milland were among the revelers. Almost everyone outside of Crosbyland, however, seemed to be rooting for Seabiscuit, who probably would have been the 1–3 favorite if there had been betting on the match. Still, he was the people's sentimental choice.

Crosby was so nervous watching the horses go down to the start that he banged his binoculars against his mouth. Jockeys Woolf and Richardson displayed no such nerves. Indeed, they both entered the starting gate loaded for bear. Taking advantage of his inside draw, Woolf, whose nickname was "Iceman," broke Seabiscuit on top and quickly took a half-length lead, which he maintained through the long, straight run past the stands. Richardson moved Ligaroti alongside the favorite heading into the first turn, with two of the nine furlongs behind them. They raced as a team down the backstretch, and that's when the fireworks began.

Both Woolf and Richardson figured that with no betting on the race, interference from the stewards would be minimal. As the two horses approached the far turn, with about three and a half furlongs to go, Seabiscuit held a lead that wavered between a nose and a head. At that point, Richardson decided to take matters into his own hands—literally. He reached out and grabbed Woolf's right arm. Woolf shook free and slashed his whip at Richardson, who gave as good as he got with his own whip. The struggle continued around the turn, depositing them into the short stretch with Seabiscuit leading by a neck. At the eighth pole, with only a furlong left to run, Ligaroti renewed his effort. With each stride he grew closer and closer to Seabiscuit as Richardson whipped his mount for all he was worth. Woolf was working equally hard on the favorite but was paying much less attention to the whip, perhaps because Richardson still had a tight hold on Woolf's right arm. For a moment it looked as if Ligaroti would prevail, but fifty yards from the line, Richardson stopped whipping his horse. Seabiscuit held on to win by a half-head, or what we would call a nose today.

As soon as he dismounted, Richardson claimed foul against Woolf. Woolf returned the favor by claiming foul on Richardson. Not to be upstaged, the stewards called for an inquiry of their own. In fact, both riders were guilty of flagrant violations of the rules of racing, rules they had both dispensed with shortly after the start. After a long consultation, the stewards, in their discretion, allowed the order of finish to stand but suspended both riders for the remainder of the Del Mar meeting, with a recommendation to the CHRB that they both be banned for the remainder of the year.[10] However, these longer suspensions could not be enforced because the CHRB, having ruled that there would be no wagering on the race, had no jurisdiction over the event. This, ultimately, was why Woolf and Richardson had ridden so roughly. Under normal circumstances, if the CHRB had been involved, both jockeys likely would have ridden a clean race, unwilling to risk a year-long suspension.

Amid all the bad feeling, Dixie Lee Crosby was left to present the winning trophy to Charles Howard as her husband and Howard's son looked on. Bing took the narrow loss with his usual equanimity. "It's no disgrace to be beaten by the world champion," the losing owner said in his most graceful, sportsmanlike manner.[11]

The race didn't take much out of either horse, despite a final time of 1:49 flat, which broke the track record for 1⅛ miles by four seconds. Two weeks later, Ligaroti would redeem himself by winning the San Diego Handicap; however, he banged his leg against the starting gate, sustaining an injury that would eventually lead to his retirement. On November 1 Seabiscuit would take another step on the road to equine immortality by defeating 1937 Triple Crown winner War Admiral in a match race at Pimlico in Maryland.

Crosby didn't lament Ligaroti's defeat for long. He knew full well that the great match had put Del Mar on the map as one of the most important racetracks in the country. The public apparently agreed with him. Attendance for the twenty-five-day 1938 meeting was 161,485, up from 102,388 the previous year. The total betting handle reached $3,920,251, up from $2,224,301 in 1937. But Del Mar still finished in the red in 1938. Seeking to recoup some of his losses, Crosby offered to sell Ligaroti to Louis B. Mayer for $75,000. The head of MGM was in the process of building what would become one of the most powerful racing stables in America, but Mayer wasn't interested in the injured six-year-old and turned Crosby down.

Business at the 1939 meeting was even worse, as the pari-mutuel handle fell a shocking 11.5 percent. It would take the advent of World War II to shake things up at Del Mar.

Del Mar Hits Its Stride

By 1940, more top-class stables were applying for stall space at Del Mar. At the same time, Crosby was nearing the peak of his unprecedented popularity. Bing was one of filmdom's top ten box office attractions in 1937 and 1940, and he would head the list from 1944 to 1948.

During the first seven months of 1940, before the Del Mar season opened in August, Crosby recorded forty-four songs, including the number-one hits "Only Forever" and "Rhythm on the River" (both written by Monaco and Burke), the second of which debuted in the Victor Schertzinger film of the same name. That year, Paramount also introduced the first of the popular Crosby-Hope collaborations, *Road to Singapore.*

Crosby had met Bob Hope in 1932 when they were on the same vaudeville bill at the Capitol Theater in New York, and although their paths crossed frequently over the next few years, they didn't work together again until July 23, 1938, when Hope appeared on Crosby's Kraft Music Hall radio show. Bing invited Bob and his wife Dolores to spend a day at Del Mar on August 6, the day before Motion Picture Day. That evening, after the races, Bing held a backstretch clambake for the stable help and selected guests. One drink led to another, and soon Hope and Crosby were trading witty barbs, to the delight of the crowd, which included Paramount producers William Le Baron and Harlan Thompson. They saw potential in the ad-libbed camaraderie between the ex-vaudevillians, and this eventually led to *Road to Singapore,* which would be followed by lucrative excursions to Zanzibar, Morocco, Utopia, Rio, Bali, and Hong Kong. In all but the last, Dorothy Lamour would tag along in a sarong or some similar mode of dishabille.

The 1940 Del Mar season was a bit more successful financially than its three predecessors. Led by Mickey Rooney, the stars continued to come out in large numbers. The irrepressible former child star turned twenty that year, but he had already made more than forty films, nine of them musicals with Judy Garland. That year also marked the release of *Love Finds Andy Hardy,* the eighth of twelve installments in the remarkably popular series that later prompted Rooney to quip: "I was a thirteen-year-old boy until I was thirty." He behaved like one at Del Mar that summer, donating a large portion of the track's $192,000 daily handle.[12]

Rooney wasn't the only movie star with an apparent gambling problem. Friends and relatives were beginning to worry about Bing Crosby's betting habits at the pari-mutuel windows. When a person spends as much time at racetracks as Bing did, the temptation to bet often and in large amounts is difficult to resist, especially when that person has deep pockets. And Crosby wasn't just a habitué of Del Mar. He still occupied his box at Santa Anita on a regular basis through the winter. With the opening of Hollywood Park in 1938, there was yet another opportunity to spend the day at the track. He was frequently up before dawn to watch his horses work at whichever track they were stabled, hobnobbing with trainers, jockeys, stable hands, and fellow owners. The conversation frequently turned to hot items on that afternoon's card. But this kind of "inside information" can lead some people down the primrose path to penury. Still, with his large and steady income, Crosby was hardly in danger of bankruptcy, no matter how much he wagered on the ponies. "To me, a racetrack is for people who can afford to go there once in a while for an enjoyable afternoon of watching good horseflesh compete and who are reconciled to losing the kind of money they won't miss," he opined.[13]

Bing had always been a gambling man, and his interests in that respect were not limited to the track. In 1934, when Notre Dame's football team made its semiannual trip to play USC in the Los Angeles Coliseum, Bing had booked bets on the Fighting Irish, who were 7-point favorites to defeat the Trojans. That particular gamble turned out to be a winning one, as Notre Dame covered the spread, shutting out USC 14–0.

Some critics blamed Bing's rather dull performance in the 1937 film *Double or Nothing* on his involvement with Del Mar. The next few years saw him devoting even more time to his myriad racing interests. During the summer of 1940, Bing's eldest brother Larry, who doubled as his publicity director, wrote to their brother Ted and expressed his concern: "Bing has put so much money into the Del Mar Racetrack, and gambling on horses, that we are having a time holding him down in order that he will have enough left to pay the Income Tax."[14]

To make matters worse, Bing was having difficulty recouping the large loan he had taken out against his life insurance policy to get Del Mar started, although the 1940 meeting eased his financial situation somewhat. The average daily handle that season grew to $192,075, up from $178,093 two years earlier. In 1941 the thirty-two-day meeting produced new records, with average daily attendance in excess of 7,500 and an average daily handle of $245,393. Del Mar was suddenly flush with cash.

One of the reasons for the upturn was the shipbuilding industry in nearby San Diego. Europe had been at war for nearly two years when the 1941 Del Mar season began, and many local companies were working overtime to supply Great Britain with war materiel. As a result, there was a trickle-down effect from workers' wallets to the track. But the war pointed its ugly head America's way in earnest on December 7, 1941. One of its first American casualties was the Southern California racing industry.

The War Intrudes

With the very real threat of a Japanese attack on the West Coast in the early days of the war, the government took every precaution to prevent a calamity. The US Marine Corps kicked the horses out of Del Mar to install a training base, while Santa Anita became a relocation center for Japanese Americans and Hollywood Park was turned into a storage depot. So racing was canceled at all three tracks. The marines moved out of Del Mar in late 1942, but the track grounds were used for the next two years as a manufacturing plant for B-17 bomber parts. There would be no horse racing in Southern California until 1945.

Crosby took the wartime closing of Del Mar in stride. In fact, he eased himself right into the war effort as an entertainer. His renditions of "The Army Air Corps Song" (better known as "Off We Go into the Wild Blue Yonder"), "Yankee Doodle Dandy," and "The White Cliffs of Dover" were played at military bases throughout America as well as in the European and Pacific theaters, keeping Allied forces in touch with the home front. When the war was over, *Yank*, the US Army's weekly magazine, hailed Crosby as the man who had done the most to lift the morale of American servicemen, although he probably took a backseat in that respect to Betty Grable and Rita Hayworth, both of whom had racing blood in their veins. Bing even had a pacifying effect on the enemy. Germans who were lucky enough to hear his radio shows beamed into the fatherland affectionately nicknamed him "Der Bingle." He sang songs in English and read propaganda messages in German.

On the racing front, Crosby, like the owners of many California stables, headed east. He sent his best horses to be trained in New York, where racing continued without interruption for most of the war. Encouraged by the success of Ligaroti, Binglin Stable continued to import horses from Argentina. One of them, a mare named Barrancosa, was good enough to finish in a dead heat with the champion American filly Vagrancy in the 1942 Beldame Stakes at Belmont. Another, Etolia, won the inaugural running of Hollywood Park's Vanity Handicap in 1940.

The biggest American victory of Crosby's career, however, came at Belmont on Memorial Day 1943, when Don Bingo, an Argentine-bred half-brother to Ligaroti, won the prestigious 1¼-mile Suburban Handicap at odds of 12–1 with Joe Renick aboard. Among the vanquished in the seventeen-horse field were Jock Whitney's 1942 Kentucky Derby winner Shut Out, along with Market Wise and Devil Diver, who would share honors as champion handicap horse that year.

The Suburban had previously been won by champions Whisk Broom, Grey Lag, Crusader, and Equipoise, so Don Bingo (obviously named after his owner) was muscling in on some high-class company, even though he carried a mere 104 pounds. Carrying 9 pounds more four weeks later in Belmont's 1⅛-mile Brooklyn Handicap, Don Bingo couldn't quite reproduce his Suburban form, finishing third behind Devil Diver and Market Wise. On July 5 in the Massachusetts Handicap at Suffolk Downs in Boston, Don Bingo was third again in a race won by Market Wise.

Peace

The war in Europe ended, and Del Mar was back in business in July 1945. The new, improved forty-day meeting actually began more than a month before Japan surrendered, but by that time, any threat of an attack on the Pacific Coast had long since evaporated. On Tuesday, August 14, Pat O'Brien made the announcement that Japan had officially surrendered, and racing was interrupted for a five-minute period of silence. President Truman declared August 15 a national holiday, prompting a throng of 20,324 revelers to turn out at the track. In a joyful and optimistic mood, they crammed a record $958,476 through the betting windows.

On Labor Day, a record 22,402 spectators poured through the turnstiles. The 1945 Del Mar season ultimately attracted record crowds of 342,498 (a daily average of 8,562) and an astonishing handle of $23,846,789 (a daily average of $596,169). America's postwar economic boom would vault horse racing into worldwide prominence that would last for at least thirty-five years.

Del Mar had become so profitable that in January 1946 the track's landlords at the 22nd District were able to repay Crosby and O'Brien their $600,000 loans, yet Bing was restless. War has a way of changing people, and 1945 America was a different place from its prewar days. Bing had also grown weary of running a racetrack. "In the end, Del Mar became a burdensome chore," he said. While the racing industry was booming, Crosby was contemplating more lucrative horizons.[15]

From Del Mar to Pittsburgh

In the summer of 1945 Crosby received an offer from John Galbreath to join him in a new venture: becoming a part owner of the Pittsburgh Pirates. The National League's perennial cellar dwellers had been put on the block by owner Florence Dreyfuss, and Galbreath was looking for minority investors to buy into the team.

Crosby had met Galbreath during his racing travels. Galbreath was the owner of Darby Dan Farm in Ohio, a breeding and racing establishment that would become prominent in international racing circles in the 1960s and 1970s. A lifelong baseball fan, Crosby liked the idea of owning a major league team, even if it was the disreputable Pirates. But there was a hitch. The rules of baseball stated that no owner of a major league team could also be the owner of a betting establishment, including a racetrack. So Bing had a decision to make.

Perhaps the almost nonstop effort required to keep Del Mar profitable had become too much for him. Bill Quigley, Del Mar's hands-on general manager and Bing's close friend, had died in 1943. A new management team had been assembled for the postwar reopening, and winds of change were in the air. On November 3, 1945, Crosby made up his mind. He announced that he was putting his 35 percent share in Del Mar Racecourse up for sale. The transaction was completed on April 17, 1946, when Arnold Grant, a lawyer with offices in New York and Beverly Hills, bought him out for the sum of $481,000.

Crosby's exit signaled a changing of the Del Mar guard, as Pat O'Brien and Charles Howard followed him out the door. Years later, O'Brien seemed to regret his decision. "The closest I ever came to being a millionaire was when Bing and myself and others organized Del Mar Racetrack. The stock became fabulous, but I sold my share to avoid becoming a millionaire." O'Brien, however, maintained his beachfront home in Del Mar and continued to patronize the track.[16]

Crosby vacated the area entirely when he sold Rancho Santa Fe a few weeks later. His deal with Grant, however, included a clause that gave his wife Dixie a seat on Del Mar's board of directors, allowing him to have some input into the track's affairs. Most importantly, the road was clear for Crosby to join Galbreath in the deal to buy the Pittsburgh Pirates. On August 8 the sale was consummated for $2.25 million, with Bing holding a 25 percent interest.

Del Mar's new management team commemorated Bing's contribution to the track by naming a race for him. The Bing Crosby Handicap, a six-furlong stakes race, has become one of the nation's most important sprint contests. He attended its first running on August 10, 1946, and then didn't set foot on the Del Mar grounds for more than thirty years.

Bing's departure from Del Mar didn't mean that he gave up racing entirely. He maintained his interest with Lin Howard in Binglin Stable, although horses as good as Ligaroti, Don Bingo, and High Strike eluded them. Bob Hope, always ready with a good-natured gibe, was forever kidding Bing about the speed (or lack thereof) of his horses. "I was out driving with Bing the other day when we saw an old nag standing in the middle of a field," Hope quipped on Crosby's radio show one night. "'That must be one of yours,' I said. 'It's stopped!'"[17]

Hope took equal delight in reminding Bing that the baseball team he co-owned, the Cleveland Indians, was much better than Crosby's Pittsburgh Pirates. The Indians won the World Series in 1948 and the American League pennant in 1954 as the Pirates struggled to escape the National League cellar. Bing had the last laugh, though, when the Pirates upset the mighty New York Yankees in the 1960 World Series. They racked up another World Series win in 1971. So Crosby's change of investment from racetrack to baseball team was at least satisfying in that regard.

Crosby's fellow Pirate owner, John Galbreath, would have much greater racing success. He seemed to develop a Midas touch when it came to Thoroughbreds. Among the champions he bred and owned at Darby Dan Farm were the undefeated Graustark and Kentucky Derby winners Chateaugay and Proud Clarion. Roberto, named for the Pirates' Hall of Fame outfielder Roberto Clemente, made Galbreath the first man to own both a Kentucky Derby winner and an Epsom Derby winner, when Roberto won that great English classic in 1972. Whenever Galbreath and Crosby got together for a Pirates game, be it at Forbes Field or Three Rivers Stadium in Pittsburgh or at Dodger Stadium in Los Angeles, the conversation was likely to turn to racing.

But for all intents and purposes, Crosby was out of racing. He would dissolve Binglin Stable in 1953 to help pay the inheritance taxes after his wife's death. Throughout the 1950s he was little more than a fan at the racetrack. He would not return to his once beloved Del Mar until 1977, a few months before his death. He would, however, return to racing and near-championship glory in Europe (see chapter 8).

4

Hollywood Park
A Racetrack of Their Own

Hollywood's motion picture tycoons are about to release the greatest
and most colossal epic of their long and interesting careers. A real
feature, a true gigantic, a production without equal, unusual, colorful
and one keenly anticipated by an anxious public.

Colonel Walter Moriarity

The Battle Lines Are Drawn

The hyperbolic and somewhat ironic Colonel Moriarity wasn't talking
about *The Adventures of Robin Hood, Marco Polo,* or *Tom Sawyer,* all of
which were released to the public on a grand scale in 1938. The "colossal
epic" he referred to was none other than Hollywood Park, which had its
much-ballyhooed premiere on June 10 of that year.

The birth had been a long and painful one, racked by greed, political
dissension, backroom scheming, and not a little race hatred. After the
successes of Santa Anita and Del Mar, it was evident that Southern
California could accommodate a third racetrack, one that could fill in the
gap to provide a nearly year-round program of horse racing in the region.
In 1937 Santa Anita had the winter dates from Christmas through April;
Del Mar had the late summer dates. In between lay a three-month period
when there was no racing. Just as the public was sinking its teeth into
what had become Southern California's favorite sporting pastime, there
was suddenly nothing to do. So Jack Warner did something about it.

At the end of the first season of racing at Santa Anita in March 1935,
Bing Crosby had matter-of-factly noted that he, along with many other
owners who stabled their horses in Arcadia, would routinely head upstate
for the spring meeting at Bay Meadows. His observation underscored the
gap in Southern California's racing schedule. Some of the horses shipped
up to Bay Meadows might not return to Del Mar in the summer. This was

an even more crucial issue with the big eastern owners, who cleared their regally bred horses out of Santa Anita as soon as the meeting ended to aim at bigger prizes in the more prestigious races in New York and Kentucky.

Warner anticipated the building of a new track in Los Angeles shortly before the first Santa Anita meeting was over. On March 5, 1935, the formation of the Golden State Jockey Club was announced. Warner, however, kept his name out of the press, putting high-rolling film director Raoul Walsh out front as the club's director. The move was a double-pronged scheme. First, it concealed the intent of the club's heavy hitters lurking in the shadows. Jack and Harry Warner of Warner Bros. and Columbia's Harry Cohn, three of the most powerful producers in Hollywood, were planning to open a new track in direct competition with Santa Anita. Walsh was well known in Hollywood as a Thoroughbred owner, a keen racing fan, and a big gambler. Horses had raced under his name at both Agua Caliente and Santa Anita, and he was frequently seen partying at Santa Anita's exclusive Turf Club. No one questioned the legitimacy of his presence at the head of the new club.

Second, the Warners and Cohn, along with several club members such as directors Alfred E. Green, Mervyn LeRoy, and Anatole Litvak, were Jewish. And they were all bridling over their exclusion from Santa Anita's exclusive Turf Club, which denied Jews membership. Jews could attend the races at Santa Anita, they could race their horses at the track, and they could enjoy the amenities on offer in the clubhouse, which shared the main building with the grandstand, where the impecunious masses watched the races. However, it was in the separate Turf Club building, beyond the finish line, where racing deals, film deals, and business deals in general were made on an almost daily basis.[1] Most of the major studio heads in Hollywood during the first few decades of the fast-growing film industry were Jewish, and it rankled that they should be banned from the hottest social and business scene in California. Jack Warner refused to sit idly by. If Santa Anita wouldn't let him in on the party, he would throw a party of his own.

Showing great resourcefulness, the Golden State Jockey Club had already selected four potential sites for its new racecourse. But the members played their hand close to the vest, keeping the sites a secret to prevent real estate prices from skyrocketing and to keep Charles Strub and Hal Roach over at Santa Anita from interfering with their plans.

On August 5, 1936, in the midst of Del Mar's inaugural season (when the news would receive the greatest word-of-mouth publicity), the Golden State Jockey Club announced that it had changed its name to the Hollywood Turf Club to better reflect its members' interests. It also named Alfred E. Green its new president. In addition to being a Thoroughbred owner, Green was a house director at Warner Bros., with successes like *Disraeli* (1929) starring George Arliss and *Baby Face* (1933) with Barbara Stanwyck to his credit.

Two days later, Warner turned up the heat when Green announced that the Hollywood Turf Club had selected as the site of its new racecourse a 228-acre tract of land centered on the corner of Sawtelle and National Boulevards in West Hollywood, about a mile east of Santa Monica Municipal Airport. It soon became apparent that Jack Warner was calling the shots at the Hollywood Turf Club. It also became known that Warner had enlisted dozens of Hollywood names to back his project. Bing Crosby, who loved all things Thoroughbred, had signed on as a shareholder, along with Warner Baxter, Ralph Bellamy, Joan Blondell, Joe E. Brown, Ronald Colman, Irene Dunne, Georgie Jessel, Al Jolson, and Edward G. Robinson.

Warner was keeping the business in the family. Jolson made Warner Bros. and himself world famous in 1927 when he starred in the first talkie, *The Jazz Singer*. Robinson made his breakthrough to stardom in 1931 with *Little Caesar*, directed by LeRoy; the pair scored again a year later with *Two Seconds*. Baxter starred in Warner Bros.' hit 1933 musical *42nd Street*, followed by Columbia and Cohn's racing film *Broadway Bill*. Colman made the world weep with his closing speech, "It is a far, far better thing I do . . .," in MGM's *A Tale of Two Cities*. And the saucy, wise-cracking Blondell, a key Warner performer if not a star in her own right, made her mark in LeRoy's racing-gambling film *Three Men on a Horse*. Producers Walt Disney, Sam Goldwyn, and Hunt Stromberg and director David Butler (who had already had a handful of winners at Santa Anita) soon joined the fold. The new Hollywood Turf Club even persuaded the previously recalcitrant and very conservative Darryl F. Zanuck, the boss at 20th Century Fox, to come on board.

Things were going smoothly. Warner had gathered a glittering, wealthy, powerful array of Hollywood names on his side, but there was trouble on the horizon. On September 18 Green announced that the Hollywood Turf Club was aiming for a June 15, 1937, opener for the new track, but a few obstacles still had to be cleared. Sadly, the club fell at the first hurdle.

Santa Anita Strikes Back

The Los Angeles Planning Commission duly approved changes to the zoning laws that would allow a racetrack to be built on the Warner group's chosen site. And that was where the Hollywood Turf Club's troubles began. There was an almost immediate outcry from every corner of West Hollywood, and all the noise was negative. Churchmen railed against the incursion of sinful gambling into their parishes. Professors and administrators at UCLA, just two miles up the road, warned of the pernicious influence of horse racing on their innocent young students. Businessmen were aghast, especially Donald Douglas of Santa Monica's Douglas Aircraft Company. He trembled at the thought of his employees losing their hard-earned wages at the pari-mutuel windows. Most convincing were pleas from the directors of a pair of veterans' homes down the block. It would be criminal, they claimed, to tempt the old doughboys to wager their meager government incomes on horse racing.

On October 1 the Hollywood Turf Club backed down. The last thing Jack Warner needed was an onslaught of bad publicity that might snuff the entire project. But in its foresight, the club had selected four potential sites, so Plan B was put into effect. The very next day, the Warner group announced that it would build its new track on 315-acre parcel in Inglewood—a swampy site that had once been a bean field—six miles southeast of its first choice and nearly ten miles south of Hollywood itself. According to Green, construction of the new track, tentatively called Inglewood Park, could begin immediately. Groundbreaking was set for October 23. All the Hollywood Turf Club needed was a green light from the California Horse Racing Board (CHRB), which had to approve its requested racing dates.

But before the month of October ended, the CHRB cried "Whoa!" Led by president Carleton Burke, the CHRB denied the Hollywood Turf Club its requested dates. Now the gloves came off. Jack Warner replaced Green as club president and assumed the role himself. He had been calling the shots for more than a year anyway. It was time to face the CHRB head-on.

Warner and the rest of the Hollywood Turf Club were convinced that Charles Strub, Hal Roach, and Gwynn Wilson at Santa Anita were behind the CHRB's rejection, and they had good reason to think so. Santa Anita had a monopoly on horse racing in the Los Angeles area, as, geographically speaking, Crosby's Del Mar was a San Diego track. Strub and Roach were not about to let another racetrack interfere with their increasingly profitable operation. On April 5 Jack Warner accused the "selfish interests" at Santa Anita of trying to sabotage his group's efforts to open a second track in the Los Angeles area. There was an economic reason behind their opposition to the new track in Inglewood, and, in the eyes of the Hollywood Turf Club, there was a hidden agenda: the desire to keep Jews from having a controlling interest in Los Angeles racing.

The extent to which anti-Semitism played a part in Santa Anita's stonewalling of Hollywood Park is difficult to gauge at this late date, but there are plenty of clues to support the supposition. These include Santa Anita's ban on Jews at its Turf Club, of which CHRB president Burke was a member. Burke was widely regarded as Santa Anita's man at the CHRB. He had already denied two licenses to potential Santa Anita rivals, and there were rumors that he and Strub provoked opposition to Warner's plans to build a new track in West Hollywood. Interestingly, not one member of the CHRB was Jewish.

Roach and Mussolini

Hal Roach, meanwhile, had tipped his political hat in the wrong direction. Even before the Santa Anita–Hollywood Park battle began, the producer of the lovable Our Gang and Laurel and Hardy films, who doubled as president of the Los Angeles Turf Club (Santa Anita), had formed an admiration for Italy's fascist dictator Benito Mussolini, whom Roach described as "the only square politician I've ever seen" (in 1930s slang, "square" meant straight or honest).[2] While Roach was traveling through Italy in 1937, Mussolini invited him to Rome to discuss a business proposition. The result was the formation of Roach and Mussolini, a production company known by the acronym RAM, and a deal to make twelve films at the sprawling, up-to-date facility in Rome called Cinecitta, built by Mussolini as his gift to Italian culture and opened on April 21, 1937. Roach was highly impressed with Cinecitta. It had been modeled after Germany's Studio Babelsberg in Potsdam, where most of the between-the-wars classics by Fritz Lang, F. W. Murnau, and G. W. Pabst were made. But when news of RAM reached Hollywood, rumblings of protest began almost immediately.

How could Roach enter into a deal with a fascist dictator who was Nazi Germany's closest ally? Roach defended himself, stating that he had received assurances from Mussolini that Italy would not apply sanctions against Jews. But Jack and Harry Warner and Louis B. Mayer were incensed. They reminded Roach that Mussolini had already banned many American films from Italian screens and that he had once sarcastically proclaimed that there were more Jews in Hollywood than in Tel Aviv.

Roach went on the defensive. The $6 million deal, he pointed out, was being backed primarily by Italian bankers. Not a single lira had come from the Italian government, although Roach himself had made a relatively small investment in RAM. The plan, he said, was to incorporate Italian talent and American technique. Four of the twelve films would be relatively big-budget projects intended for international release; the other eight would be for Italian release only, starting with a production of Giuseppe Verdi's opera *Rigoletto,* with a skimpy budget of just $40,000.

On September 25, 1937, while the Hollywood Turf Club's bid to build a racetrack in West Hollywood was being considered by the CHRB, Roach welcomed Mussolini's son Vittorio to his studio in Culver City. The movie-mad Vittorio, already an adviser to his father, was photographed with Spanky and Alfalfa of Our Gang, with cute little Darla shaking his hand. The purpose of Vittorio's visit was ostensibly to learn American production techniques. Two days after Vittorio's arrival, Roach threw a lavish twenty-first birthday party for the son of the dictator.

The howls of protest and warning from Hollywood and elsewhere increased; they were especially loud from Hollywood's Far Left Anti-Nazi League. Roach's attempts to defend himself became clumsier and clumsier. "Il Duce is a pacifist," he proclaimed, seeming to forget Italy's 1935 invasion of Ethiopia and the downfall of Addis Ababa on June 5, 1936. Roach, whose maverick qualities had always been an asset in his film and racing endeavors, put his foot further into his mouth when, on October 5, he told syndicated Hollywood columnist Sheilah Graham, "If one day Mussolini adopted Hitler's racial policy, a man close to him (meaning Roach himself) could be of great use. I'm convinced that my association with Mussolini is the finest thing that could have happened for the Jews. If they're smart, they'll stop antagonizing Mussolini."[3]

But RAM fell apart at the seams in mid-October when an Italian businessman, Dr. Renato Senise, claimed that he had brokered the deal between Roach and Mussolini but had been denied a share of the spoils. Senise sued Roach and MGM, with which the Roach studio had a distribution deal. This was exceedingly embarrassing to Mayer, but the top man at MGM never lost his cool. MGM executives negotiated a deal that allowed Roach to back out of RAM by paying Vittorio Mussolini 500,000 lira, or a mere $26,000.

Roach was off the hook, although the contretemps eventually cost him his distribution deal with MGM, which later took over production of both the Our Gang and the Laurel and Hardy pictures. However, Roach never apologized for his egregious moral error. Although he showed true patriotic zeal by turning his studio into Camp Roach during the war, Roach proudly displayed a signed portrait of Mussolini in his living room for the rest of his life.

Leopards don't change their spots, politics makes strange bedfellows, and anti-Semitism in the 1930s and 1940s was a gentleman's game, as illustrated by Elia Kazan's 1947 film *Gentleman's Agreement,* produced, ironically, by 20th Century Fox's Darryl F. Zanuck, the only non-Jew in charge of one of the Big Five Hollywood studios. Ultimately, Roach's flirtation with fascism lends credence to the belief that Santa Anita's management was anti-Semitic. Throughout the affair, no member of Santa Anita's Los Angeles Turf Club publicly criticized Roach for his dealings with the Mussolinis.

Hollywood Hits the Homestretch

The Mussolini business earned the Hollywood Turf Club a lot of sympathy in its fight with Santa Anita and the California Horse Racing Board. Several new shareholders came on board, including budding Thoroughbred owner Don Ameche; gambling-mad Chico Marx, who had scored big with his brothers in *A Day at the Races;* Thoroughbred breeder Barbara Stanwyck; and Lois Pantages, owner of Hollywood Boulevard's Pantages Theatre. Even Oliver Hardy, a bit of a gambler himself, crossed over from the Santa Anita side to buy shares in the Hollywood Park venture.

More importantly, the Hollywood Turf Club found strong new allies in the business and political communities. They included Walter McCarty, a Beverly Hills real estate developer and owner of the Beverly Hills Hotel, and Earl Gilmore, owner of the Hollywood Stars minor league baseball team and founder of the Farmers Market. Meanwhile, Carlton Burke defended his rejection of the Hollywood Turf Club's request by claiming that he was protecting the Los Angeles area from too much racing, but he was losing ground.

The Hollywood Turf Club used its influence to get a hearing before the state legislature in Sacramento, where Charles Strub himself was called to testify. Strub claimed that Santa Anita had never done anything to *formally* block a new Los Angeles racetrack. Informally, Santa Anita seemed to be interfering everywhere. Moreover, Strub, a San Franciscan, was overseeing the Bay Area's two tracks, Bay Meadows and Tanforan, which had been prospering for three years in a region with less than half the population of Los Angeles.

In late 1937 the Assembly Audit Committee in Sacramento ruled that the CHRB had acted improperly in denying the Hollywood Turf Club's request for racing dates. Things seemed to be rolling in the Warner group's direction, but it would take a racetrack incident to break the political logjam.

Norman Church, a prominent San Jose businessman who owned a string of horses in training at Santa Anita, was firmly on the side of the Hollywood Turf Club. He was outspoken in defending the Warner group against the unjust attacks by Strub and Burke, earning the ire of the powers that be at Santa Anita. One of Church's horses, Proclivity, won a race at Santa Anita but was subsequently disqualified by the CHRB when he allegedly tested positive for a banned substance. Church went on the offensive, called for Burke's dismissal from the CHRB, and promised to take the case for Proclivity's reinstatement all the way to the Supreme Court if necessary.

Church didn't have to go that far. He hired legal-eagle Senator Burton K. Wheeler of Montana to plead his case in the California Supreme Court. Waxing lyrical, Wheeler accused Burke of either "fraud or ignorance" in his handling of the Proclivity case, and the court reversed the CHRB's decision. Proclivity was reinstated as the winner. Seeing which way the wind was blowing, California governor Frank Merriam cleaned house at the CHRB. Although he left Burke at the helm, he filled the racing board with men who were sympathetic to the Warner group. In October the CHRB granted the Hollywood Turf Club a "provisional permit" to race. The Hollywood Park finish line was in sight, but there were still problems to overcome.[4]

As construction of the track neared completion in late 1937, there was a cash shortfall, and Jack Warner was forced to come to the rescue with a $250,000 loan. Originally expected to cost $2 million, the price tag for Hollywood Park would ultimately rise to $2.8 million. And it turned out that Burke wasn't through fighting. On October 26 he took matters into his own hands and unilaterally withdrew the Hollywood Turf Club's provisional permit, creating a panic among the club's shareholders. The yelping was heard all the way up in Sacramento, where Governor Merriam once again intervened and reversed Burke's decision.

Victory

On January 4, 1938, the CHRB granted the Hollywood Turf Club a license to conduct racing at its new racetrack and awarded it a thirty-three-day meeting to commence on June 10 and end on July 23. The business-savvy Walter McCarty was named the club's new president. Raoul Walsh and Alfred E. Green, who had both served stints as Warner's point man, were named to the board of directors, as was Al Jolson. Ninety percent of the track's stockholders had some connection to the film industry, and most of them were in attendance that first day. Bing Crosby almost missed it. In the middle of making *Sing You Sinners,* the crooner had been told by his Paramount bosses that on no account was he to skip work on June 10, which fell on a Friday. Crosby replied that if he wasn't given the day off, he would take it off anyway, and that is exactly what he did.

Before the end of June, Inglewood Park's name would be changed to Hollywood Park, thus simplifying matters. After all, the Warners, Harry Cohn, and Darryl F. Zanuck wanted the world to know that this track was being run by Hollywood, the center of the film world, even if it was located in unfashionable Inglewood. The track had a built-in publicity machine in the Warner Bros. public-relations department. During the run-up to opening day, a deluge of press releases reported on the progress of construction and owners' and trainers' plans for the inaugural meeting.

Typical was a radio show called *George McCall's Old Gold Program* (named for its sponsor, Old Gold cigarettes), broadcast in Los Angeles on CBS affiliate KNX. On the evening of June 9, McCall (known in radioland as "that man about Hollywood") broadcast his show from the new track's Turf Club. He began with a glowing five-star review of the new Warner Bros. musical comedy *Cowboy from Brooklyn,* directed by Lloyd Bacon. In the absence of the film's leading lights Dick Powell and Pat O'Brien, McCall trucked out its costars, Rosemary Lane, Dick Foran, and Arthur Treacher, as well as local trainer John Kermuth, all of whom picked their favorite horse in the next day's fifth race. When McCall asked Miss Lane what she would be wearing for the opener, she coyly demurred. "I'd rather keep it a secret," she cooed, "until I burst upon the scene in all my glory," surely prompting the appearance of a few dozen extra Rosemary Lane fans at the track.[5]

The weather in Los Angeles in mid-June is almost always perfect, with an average high of 79 degrees and rarely any rain. But on June 10, Strub and Burke enjoyed one last little victory when the day dawned raining. It was still drizzling at post time, but, defying fate, an official crowd of 25,258 poured through the gates, and they would wager $512,942, considerably more than the $264,000 bet at Santa Anita's 1934 opener. Among the revelers were Milton Berle, Claudette Colbert, Howard Hawks, Bob Hope, Barbara Stanwyck and her horse-breeding partner Zeppo Marx, George Burns, and Joan Crawford. Harold Lloyd also put in an appearance, but he kept his bets down to the track minimum of $2 per race, perhaps because all his ventures into the talkies had been flops.

Track announcer Joe Hernandez, moonlighting from his regular job at Santa Anita, spoke his immortal words of introduction: "And now, ladies and gentlemen, Hollywood Park belongs to you." In spite of the rain, the track remained fast throughout the day. Air Chute, owned by aircraft manufacturer William Boeing (clearly not as skittish about horse racing as his business rival Donald Douglas), won the featured $2,500 Hollywood Premiere Handicap by four lengths. Barbara Stanwyck presented the trophy in the winner's circle. Hollywood, both the track and the film community, was off and running. And the track would keep running, despite an inordinate amount of bad luck throughout its seventy-seven-year history.[6]

Day two at Hollywood Park was a Saturday, so Crosby didn't have to play hooky from Paramount. He joined the crowd of 22,412 and relaxed under sunny skies. Crosby was rewarded when his gallant Argentine-bred Ligaroti won the featured Inglewood Handicap; Ligaroti followed up with victories in the American and Sunset Handicaps later in the meeting. As the owner of Del Mar and a shareholder and boxholder at both Santa Anita and Hollywood Park, Crosby was the film industry's most visible face in the racing world.

And the stars came out in force. On June 13 comedian Joe E. Brown landed a famous double when his horse Kay Em Bee won the second race and his Barnsley took the sixth. On the same day, screenwriter Robert

Riskin, author of several Frank Capra–directed hits as well as John Ford's *The Whole Town's Talking,* won the featured Pasadena Stakes with Dogaway. And Crosby's High Strike (at 2–5 odds) chimed in to win the fifth race. The movie trade paper *Boxoffice* dubbed Hollywood Park "the Inglewood subsidiary of the Warner film-making emporium in Burbank."[7]

The ubiquitous Seabiscuit gave Holly Park (as it came to be known in newspaper headline slang) his seal of approval when he won the inaugural $50,000 Hollywood Gold Cup on July 16. The overflow crowd of 55,000 that day included William Powell and Warner Baxter, who shared a box. Specify, winner of the Hollywood Derby a few weeks earlier, drew off to an eight-length lead on the far turn, but the 7–10 Seabiscuit, who was carrying 133 pounds (most of that jockey George Woolf) and spotting his rivals 13 to 28 pounds, reeled him in midstretch to prevail by a length and a half, as Whichcee lost second on the line, with Crosby's Ligaroti fourth.

The Gold Cup was Hollywood Park's signature race from the start. Over the years, it would be won by a number of Thoroughbred greats, including Calumet Farm's Triple Crown winner Citation (1951), Kentucky Derby winner Swaps (1956), 1958 Horse of the Year Round Table (1957), Belmont Stakes winner Gallant Man (1958), and Triple Crown winner Affirmed (1979). Native Diver won it three times from 1965 through 1967, earning him a burial place at the track. The film world had its say in the Gold Cup as well, with Fred Astaire's Triplicate winning it in 1946 and Ack Ack, owned by Mrs. and Mrs. Buddy Fogelson (the latter better known as Greer Garson), taking it in 1971.

Crowds swelled as America prospered during the postwar period. Average attendance boomed to 34,516 in 1965, and the quality of the racing was as high as that at Santa Anita. In 1984 Hollywood Park was honored as the site of the first Breeders' Cup, an event that immediately established itself as the season-ending championship of American Thoroughbred racing.

Trouble

In spite of its financial and artistic success (its beautifully sculpted infield earned it the nickname the "Track of Lakes and Flowers"), Hollywood Park might be the unluckiest racecourse of all time. It continued to be harassed by the Santa Anita set. Hollywood Park supporter Norman

Church (of Elgin wristwatch fame) had donated heavily to get his man Cuthbert Olson elected governor in 1939. Suddenly, the political winds favored Hollywood Park over Santa Anita. A war over which of the two tracks would get the prime racing dates and the most racing dates ensued, with Hollywood Park the clear winner. Santa Anita's 1940 winter meeting was reduced from sixty-five to thirty-five days, while Hollywood Park's thirty-three-day meeting was increased to forty-one days. Charles Strub and Hal Roach fumed, but this time, they were outnumbered. In any case, both tracks, along with Del Mar, took a hit when Olson wangled a new deal that would increase the state's share of pari-mutuel wagering to 4 percent.

When World War II broke out, Hollywood Park, like Santa Anita and Del Mar, was lost to racing. The track was leased to North American Aviation and served as a storage depot for three years, through November 1944, when the situation eased in the Pacific. Jack Warner pulled some strings with the military and got permission to run a thirty-four-day War Charities Meeting at the track. The government complained that racing would result in absenteeism from the numerous aircraft industries in the region, but those fears proved unfounded. More importantly, the War Charities Meeting produced $1,013,967 for war relief services, plus an additional $1 million in war bond sales.[8]

The postwar years at Hollywood Park were dominated by Louis B. Mayer, whose phenomenal fillies Busher and Honeymoon defeated colts to win the Hollywood Derby, and the rising owner-trainer team of Rex Ellsworth and Mesh Tenney. The track's keystone event, the Hollywood Gold Cup, was won by Fred Astaire's Triplicate in 1946 and by the Mayer-bred Cover Up a year later. Shannon, owned by MGM lawyer and Mayer's chief racing adviser Neil McCarthy, won the Gold Cup in 1948. Hollywood seemed to be in charge of Hollywood Park, but then disaster struck.

Shortly before midnight on May 5, 1949, just twelve days before the scheduled start of Hollywood Park's spring-summer meeting, a fire broke out and was soon raging the length of the quarter-mile grandstand. More than a dozen fire companies from the surrounding area answered the call, but it was hopeless. The structure was razed, though fortunately, no one was killed in the worst disaster in California since the 1906 San Francisco earthquake. The fire department determined that the blaze had been the result of spontaneous combustion, perhaps caused by some oily rags left in a storage closet near an elevator shaft after the repainting of the grandstand earlier that spring. But not everyone bought that story. Suspicions linger to this day that the fire was started by a disgruntled ex-employee, but nothing was ever proved.

Jack Warner was put in the embarrassing position of having to ask archenemy Charles Strub if he could move Hollywood Park's meeting to Santa Anita, which had concluded its own winter-spring meeting just a few days earlier. With an opportunity to play the white knight, Strub came to Hollywood Park's rescue, and the transferred meeting went off without a hitch. It even introduced future all-time great jockey Bill Shoemaker to Southern California racing fans.[9]

Jack and Harry Warner lost no time in rallying their considerable forces to the task of rebuilding the grandstand. Such was the power, ingenuity, and wealth of the film community that the new Hollywood Park was open for business a year later on June 27, 1950. Even though Warner Bros.' net profits had declined from $22 million in 1947 to $10 million in 1949, Jack and Harry had money to burn on their burned down racetrack.

The Hollywood Phoenix Fizzles

It can be argued that Hollywood Park's history is more storied than that of Santa Anita or Del Mar, and executives and employees of the Inglewood track would certainly agree. The names of the great horses, jockeys, trainers, and Hollywood personalities that graced the place over the years would fill an encyclopedia. Yet after the first Breeders' Cup in 1984, Hollywood Park suffered more than usual from the general malaise that had begun to plague horse racing in America.

Successive administrations under Marje Everett, Cal Hubbard, Churchill Downs Inc., and Bay Meadows Land Development couldn't prevent Holly Park's long, slow decline. After a peak of 34,516 in 1965, average daily attendance dropped to 25,677 in 1984 and then plunged to 3,800 in 2013, the track's last year of operation. Track bosses tried everything. Hollywood Park was the first racecourse in America to offer exacta and pick-six wagering, and it was the first to schedule Friday night and Sunday racing. None of these innovations had a positive long-term effect. Postrace rock concerts failed to waken the younger generation to the beauties of the sport. And then there was the transformation of the surrounding area. By 1990, Inglewood had become a crime-ridden neighborhood in decline.

Things only got worse until Bay Meadows Land Development closed the track for good on December 22, 2013. There was no Jack Warner or Bing Crosby to bail out the old track. On May 31, 2015, the Hollywood Park grandstand was demolished to make way for a new football stadium that would be home to the Rams and the Raiders. Professional football had long since supplanted horse racing and baseball as America's favorite sport. Now the lords of the National Football League would be erecting their new playpen on the graveyard of Hollywood Park.

Racing Goes to the Movies

With three racetracks operating in the region in 1938, Hollywood began to reflect its newfound passion on the screen.

Even in its infancy, the cinematic world had been drawn to horse racing, probably because the new art required moving objects, and racehorses certainly moved. In 1872 Eadweard Muybridge had proved through photography that horses did indeed lift all four hooves off the ground at the same time when in full gallop. In 1896 Englishman Robert W. Paul had rushed his brief footage of that year's English Derby into theaters in Piccadilly and Leicester Square, qualifying his little film as the first newsreel in history. And in 1909 film pioneer Francis Boggs had made *The Heart of a Race Tout.* Shot in downtown Los Angeles and at the original Santa Anita Park, it was the first film made entirely in California.

With the formalization of film production and distribution following World War I, Hollywood started to produce racing pictures on a regular basis. The studios were not only reflecting a major American pastime but also promoting the sport that was nearest and dearest to Americans' hearts. Even during the silent era, when there was no racing in Southern California, Hollywood produced an average of two racing films per year, no doubt inspired by the success of the Hipodromo de Tijuana. Horse racing was, after all, very popular east of the Mississippi, especially in the key film markets of New York, Chicago, New Jersey, and Florida.

One of the earliest feature racing films, 1915's *Wildfire,* starred the legendary Lillian Russell, reprising her stage role. A youthful-looking, thirty-six-year-old Lionel Barrymore was cast as the villain of the piece. Directed by Edwin Middleton (who would later direct W. C. Fields in his cinematic debut, *Pool Sharks*), the film was named for the horse that wins the climactic race, despite Barrymore's attempt to bribe its jockey.

Crooked jockeys and fixed races were a staple of early racing films, especially in the sport's birthplace, England, which regularly churned out silent films with lurid titles like *A Turf Conspiracy, A Reckless Gamble,* and *A Dead Certainty.*

The ascent of Man o' War to superstar status in 1920 spurred the production of racing films. America's first truly great Thoroughbred became a household name, and although Hollywood never filmed his biography, his exploits brought the sport to the attention of millions of Americans— all potential filmgoers that the studios hoped to draw into their theaters. John Ford himself chipped in with *Kentucky Pride* (1925) and *The Shamrock Handicap* (1926). And the nation's most popular screen star, Mary Pickford, was the driving force behind the 1923 production of *Garrison's Finish,* a fictionalized account of America's most famous nineteenth-century jockey, "Snapper" Garrison. Her younger brother Jack played the title role.

With the return of racing to Santa Anita in 1934 and the subsequent successes at Del Mar in 1936 and Hollywood Park in 1938, interest in racing movies peaked. Films about fixed races, crooked jockeys, and gambling coups, as well as sporting-related historical dramas, were released with increasing frequency throughout the second half of the 1930s. Hollywood produced at least eight racing-themed films per year over the last half of the decade.

Perhaps the most popular story line was the tale of the impossible longshot that overcomes numerous obstacles to win the big race. This kind of equine fairy tale came to life in Seabiscuit, the cheap, undersized claimer that rose to the top of the Thoroughbred world in the late 1930s. It was the Depression, after all, and war clouds were gathering in skies both East and West. Transformative stories of losers becoming winners distracted Americans from their everyday fears and worries and gave them hope for the future, however brief or illusory. In movies like *Broadway Bill, A Day at the Races, Stablemates,* and *Sing You Sinners,* Hollywood provided Americans with fictional versions of Seabiscuit's real-world accomplishments.

No one will ever proclaim horse racing movies an important film genre. Far from it. They will always be also-rans behind film noirs, screwball comedies, and musicals, even though racing films frequently incorporate all three of those genres. The *Ex–Mrs. Bradford* and *Charlie Chan at the Race Track* are early examples of film noir. The Marx Brothers classic

A Day at the Races and Mervyn LeRoy's *Three Men on a Horse* stand up as screwball comedies, despite their racing and gambling scenarios. And *Broadway Melody of 1938,* with Eleanor Powell tap-dancing her way from 45th Street to Saratoga, joins the Dick Powell–Louis Armstrong vehicle *Going Places* in successfully marrying the racing film to the musical. By 1938, a pair of racing films actually slipped onto the list of top twenty box office draws. MGM's *Stablemates,* starring Wallace Beery and Mickey Rooney, was in eighteenth place, and 20th Century Fox's big-budget Technicolor historical extravaganza *Kentucky* was in twentieth.

The 1930s were halcyon days for the racing film. With three new tracks in California, almost everyone in Hollywood was involved in the sport, whether as track shareholders, Thoroughbred owners, or fans. Studios used attendance at racetracks to promote new films or budding young stars. When a movie was scheduled for release, the studio would send the leading players out to the track. Being photographed at Santa Anita, Del Mar, or Hollywood Park was good publicity, whether the film was a racing picture or not. And in the case of Warner Bros., that sort of publicity also promoted their track down in Inglewood.

Among the studio heads, Jack Warner and Louis B. Mayer were most involved in horse racing, and they didn't stint on films of a racing nature. Warner Bros. led the 1930s in racing film production, while Mayer's MGM produced some of the best in the genre. By 1937, Mayer began to develop one of the most powerful racing stables in the nation, one that would challenge the Vanderbilts, the Whitneys, and Calumet Farm, culminating in the 1945 Horse of the Year, Busher. From producer to director to major star to bit player, from the studio to the track and back again, Hollywood had gone gaga over the gee-gees.

5

The Stars Come Out
Racetrack Society in the Golden Age

Hairdressers report that every girl in town insists on having her locks curled in the morning, because they go to the race track in the afternoon.

Ed Sullivan

A Day at the Races

Attending the races is not quite the same as going to a ball game, be it of the foot-, base-, or basket- variety. At the ballpark, you plunk yourself down in your assigned seat and sit there for two or three hours. Some baseball fans spend much of their time scratching out the arcane brand of Morse code known as keeping score. Football fans spend a lot of time trying to figure out exactly where the ball is. At halftime or during the seventh-inning stretch, fans might rise from their seats and head over to the concession stand for a beer or a hotdog, but they are more likely to sit and wait for a vendor to come by. This is why football, baseball, and basketball are called spectator sports: the people who attend them spend almost all their time spectating.

It is a different story at the racetrack, for horse racing is both a participatory sport and a spectator sport. The money wagered at the pari-mutuel windows is the sport's lifeblood, accounting for a very large portion of the purses that give the races their prestige and the owners, trainers, and jockeys their incomes, making horseplayers every bit as important to the game as these other participants are. But there is an even more crucial difference between going to the track and going to the ballpark. While sports fans spend most of their time sitting on their duffs and stuffing their faces with peanuts and Cracker Jack, racegoers are active participants in the day's events, for the racetrack is like a microcosm of a city, and a city cannot be fully appreciated or understood unless it is fully explored.

A racegoer might start his day at the track by buying a program at the entry gate. He then visits the board where the day's changes are posted: horses scratched, jockeys or weights changed, blinkers on or off, or switches in racing surface (such as a move from turf to dirt because of rain). He goes to the betting window to place a bet on the first race, but not before checking the tote board to determine the odds on each horse. He then takes a seat in the grandstand to watch the race, after which he might watch the replay on one of the TV screens posted throughout the track.

Between races, he might stop at the bar for a drink or buy a snack at a concession stand. He might even go up to the track restaurant for lunch. But wherever his travels take him, a wise racegoer will have a copy of the *Daily Racing Form* handy to check the form of the horses running in the next race. A prerace trip to the paddock can provide information about the condition of the horses that might escape a more sedentary fan. After a return to the betting window and a last-minute check of the odds, it's back to the grandstand to watch the next race. If a winning wager has been placed, the lucky bettor might want to go down to the winner's circle to share in the festivities.

A day at the races is as much a social occasion as a sporting event, and this was appreciated by the Hollywood film community. Actors are a sociable breed. They enjoy the camaraderie a racetrack can offer, be it in the stands, in the restaurant, or under the trees in one of the track's gardens. Each way station at a racetrack—the paddock, the bar, the line at the betting windows, the winner's circle—is an opportunity to greet friends, exchange opinions on the next race, or complain about the jockey's horrible ride on the favorite in the previous race. To that extent, racetracks seemed purpose-built for Hollywood, where a good conversation—or a juicy piece of gossip—never went unheard.

And of course, there was the betting. Anyone who worked regularly in Hollywood had reserves of cash that they were just itching to pour through the pari-mutuel windows at Santa Anita, Del Mar, and Hollywood Park—the only places in Southern California where wagering was legal. During the 1940s, the entertainment trade paper *Variety* printed the selections of racing experts from around the country, compiled from no fewer than six different newspapers. The publicity value of being seen at the track was immense, so it is little wonder that Hollywood led the way in making horse racing the most popular pastime in the region—outside of going to the movies, of course.

In 1939 Ed Sullivan—who, in the 1950s and 1960s, would host the most popular variety show in the history of television—documented the change in Hollywood's social and sporting scene. He wrote for the movie trade paper *Silver Screen,* which frequently ran photos with captions that read, "Anita Louise follows the horses but bets wisely" and "Maxie Rosenbloom (looking forlorn) picks another loser." In those same pages, Sullivan opined, "In the past when Louis Mayer or Harry Warner or Bing Crosby or Mervyn LeRoy invited you to their home they'd show you their latest film. Now they take you out to the barn to show you their new yearlings."[1]

Linda LeRoy's Disappointing Day at the Races

The extent to which horse racing is a participatory sport is illustrated by the heartbreaking story of little Linda LeRoy's first trip to a racetrack. Her father, director Mervyn LeRoy, was instrumental in the development of Hollywood Park, and in 1941 he was appointed a member of the track's board of directors. After marrying Harry Warner's daughter Doris, he ran a successful racing stable, W-L Ranch, through the 1940s and 1950s with his father-in-law.

Linda, born in 1935, was his first child with Doris. Like any proud papa, LeRoy wanted to show her off to his friends, as well as introduce her to his beloved pastime. So he arranged a father-daughter outing at his favorite hangout, Hollywood Park, during the track's third season in the spring of 1940. By his own account, Linda was enthralled by everything she saw: the magnificent grandstand, the garden-like infield, the jockeys wearing their colorful silks. It all seemed like a trip to fantasyland to the little girl, but then her daddy, producer of *The Wizard of Oz,* was adept at putting on a show.

But what caught Linda's eye most of all were the horses. Before the first race, LeRoy took her to the paddock for a closer look at the runners. "Which one do you like?" he asked her. "That one," she answered, pointing to a leggy chestnut filly. "All right!" her daddy said. He pulled $2 out of his wallet and bet on the filly to win. Linda beamed as he handed her the pari-mutuel ticket, which seemed to her like a passport to paradise.

She was part of the action—real, grown-up action on a stage the likes of which she could never have imagined.

And then she was hit with a major dose of beginner's luck, that mysterious good fortune that strikes so many first-time visitors to a racetrack. Her filly won the race, and little Linda was over the moon, her smile illuminating an already beautifully sunlit day. Hand in hand, father and daughter cheerfully walked down to the winner's circle in front of the grandstand. When they got there, Linda's winner was already having her picture taken, and the little girl asked her father, "Where are we going to keep her when we get her home, daddy?" LeRoy's face fell when he saw the look of bliss on his daughter's. In her innocent excitement, she thought that by backing the winner she had won the horse itself, that the filly now belonged to her. LeRoy had to explain the reality of the situation. In a twinkling, Linda's joy changed to deepest disappointment; her face darkened, and she broke down in tears. In its long history, horse racing has produced more sorrow than joy, but no sorrow ever exceeded that of Linda LeRoy on her first day at the races.[2]

The Mean-Spirited Mr. Hardy

There is a photograph from the late 1930s that shows Cary Grant sitting in the grandstand at Los Alamitos, one of the lesser racetracks in the Los Angeles area that filled the gap between the close of Del Mar at the end of August and the opening of Santa Anita at Christmas. Grant, who loved horse racing, is seen grinning ear to ear as he engages in conversation with a young female admirer. This was before the star of *Bringing Up Baby* and *Holiday* began to charge his fans 25 cents for an autograph. Here, Grant seems to be at ease with the public, happy to curry favor with even a single fan.

Oliver Hardy could have taken a lesson from Grant's charm. Beloved the world over as the fat man partnered with skinny Stan Laurel, Hardy was not easy to get along with. Problems with his wife, Myrtle, had started during the silent era, when she became an alcoholic and he a hard-core gambler. Hardy once dropped $30,000 in a single day's racing at Agua Caliente, and he was no less profligate once Santa Anita opened. Perhaps weary of losing money betting on horses, he tried owning them in 1935. He had a stable of ten, but none of them was any good. "His horses seem so fond of the starting post," a Hollywood columnist wrote, "that they invariably stay there."[3] It is estimated that he spent $50,000 to buy them and more than that in training fees, but not one ever crossed the finish line first. Hardy would attend the races disguised as "Babe," an overweight tough guy, to drown his sorrows in gambling, then show up the next day on the set of the Hal Roach Studios as the affable Ollie.

On January 4, 1936, ace Hollywood reporter Aggie Underwood was in the Turf Club lounge at Santa Anita looking for a story. Across the room she spotted Hardy leaning against the bar, immersed in his copy of the *Racing Form*. Accompanied by photographer Perry Fowler, she made her move. Fowler politely asked if he could take Hardy's picture, to which the actor brusquely replied, "No, I'm busy!" When Underwood explained that they were from the *Los Angeles Herald-Express*, Hardy changed his tune. He was, after all, at Hal Roach's racetrack, and Roach was his boss at the studio. Moreover, it would be good publicity to smile for a few harmless pictures in the wake of Stan and Ollie's recently released comic operetta *The Bohemian Girl*.

But then Fowler made the mistake of asking Hardy if his wife was around and suggesting that she might join him in the photo. He and Underwood were certainly aware that Hardy's marriage was in tatters and that divorce proceedings were under way. Hardy saw red. "Don't ask so goddam many questions!" he snapped. Fowler bristled and cautioned Hardy to mind his manners, pointing out that there were ladies present. Hardy responded by slamming Fowler in the shoulder. "Put down that camera or I'll throw you over that rail and break your goddam neck!" Hardy screamed. Having succeeded in getting himself into another fine mess without any help at all from Stan, Hardy stormed off. Fowler never got his picture, and Underwood, figuring that discretion is the better part of valor, didn't report the incident in her column. Lawsuits were threatened on both sides, but Roach Studio executives and *Herald-Express* editors managed to smooth things over.

In his "Babe" persona, Hardy can be seen in the 1938 short *Hollywood Handicap*, a ten-minute quickie slapped together by Buster Keaton, who was still hanging around MGM as an idea man. Much of the film consists of A-list stars such as Bing Crosby, Mickey Rooney, Al Jolson, and Dorothy Lamour and B-listers Charlie Ruggles, Stuart Erwin, and Charles Butterworth hanging around the newly opened Hollywood Park, waving at the cameras. Rooney hogs the newsreel footage touting the number-two horse, but Crosby's Rhythm King carried the day. It is doubtful that Hardy backed the winner.[4]

The Stars' Winning Systems

Oliver Hardy relied on the *Racing Form* to help him pick winners, not that it did him much good. All racetrack regulars eventually develop systems for selecting winners. In most cases these systems consist of rational handicapping based on past performance, quality of competition, trainer, jockey, breeding, ground conditions, distance, and so forth—the criteria used by racetrack professionals. Some people, however, come up with formulations that bear no relation to the business at hand.

By all accounts, Fred Astaire was a rational man. His dancing was of the highest Apollonian order—logical and balanced. George Balanchine, the great choreographer and founder of the New York City Ballet, called him "the greatest dancer in the world," to which Astaire logically replied, "Undeniably erroneous." Yet Astaire, who was as prominent trackside as he was in the immortal musicals *Top Hat, Swing Time,* and *Shall We Dance,* often reverted to a betting system that defied all logic.[5]

Early in his career during the Roaring Twenties, Astaire had been introduced to the pleasures of the turf in England while performing in London's West End in shows such as George and Ira Gershwin's *Lady, Be Good!* and *Funny Face.* Almost everyone in the West End had themselves a daily "nap"—that is, a horse that couldn't lose—and few were loath to keep their good thing to themselves. Astaire was soon bitten with the punter's bug ("punter" being British slang for bettor).

One night after a performance of *Lady, Be Good!* at the Empire in Piccadilly, Astaire was visited backstage by a jockey named Jack Leach. The son of prominent Newmarket trainer Felix Leach and the brother of jockey Chubb and trainer Felix Jr., Jack had racing in his veins. Astaire was duly complimented when Leach told him over drinks that he was a "good mover," a term normally reserved for Thoroughbreds with an easy, fluid action. From time to time they would run into each other at nearby racecourses such as Sandown, Lingfield, Kempton, or Ascot—site of the annual four-day garden party and racing extravaganza known as Royal Ascot.

Astaire soon invested in a small string of modest horses trained by Felix Jr., but he was having little luck with the bookies. One day he noticed his English chauffeur, George Griffin, poring over a copy of *The Sporting Life,* the British racing daily, as if his life depended on it. Griffin explained that he was applying his handicapping system to the big race at Newmarket.

Handicaps in England are the most difficult races to figure out. They frequently consist of at least twenty and as many as thirty-six runners. The horses are never top class, and their form is ever changeable. Moreover, the difference between top weight and low weight can be as much as 30 pounds, with any number of modest horses carrying light weights and an equal number of well-intended horses saddled with heavy weights designed to stop them in their tracks.

Sometimes it just doesn't pay to wade through the minutiae required to find the winner of such a race. Rather than using the hatpin method, Griffin had developed a system all his own. He went directly to the bottom horse on the race card, the horse carrying the lowest weight. Then he counted the number of letters in that horse's name and counted up that number on the race card, starting with the bottom horse. For example, if the bottom horse had twelve letters in its name, Griffin would count up twelve horses. If there were thirty horses in the race, he would count up to horse number nineteen and bet on that horse.

Astaire was impressed, or perhaps he was mystified. He tried the system himself the next time he went to the track, and lo and behold, it worked! For the rest of his life, Fred Astaire, a dancer with the most logical of artistic minds, swore by this system. He claimed that it worked most of the time, although he admitted that it could be used only in large fields of sixteen or more.[6]

"If you can't get your name on a marquee, get it on a racetrack program."[7] So said Pat O'Brien, who made a career out of playing the Irish American homeboy. A Thoroughbred owner, inveterate racegoer, and cofounder of Del Mar (with Bing Crosby), O'Brien was only a modest gambler. Like Jimmy Durante, Betty Grable and Harry James, and Lucille Ball and Desi Arnaz, O'Brien was so enamored with racing, especially with the seaside delights of his beloved Del Mar, that he bought a beachfront house near the track to use as a summer getaway. "It wasn't just the gambling," he explained in his autobiography, *The Wind at My Back*. "It was the crystal atmosphere warm with life. Long golden days with the deep blue shadows coming in over the grandstand; the color of the holiday-held crowd milling around, the slight salty breeze on the banners, and the tang of the best horses and the pungent whiffs of stable life."[8]

When O'Brien wasn't waxing poetic about the charms of Del Mar, he was busy figuring out ways to pick winners. One August weekend he was hosting Ed Kelly, the all-powerful mayor of Chicago, and his wife Margaret. Afternoons at the track were, of course, de rigueur. One day, O'Brien noticed that another mayor of note, Jersey City boss Frank Hague, was mingling with patrons in the clubhouse. The presence of two prominent mayors, each the leader of his city's Democratic machine and far from the mundane concerns of City Hall, seemed rather unusual, and O'Brien sensed something in the air. There was a horse running in the sixth race named Hizzoner, and O'Brien had a hunch. Chastened somewhat by Hizzoner's long odds, he placed a small bet and was rewarded with a 35–1 payoff. Irish eyes were smiling for the remainder of the afternoon.[9]

If politics could work as a handicapping tool, why not religion? Frankie Chojnacki was a regular rider on the Southern California circuit. One day at Del Mar, O'Brien's wife, Eloise, took a fancy to a horse he was riding at 60–1 and made an across-the-board bet—$2 each to win, place, and show, for a total of $6. When Chojnacki booted the horse home in front, Pat gasped in disbelief. "How could you possibly bet on that horse?" he asked. To which Eloise reverently replied, "I saw that little jockey at Mass Sunday, so I figured I'd encourage him with six dollars."[10]

Keye Luke was not a big movie star, but he probably should have been. As an artist, he contributed some of the murals at Grauman's Chinese Theatre, but his biggest claim to fame was his role as Number One Son in eight installments of Warner Oland's Charlie Chan series, among them *Charlie Chan at the Race Track*. To American audiences at the time—who were used to sinister Chinese underworld characters or Chinese servants who spoke silly pidgin English—Luke must have been a revelation. His rat-a-tat dialogue, delivered at a machine gun pace, rivaled that of the Dead End Kids or any fast-talking cinematic newspaper reporter.

Born in China but raised in Seattle, Luke brought a decidedly Chinese attitude to the races. In China, unlike in the West, there is no sinfulness attached to gambling. Ask any racegoer at Sha Tin or Happy Valley, the fabulously profitable racetracks in Hong Kong, and they will tell you, "We make our own luck."

It was an early spring day in 1938 that Keye Luke made his own luck at Santa Anita. He noticed a horse on the card with the familiar name of Charlie Chan. Nobody was betting on Charlie Chan because the poor thing had won only once in forty-seven previous starts, but Luke was not deterred. He bet on his screen father's namesake to win, and the old boy romped home by seven lengths! Afterward, the calculating Luke denied that it had been a hunch bet. "It was cold figures. Careful analysis showed the horse couldn't lose," he said sheepishly.[11]

Clubhouse Romance

Racetracks, particularly those in Southern California, were well suited to social life. A favorable climate produced one sunny day after another. The lovely tree-lined paddocks, the outdoor bars, and the restaurants over-looking the finish line were all spurs to congenial conversations that might shift from the topic of the next race to something more intimate in the blink of an eye. Whenever like-minded people engage in shared interests, romance can bloom.

It happened to Betty Grable and Harry James in a big way. The highest-paid actress in the world (in 1947 her salary was pegged at $300,000), she was the pinup girl with the "million-dollar legs," the heartthrob of millions of GIs around the world. He was one of the most popular bandleaders in the land, the brassy sound of his trumpet making him a 1940s big-band version of a 1960s rock star. They first met in 1940, shortly after Betty had finished working with Don Ameche on the musical racing film *Down Argentine Way* and Harry's version of *Ciribiribin* had sold a million copies with Frank Sinatra on vocals. But their initial meeting at a Hollywood party didn't pan out. Harry's inherent shyness left the vivacious Betty rather cold.

At the time, she preferred the company of George Raft, with whom she shared a love of both racing and dancing. The couple became an item at nightclubs and racetracks, where they occasionally bumped into James, who kept a small string of horses at Santa Anita. "He's a swell guy," Betty said of Raft, as the Hollywood gossip machine predicted a walk down the aisle for the couple, "but there is no news about us. If there were, I couldn't keep a thing like that secret." These were turbulent times for the marriage-shy Raft, who had turned down roles in *High Sierra, The Maltese Falcon,* and *Casablanca,* which then fell into the lap of Humphrey Bogart. More of a homebody, Betty eventually grew tired of Raft's act and began to take notice of James, who introduced her to life on the backstretch. On July 5, 1943, they tied the knot. They bought a 109-acre tract in Calabasas, named it Baby-J Ranch, and took up breeding Thoroughbreds.[12]

After the war, Harry and Betty bought a house on the beach at Del Mar, where they spent the entire August race meeting and declared all talk of movies and music taboo. "That's why I like Del Mar," Betty said. "I never let anything interfere with having a month with Harry, Vicki and little Jess (their two children). We have never gone to Europe because we can never tear ourselves away from Del Mar. The beach is here, golf, tennis, racing and everything we want. What more can anyone ask?"[13]

Indeed, Betty and Harry could usually be seen riding along the beach in the morning in the shadow of the Del Mar grandstand. Later, they would drive over to the track for the afternoon's races. Betty was so into the game that she had her dressing room decorated in their racing stable's colors: red and white. During the winter, they always took a suite at the Westerner, a hotel in Arcadia just minutes away from Santa Anita, to be close to the action. When the 1950s brought a decline in her cinematic fortunes, Betty rolled with the punches. "I'll go out there like Citation, win or lose—I'll arch my back and take my bow, now that I know how."[14]

The studios were well aware of the pull racetracks were exerting on their star players, and they capitalized on that attraction whenever the opportunity arose. The opportunity arose rather frequently during the tempestuous marriage of Joan Crawford and Franchot Tone. Tone was a good-time guy who loved to go to the track and bet on the horses. When they began dating in 1933, both their careers were in high gear, and Tone's predilection for the ponies made them regulars at the races. It was an affair that produced seven cinematic collaborations, including *Dancing Lady*. They married in 1935, and MGM executives, ever sensitive to the rumor mill, made sure their stars were presented in the best possible off-screen light. A semistaged photo shoot at Santa Anita or Hollywood Park might keep their fans from noticing that there was trouble in paradise, but the illusion couldn't last. Tone's gambling problem rankled Crawford, and after four years of on-and-off wedded bliss, the glamour couple went their separate ways.

Sex siren Lana Turner and crooner Tony Martin met on the set of *Ziegfeld Girl* in 1940, and the attraction was mutual and magnetic. Turner was on the rebound after a brief but stormy liaison with bandleader and clarinetist Artie Shaw, and Martin's relationship with actress Alice Faye was in melt-down. They liked to drown their mutual sorrows together at Hollywood Park, and the gossip columnists figured they were on to a good thing. But this time, they were wrong. Hollywood's latest daily double proved a bust, as Turner quickly moved on to Steve Crane, the second of her seven husbands.

When it comes to Hollywood aristocracy, Barbara Stanwyck and Robert Taylor were the most royal of racing couples. Their romance started in 1936 on the set of W. S. Van Dyke's MGM romance *His Brother's Wife*. After a long love affair, during which they moved in together (much to the displeasure of Louis Mayer, who was always sensitive to his stars' public displays of affection), "Stanny" and Bob were finally married on May 14, 1939, with a relieved Mayer arranging the low-key wedding.

Barbara had been introduced to the races by Marion Marx, the wife of Marx Brothers straight man Zeppo. Barbara partnered with Zeppo, and the two of them consulted Kentucky trainer Harry Hart, who advised them on a 130-acre property in Northridge in the San Fernando Valley. Barbara and Bob purchased the property for $200,000, and she and Zeppo christened the place Marwyck Ranch. It was designed along the lines of a proper Kentucky breeding farm, and Hart was hired as manager.

The facility held twenty broodmare barns and a six-furlong (three-quarter-mile) training track. No expense was spared. Stanwyck had hopes of challenging Kentucky's Thoroughbred empire, which would have been like Luxembourg challenging Germany for European military superiority. Of course, it couldn't be done, but Taylor and Stanwyck earned an A+ for effort. They both took an active part in running the ranch, as well as consulting on matings and new purchases.

The top stallion at Marwyck was The Nut. He was a son of Mad Hatter, who had been America's champion older horse in 1921 and was descended from the female family of champion colts Whisk Broom II and Crusader, as well as champion filly Top Flight. But Thoroughbred breeding is more art than science, and while The Nut and Marwyck's mares produced a number of winners, there were no champions—or even near champions—among them. Taylor and Stanwyck sold horses to Harry Warner (Co Step) and his son-in-law Mervyn LeRoy (Mad Sue), as well as to Spencer Tracy and Wallace Beery; others they retained to race. They always finished the year in the black. The surest money in the Thoroughbred world has always come from the breeding end of the game.

Stanwyck recalled as early as 1938, "We haven't made a lot of money, but probably about as much as we could have got in interest from the bank." Later, during the war, when racing in Southern California was shut down, Marwyck ceased breeding operations and became a Thoroughbred boarding facility. In 1943 Stanwyck and Taylor sold their interest in the ranch to Marx. But both before and after the war, the couple attended every important race day on the Southern California circuit: opening days at Santa Anita in December, at Hollywood Park in May, and at Del Mar in late July, along with the Santa Anita Handicap and the Hollywood Gold Cup. Stanny and Bob could be seen together in their box seats until their amicable divorce on February 25, 1952.[15]

Racetrack Catwalk

The racetrack as fashion showcase where ladies display the latest styles began in the mid-nineteenth century at Royal Ascot, the four-day, mid-June cornucopia of high-class racing that is the single most important event on England's social and sporting calendar. Women from every walk of life—from the queen to the lowly office clerk and housewife—use the occasion to show off the newest summer fashions. The custom spread to France, where on Prix de Diane (French Oaks) Day, *les jeunes filles* and *les vielles filles* alike turn the Hippodrome de Chantilly into an open-air fashion show. The tradition continues at Churchill Downs on Kentucky Derby Day and at Santa Anita on its December 26 opener, when those tracks are turned into one-day American versions of Royal Ascot.

Hollywood has long used its local tracks for much the same purpose. It wasn't only reporters from the *Daily Racing Form* or *Variety* who went to Hollywood Park, Santa Anita, and Del Mar looking for stories. The fashion editors of every newspaper in the nation knew that starlets were eager to present themselves trackside in their latest finery. The studios knew it too, and they would arrange photo shoots for their fetchingly arrayed femmes fatales in the clubhouse, in the paddock, or along the rail.

In 1941, following a seven-year absence from the screen, silent film siren Gloria Swanson was attempting a comeback in RKO's *Father Takes a Wife* with Adolphe Menjou. On June 9 studio publicists chauffeured her down to Hollywood Park in full regalia, confident that every fashion editor in Southern California would be eager to publish the RKO house photographer's pictures. The next day, the photos appeared in a dozen Southern California papers, each one accompanied by the caption supplied by the RKO public-relations department: "Glamorous Gloria Swanson, whose new RKO picture will soon be released, is shown descending from the stairs in the exclusive Turf Club at Hollywood Park. Famous as one of the best dressed women in the nation, Miss Swanson wore a black crepe dress with a neckline of yellow waffle crepe. Her broad-brimmed sailor cap of matching crepe is floated with a sheer black lace veil."[16] Alas, in spite of the trackside buildup, *Father Takes a Wife* was a flop. No longer quite as glamorous as she had been, Gloria Swanson wouldn't appear in another film until 1950, when she emerged from oblivion in the persona of Norma Desmond and walked away with Billy Wilder's *Sunset Blvd.,* which needed little publicity.

A week earlier, Hollywood Park had been the scene of an equally glamorous—and more successful—fashion shoot featuring Susan Hayward. The twenty-two-year-old Brooklyn girl with the perfect profile was a rising star in the Paramount galaxy. Her supporting role behind Gary Cooper and Ray Milland in William Wellman's *Beau Geste* had caught many an eye, but her first starring role would be in the Southern Gothic suspense film *Among the Living.*

Paramount used the same formula as RKO, sending a blast of photos and press releases to every newspaper in the country. The caption for the photo of the vivacious brunette read: "Pert and pretty is Susan Hayward, who is shown in the Turf Club at Hollywood Park. She wears cocoa brown crepe, coin-dotted in white, and a white shantung jacket with turn-back sleeves of print fabric. Her off-the-face toyo hat in white completes her accessories."[17] It appeared in at least three dozen local papers over the next two weeks and in countless more around the country.

The B feature *Among the Living* was only a modest success, but it proved to be a stepping-stone that helped catapult Hayward to stardom and five Oscar nominations, culminating in her victory for *I Want to Live* in 1958. Her early public-relations training at Hollywood Park stood her in good stead. Hayward became a gifted self-promoter, battling more tenaciously each time she was nominated for the Academy Award until she finally achieved her coveted goal.

Huston, We Have a Problem

One day, director John Huston invented a new way of losing at Hollywood Park. It was his custom to arrive at the track early so he could discuss the card with his friend and fellow art collector, jockey Billy Pearson. On this particular day, Huston was late and had to forgo his usual handicapping session. He didn't take his seat in the grandstand until the horses were coming out onto the track. Catching the eye of Pearson, who was perched atop a formless longshot, Huston waved hello to his friend. The jockey returned the greeting with a nod of his head, a gesture that Huston interpreted as a signal that he should bet on Pearson's mount. Huston ran to the $100 windows and plunked down a couple of thousand on Pearson's horse to win, then watched, crestfallen, as the nag failed to pick up his feet and finished dead last.

Later, Huston confronted Pearson, demanding to know what had gone wrong. Aghast, Pearson asked, "You bet on that dog?"

"Sure," Huston replied, "you gave me the nod."

"Hell, John," came the response, "I was just saying 'Good morning!'"

And so Pearson's "hello" became Huston's "good-bye" to every cent he had in his pocket.[18]

I Love Lucy . . . Sometimes

Any American living in the 1950s took it for granted that if Lucy and Ricky on the fabulously successful sitcom *I Love Lucy* were the perfect television couple, then Lucille Ball and Desi Arnaz must be the ideal American couple in real life. In 1960, three years after *I Love Lucy* ended its six-year run on CBS, Lucy and Desi shocked the nation with a very public divorce. Looking back, their split can be seen as a dividing line between the comfortable, happy 1950s and the turbulent, revolutionary 1960s. Nothing would ever be the same again.

Lucy and Desi met in 1940 on the set of *Too Many Girls*, an RKO musical comedy directed by George Abbott. Desi was reprising his Broadway role as a singing football player, and his dark good looks immediately knocked Lucy cold. A few weeks after production ended, they tied the knot. "You could tell that sparks were flying with Lucy," said their costar Eddie Bracken. "It happened so fast, it seemed it wouldn't last. Everybody on the set made bets about how long it would last." Bracken, who would reach his apogee three years later in a pair of Preston Sturges comedies, *Miracle of Morgan's Creek* and *Hail the Conquering Hero,* won the bet, having guessed the longest time: six months. He was only off by nineteen and a half years![19]

Those years were marked by trouble and strife in the on-again, off-again romance that never really came to a conclusion. Most of the problems stemmed from Desi's womanizing, drinking, and gambling. Lucy first filed for divorce in 1944. The legalities were on the brink of being finalized when they kissed and made up, paving the way for the couple to make television history.

Desi Arnaz was a drinker and a gambler with a short fuse. As a boy, he had been introduced to horse racing at Havana's Oriental Park. He resumed his Thoroughbred studies at Hialeah, after his well-to-do father brought the family to Miami in 1933 to escape Cuban dictator Fulgencio Batista. Twenty years later, Desi was riding the *I Love Lucy* crest. Meanwhile, his old friend Eddie Bracken had returned to Broadway, after opportunities in Hollywood dried up. One day, Desi invited Bracken to spend the day at Jamaica Park, then a well-known racetrack in New York City. Located in the heart of Queens, Jamaica Park was an odd racecourse by American standards. It was one of the few tracks in the country that was not a perfect oval. Its narrow first turn fanned out onto a backstretch that led to a very wide second turn, making it an ideal track for closers—horses that come from behind to win.

Arnaz was a hardened veteran of the betting window wars, while Bracken was a weekend warrior who made small wagers whenever he ventured out to Santa Anita or Hollywood Park. Bracken got lucky and backed the winners of the first two races, raising the ire of the luckless Desi, who was downing highball after highball at their table in the track restaurant. Desi suggested a small side bet on the next race, and Eddie accepted. Eddie placed a modest wager on his selection, while Desi (perhaps taking a page from the playbook of his Del Mar buddy Jimmy Durante) placed $100 bets on each of two horses to win. Desi's two horses hit the homestretch together, battling for the lead. Desi looked like a sure winner until another horse came up the rail and drifted out, forcing the Desi-backed pair wider and wider and allowing Bracken's horse to scoot up the inside and claim victory. No sooner had the horses crossed the finish line than Desi snapped. He threw chairs around the restaurant, smashed plates and glasses, and screamed, "Nobody likes me because I'm Cuban!" With Bracken's help, track security managed to calm him down, and no charges were pressed. Desi paid for the damage.[20]

Richard Keith, who played Lucy and Desi's son, Little Ricky, on *I Love Lucy,* could attest to Desi's temper as well as the precarious state of the Lucy-Desi marriage. "At their home there was always tension. One time Desi Jr. and I were playing in the backyard, and they were in the guest house. We heard a lot of loud arguing and cursing and glass shattering, and we were scared. Desi Jr. turned to me and said, 'There they go again.'"[21]

Lucy and Desi owned a house in Del Mar, next door to Jimmy Durante's place, for thirty years. Desi joked that when they weren't studying the racing form for the next day's races, Durante was helping him with his English. "That's why I speak the way I do," he laughed. The two men would remain close friends until Durante's death in 1980, by which time drink and gambling had reduced Desi to a shell of his former self. "When Jimmy died," recalled comedian Jack Carter, "his widow Margie asked Desi to help with the funeral. They were old friends from the Del Mar Racetrack days. Desi was so out of it that he kept inviting people who were dead. He kept calling up that old racetrack crowd, but they were all gone. He was thinking of people from 30 years ago when they were kids. At the funeral Desi stood at the back stammering. He didn't know where he was. He was even bombed that day." Desi didn't get it entirely wrong, though. Among the mourners at Jimmy's funeral were Bill Shoemaker and his Del Mar neighbor Harry James. By then, Desi's marriage to Lucy was long over, but he kept her in his heart until the day he died. "I loved her very much," he said late in life, "and, in my own peculiar way, I will always love her."[22]

Terror at the Track

Losing a big bet at the track can be a traumatic experience. It has been known to cause grown men to weep and reduce them to a steady diet of Campbell's soup for a week or two. Normally, however, a racetrack is as safe as Fort Knox. With all the money on hand and all the valuable horseflesh on display, racetracks come fully equipped with first-rate security teams to protect the spectators, the money, and the horses.

But the temptation of all that cash passing back and forth through the windows can be irresistible. Stanley Kubrick realized as much with his spellbinding 1956 film *The Killing*, in which Sterling Hayden masterminds a successful racetrack heist, only to lose it all when the bag carrying the loot splits open on the airport runway and is blown away by the blast from the airplane's engines moments before he can make his getaway.

Life imitated art on July 27, 1976, closing day of Hollywood Park's summer meeting, when a nervous thief caused a riot at the pari-mutuel windows in Inglewood. Knowing that a big crowd meant that the cashiers' boxes would be stuffed full of bills, the fellow reached under the cage of a

$10 window, scooped up $4,700, and made a run for it. A security guard who must have been schooled on the USC defensive line stopped the guy with a flying tackle, the impact causing the money to fly off in every direction. Bettors—both winners and losers—went diving, trying to catch the loose bills. Then someone yelled "Bomb!" at which point everyone scattered, some panicking so badly that they ran across the track and onto the infield. It is unknown how much the false alarm shouter made off with, once he had a clear field, but he surely did better than the thief—or the luckless Sterling Hayden.

Terror of a more serious brand struck Santa Anita on May 3, 1951, when Paul Salzburg, a deeply troubled, forty-eight-year-old cabinetmaker, approached a pari-mutuel window before the first race and slipped two letters to the surprised clerk. The writing was incoherent, but the gist of the first message was that Salzburg was broke, had lost his self-respect, and needed a few thousand dollars to buy a new house for his wife and kids. The second letter was more explicit. It read: "I'm going to blow the whole place up. There'll be no racing at Santa Anita today." The clerk immediately informed security, but Salzburg took off running. Soon there were guards and police scouring the grounds, searching for the bomber, but he had lost himself in the crowd.

Present that day in his clubhouse box near the finish line was MGM chief of production Louis B. Mayer, enjoying a day at the races with producer and agent Jess Orsatti. Spotting Hollywood's most powerful executive shortly before the start of the fifth race, Salzburg calmly walked into Mayer's box and took a seat next to him. Mayer recalled, "He drew back his jacket and said something about 'They're after me! They're after me!' He said he didn't want to hurt me but he wanted to get everybody else." Salzburg gave Mayer a brief glimpse of a gadget in his shirt pocket that had wires protruding from it. Then he said, "Anybody close to me and I'll touch these wires." Orsatti later told police that he asked the troubled man, "What do you want, money? But the guy just kept on yakking away. Then I saw someone throw a chair and hit him, and the cops came."[23]

An alert racegoer had knocked Salzburg unconscious with a folding chair. Salzburg was identified as a longshot player and a regular at Santa Anita and Hollywood Park. The "bomb" in his shirt pocket turned out to be an utterly harmless device—a battery with a couple of wires attached, placed in a cigarette pack. After Salzburg was removed, racing continued without a hitch.

6

The Gamblers
The Downfall of Mickey, Chico, and Others

Sticking to two-dollar bets, I won a few and lost more than a few. That first afternoon I lost sixteen dollars. I've spent the rest of my life (and millions of dollars) trying to win that sixteen dollars back.

Mickey Rooney

The Downside of Horse Racing

Mickey Rooney's recollection of his first racetrack experience at Agua Caliente in 1934 at the tender age of fourteen became a stock joke that went through various permutations during his long and colorful career. Sometimes the story was about the $5 he had lost at Santa Anita forty years earlier and the $2 million he'd spent trying to win it back. Regardless of which track and exactly how much money were involved, as his fortunes on screen, stage, and television rose and fell and rose again, Rooney was always playing catch-up with the horses. He never came close to getting even, but more importantly, he never learned when to stop.

Anyone who frequents racetracks, be they moneybags like Louis B. Mayer and Joe Schenck or $2 bettors like young Mickey, should ask themselves one simple question every time they step up to a pari-mutuel window: if I lose this bet that I am about to place, will it hurt me? If the answer is no, proceed to the window, but if the answer is yes, put the money back in your pocket and go home.

Rooney never went home. Neither did Chico Marx or Bud Abbott, whose gambling problems left them near paupers late in life. Psychologists can provide any number of reasons why some people become addicted to gambling: to deal with depression, as a substitute for sex, or due to an inability to face responsibility. The phenomenon of problem gambling in Hollywood also had something to do with the vast sums of money people were making. And in Rooney's case, it had something to do with the fact that no one ever told him no.

Mickey Rooney: Onscreen Jockey, Offscreen Gambler, and Hollywood's Favorite Husband

Mickey Rooney, born Joe Yule Jr., was the epitome of the Hollywood child prodigy. The son of vaudevillians, five-year-old Joe Jr. was brought to Hollywood in 1925 by his mother, Nellie, who had recently separated from his father. He made his first screen appearance a year later in a comedy short, *Not to Be Trusted.* Hal Roach, always on the lookout for potential child stars, took notice and tried to get Joe to join Our Gang, but he made his mother an offer she *could* refuse. Nellie was insulted by the $15 a week for her prized possession and told Roach where he could go.

A low-budget studio called Film Booking Offices of America (it would later be absorbed by RKO Pictures) ran an ad seeking boys for a prospective series of comic shorts, and Nellie was pleased to present Joe Jr. He was immediately hired as the lead in the Mickey McGuire comedies, adopting the character's name as his own. The series ran in direct opposition to the more successful Our Gang comedies, but whereas Our Gang was a team of ensemble players, there was no denying that the energetic Mickey was the star in all seventy-eight episodes of the Mickey McGuire series, which ran through 1936.

With the money rolling in, Rooney could hardly repress his hyperactive personality. He was always "on," even when he was supposed to be off. Between scenes on the Mickey McGuire set, he would challenge his fellow child actors to games of marbles, but they were playing for more than just marbles. The teenaged Rooney would sometimes be called away from the game to take a phone call from his bookie. He had already discovered the delights of betting on the horses down in Agua Caliente.

Rooney's first break into serious cinema came when the highly respected Austrian director Max Reinhardt cast him as Puck in Warner Bros. glamourous but stilted 1935 production of *A Midsummer Night's Dream.* But in the middle of shooting, the irrepressible kid broke his leg in a tobogganing accident, throwing the production schedule into disarray. Harry Warner was incensed: what was this brat doing on the slopes when he should have been home studying his lines? Warner was so angry that he threatened to break the other leg.

Always looking for an angle, Mickey made the best of his stay in the hospital. Doctors and orderlies would leave copies of the *Daily Racing Form* lying around in the lounge, so Mickey began to study it, testing his acumen through imaginary bets. When he noticed that, on paper, he was winning more often than he was losing, he took to booking bets for the doctors, leaving himself considerably better off financially—and the staff worse off—than when he checked in. At age fifteen, Rooney had become a professional bookie.

Because of his height—he stopped growing at five feet three inches—Rooney was a natural choice to portray jockeys in the increasingly popular genre of racing films. He prepped for those roles in Universal's 1932 production of *Fast Companions,* in which he plays opposite Maureen O'Hara as an orphan who idolizes a crooked jockey.

"I got familiar with horses when I made several horse pictures early in my movie career," Rooney recalled in 1982. "I did *Down the Stretch* and *Thoroughbreds Don't Cry.*" In *Down the Stretch* he appears for the first time as a jockey, and a crooked one at that. The story is a loose adaptation of the life of Lester Reiff, an early-twentieth-century American rider who became highly successful in England but was eventually ruled off for life for throwing a race at Manchester and letting his younger brother, John, win. MGM's *Thoroughbreds Don't Cry* was a step up in class, and it was the first of seven MGM pairings of Rooney and Judy Garland. Judy takes a supporting role, limited to a couple of songs as an onlooker while Rooney teaches English rich kid Ronald Sinclair how to race ride.[1] "He likes movies about horses," Rooney said of MGM boss Louis B. Mayer, "provided the animals were free of hoof-and-mouth disease and closed fast in the final eighth."[2]

With pots of money in the bank, Rooney's appetite for the real thing seemed to be enhanced. He became so adept at cinematic race riding that he once galloped Seabiscuit during a morning workout at Santa Anita. "I weighed 108 pounds when I got on Seabiscuit," he remembered at age fifty-two. "I'm 165 pounds now. No horse would have me."[3]

By this time, Rooney was Hollywood's most prominent cinematic jockey, although Frankie Darro, one of the original Dead End Kids, holds the record for the most appearances as such. Darro played a jockey at least a dozen times, including in *Thoroughbreds Don't Cry.* In that film, he plays the crooked rider who gets his comeuppance in the climactic race when he crashes to the ground in one of the toughest, most realistic racing scenes ever filmed.

Rooney became so enamored of the racing game that he made the 200-mile round-trip between Los Angeles and Del Mar every day of Del Mar's twenty-three-day August meeting in 1940, flying his own Piper Cub. At twenty years old, most boys his age were still trying to figure out how to drive a stick shift. His aerial efforts came to naught in the long run, however. "Del Mar was a toilet," he said, referring not to the racecourse itself but to the large amounts of money he flushed away that summer.[4]

But to the filmgoing public, Rooney was still the cute little Mickey McGuire who grew up into the charming Andy Hardy. None of Rooney's racetrack escapades ever became common knowledge outside a small coterie of MGM insiders and, of course, his fellow racegoers. It was Mayer's policy to shield the American public from the proclivities of the studio's big-name players and to protect his stars from bad publicity. Image was everything to the boss, and he couldn't have the star of *Boys Town, Strike Up the Band, Babes on Broadway,* and the ever-popular Andy Hardy series portrayed as a high-stakes racetrack gambler, even if that's what Rooney was. It was all right to show Mickey playing golf or lounging poolside with Judy, but for someone with his all-American image, racetrack publicity was taboo.

Yet Mickey never hesitated to brag about his gambling adventures. In a 1981 conversation with Lucien Laurin, the trainer of Secretariat, he claimed that he had placed bets at every racetrack in the country and at a lot of those in Europe. He had once been banned from entering Hialeah because he was only seventeen years old, even though he "had been making bets for eleven years already by then."[5]

Like many successful Hollywood stars, Rooney had a fling at racehorse ownership, and it was the fatherly Mayer who got him involved. In 1937 Mayer entered the international bloodstock market in a big way, buying horses of racing and breeding age at all the important sales venues, including Keeneland in Kentucky, Saratoga in upstate New York, and Newmarket in England, the birthplace of Thoroughbred racing. On Mickey's eighteenth birthday, Mayer gave his diminutive box office gold mine a mare named Stereopticon, who was in foal to the well-bred but rather unsuccessful stallion Port O'Prince. Instead of giving Mickey a ready-to-run two-year-old, the wise Mayer presented him with a budding Thoroughbred family. Rooney would have to oversee the mare's pregnancy, wait patiently for the foal's birth, and wait even more patiently until the foal—a colt Mickey named Inintime—was ready to race.

Two years later, that day came. On May 27, 1941, Mickey entered his young charge in a six-furlong maiden race at Hollywood Park. He had procured the services of Johnny Longden, at the time the most coveted rider on the West Coast, and his hopes were high. Inintime busted out of the gate on top and opened a seven-length lead at the halfway mark, heading into the far turn. Could this be the makings of another Seabiscuit? Rooney asked himself. And then all his hopes went up in smoke. Inintime quit. The field passed him as if he were standing still and he finished dead last, in thirteenth place.

Inintime was nothing more than cheap speed, flashy on the front end but utterly lacking in talent. Subsequent efforts proved equally disappointing. Only once did he manage to pick up a small check. Rooney had no choice but to unload the nag. He would own racehorses from time to time over the next forty years, none of them successful.

During his life, Rooney devised a number of betting systems, but like his horses, none of them ever amounted to much. He revealed some of his less feasible ones in 1982 at Del Mar, where he had squandered nearly $1 million in 1940. It is generally accepted that favorites win 30 to 35 percent of the time, but according to Mickey, they win only 15 percent of the time in the first race on the card. Before he could be asked to explain that claim, Rooney changed the subject, declaring that when late wagering on a race creates a new favorite just before post time, that new favorite loses nine out of ten times. He said he had done a great deal of research on such topics, but these off-the-wall statements sound like the proclamations of a deranged gambler. They never did him—or anyone else—any good.[6]

Rooney always adamantly refused to admit that he liked to gamble because he hoped to make money. He was already rich, and he claimed that he bet solely for the pleasure of victory. That search for victory cost him a small fortune, but that amount paled compared with the money he lost as a serial husband. Matrimony is always something of a gamble, and in eight tries at the marriage-go-round, Mickey Rooney finally found enduring happiness with the last of his brides, Jan Chamberlin.

Rooney's attraction to his first wife, Ava Gardner, was strong, but perhaps not as strong as his attraction to the *Daily Racing Form*. After two years, she grew tired of him and went off in search of bigger things. Ironically, it was Ava's memorable appearance in the B racing picture *She Went to the Races*—she knocks everyone else off the screen whenever she's on—that led MGM to cast her in her breakthrough film, *The Killers,* in which she sets the screen on fire playing opposite Burt Lancaster.

Rooney made one of his most popular films at the tail end of his marriage to Ava. In *National Velvet,* he plays an ex–jumps jockey who is afraid to ride after causing an accident in which a fellow rider was killed. With young Elizabeth Taylor in the title role, *National Velvet* charmed filmgoers around the world, despite its preposterous story of a twelve-year-old girl winning the Grand National Steeplechase without any previous race-riding experience.

Mickey robbed the cradle when he married wife number two, Alabama beauty queen Betty Jane Rase, but she was a homebody who resented her husband's public lifestyle. He hopped back into the spotlight with number three, the beautiful actress Martha Vickers, who made an impression swooning into Humphrey Bogart's arms in *The Big Sleep.* After Vickers, gossip columnist Earl Wilson wrote that actress Jane Kean would be Mickey's next wife, but Rooney denied the reports. Jane was merely a race-loving girl who kept him company at the track.

Bride number four was beauty queen and model Elaine Mahnken. However, Rooney's gambling frightened her, given that her first husband had been knocked off by Vegas mobsters for failing to pay his debts. Rooney was happy for a while with wife number five, another beauty queen named Caroline Mitchell. But he declared bankruptcy mid-marriage in 1962, and they cheated on each other with mutual affection until Mitchell was murdered by one of her lovers. Wife number six, Marge Lane, was a close friend of number five and served as a temporary stop-gap. Number seven, Carolyn Hockett, was not in show business, and Mickey once called her "the best wife I ever had."[7] She spent most of their six years together worrying about the family finances until life with Mickey grew too expensive.

Finally, after three years of bachelorhood in the late 1970s, Rooney married Jan Chamberlin. By this time, Mickey's libido had quieted, and he managed to keep his gambling more or less in check. Jan had a chastening influence on him, and the marriage lasted thirty-six years until his death in 2014.

When bankruptcy brought Rooney to a low point in his career in the early 1960s, he managed to turn in what might be the best dramatic performance of his life. *Twilight Zone* producer Rod Serling wrote an episode titled "The Last Night of a Jockey" just for him. It aired on October 25, 1963. The one-man tour de force is about a rider who has been banned for doping horses. He lives in a tiny one-room apartment and spends most of his time on the phone begging trainers and owners to give him one last chance, a situation not too far removed from the actor's real-life dilemma at the time. Rooney's character bemoans his fate as a "little man" and wishes to heaven that he could be big. When his wish is granted, it plunges him into a hellish nightmare of his own making.

Rooney liked to recount the story of Eddie Arcaro, one of the greatest jockeys of all time, a man who piloted more Kentucky Derby winners (five) than any rider in history. When asked late in his career why he continued to risk life and limb on the racetrack every day, even though he didn't need the money, Arcaro replied, "Because if I quit riding I'd be just another little man."[8] That was the problem facing Rooney's character in "The Last Night of a Jockey," and it was the dilemma he faced throughout his adult life. To his credit, Mickey Rooney never quit, but he lost a lot of money along the way. All that alimony and child support (Rooney sired eleven children) ran into the tens of millions of dollars, not to mention gambling losses, taxes, and poor investments. When Rooney died, he left an estate of just $18,000 and a mountain of debt.

Chico Marx Taps Out

Of all the sad Hollywood tales of fortunes lost at the betting windows, gaming tables, and backroom card games, none is more tragic than that of Chico Marx. The "Italian" and eldest member of the Marx Brothers, Chico was famed for his finger-pointing piano technique and mastery of the lunatic double entendre. He caught the gambling bug as a boy growing up in Manhattan's unforgiving Lower East Side during the (not so) Gay Nineties. He quit school in the second grade, and at the age of twelve he lost his first job at a lace factory for running crap games under a sign that read, "NO GAMBLING ALLOWED." As a teenager, he would disappear for days at a time, afraid that local thugs would come looking for him at home to collect overdue debts. Once, when he lost money in a card game, he stole the pinking shears from his father's tailor shop and hocked them to cover his losses.

Chico still managed to become a successful vaudevillian with his brothers: the protective Groucho, the disapproving Harpo, and the sly Zeppo. All four of them were gamblers, and they were especially adept at card games such as poker, gin rummy, pinochle, and bridge. Chico and Zeppo excelled in large part because they were good cheaters, having develop a subtle system of hand and face signals. During his early days onstage in New York, Chico was wiped out betting the horses, and his bookie, a character named Nick the Greek, wasn't happy about his client's lack of payment. One night, Chico disappeared in the middle of a show, leaving the brothers to improvise during his absence. They also had to improvise payment to Nick the Greek. When the Marx Brothers got their big break in the movies and the big money started rolling in, Chico's share rolled out just as quickly, much of it through the pari-mutuel windows at Santa Anita, Del Mar, and Hollywood Park.

The presence of three racetracks in the Los Angeles area only made it easier for Chico to place a bet, not that he ever had any qualms about less legal forms of gambling. In 1935 Chico became involved with a crooked gambler named Jimmy "The Weasel" Fratianno, who was running a sting operation at the Fair Grounds racetrack in New Orleans. Fratianno had set up a wiretap across the street from the track, enabling him to get the results of a race seconds after the finish. He would then call his cronies at El Rancho Casino in Las Vegas, where the Marx Brothers were holding court. Chico would answer the phone, get the name of the winner, and quickly place his winning bet before the casino received the official results. It was one of the few times in his life that Chico profited from a scam he was working.

Chico put his knowledge of betting scams to good use in *A Day at the Races,* in which he cons Groucho out of his betting money. Posing as an ice cream vendor, Chico spots the clueless Groucho—cast for the only time in his career as a gullible rube—wandering around in front of the betting windows. He's hoping to place a winning bet and thus save his quack psychiatric hospital, which is under threat from developers. Chico sells Groucho a slip of paper on which is printed the indecipherable code ZYBXRPL. Chico then cons Groucho into buying one handicapping book after another, each one supposedly decoding the message and leading to the name of the winner. Thoroughly confused and wobbling under the weight of his useless new library, Groucho is left penniless.

"Going to the races with Chico was quite an adventure," recalled his daughter Maxine. "His pals called him 'The Asking Handicapper' because he collected sure tips from the mouths of trainers, jockeys and, I suspect, even from the horses. There was no way for him to come out ahead betting on horses, but as long as he got to cheer home a winner now and then, his enthusiasm didn't waver."[9]

That was the thing about Chico. He never complained about his gambling losses, but he did use his happy-go-lucky charm to bilk his friends, taking their money to bet on horses that rarely won. Eventually, his addiction caught up with him. After the Marx Brothers announced their retirement from film after *The Big Store* in 1941, Chico's stash quickly dried up, but his gambling habit didn't. With Chico nearly broke, Groucho and Harpo took pity and agreed to make two more pictures with him, *A Night in Casablanca* (1946) and *Love Happy* (1949). The boys were hardly at their best in either film, but at least Chico had a source income, one that Groucho and Harpo controlled by putting their elder brother on a strict allowance.

But it didn't matter. Chico Marx was a lost cause. He would bet on anything that moved, including raindrops dripping down a windowpane. In 1952, while visiting producer, friend, and fellow horseplayer Bert Friedlob in the hospital, Chico wasn't surprised to see a copy of the *Racing Form* on the bed. Friedlob, who later produced Fritz Lang's last two American films, *While the City Sleeps* and *Beyond a Reasonable Doubt,* was busy placing bets by phone. During one of these calls, a trainer friend supplied him with a hot tip at Santa Anita for later in the week, but Friedlob wouldn't reveal the name of the horse to Chico. "You'll only blab it to everyone and knock down the odds," he complained. "Come back on Wednesday. We'll go out to the track and keep it to ourselves."[10]

Chico went into action and began hustling anyone and everyone in his acquaintance, finally managing to come up with $700—an amount that would have been pocket change for Groucho or Harpo. On the day of the race, in the car on the way to the track, Chico's charm got the best of Friedlob, and he told his friend the name of the supposed sure thing: Rice Crop in the second. He warned Chico not to reveal the information to anyone, on pain of death. But Chico couldn't help being Chico. No sooner had they arrived at Santa Anita than he began taking all and sundry aside—friends, acquaintances, complete strangers—and telling them the good news. Soon half the track was under the confirmed impression that Rice Crop couldn't lose. After all, they had heard it from the great Chico Marx himself.

By post time, the odds on Rice Crop had been banged down to 8–5. Chico put his $700 through the window, happily took his place next to Friedlob in the clubhouse stands, then watched forlornly as his sure thing came home next to last. Friedlob blew the loudmouth off, leaving a dazed and confused Chico penniless and with no way of getting home to Beverly Hills. He managed to hitch a ride with a truck driver, who casually asked him where he was coming from. "The track," Chico answered sharply, not wanting to talk about it. "Really?" the trucker said. "How did Rice Crop do in the second?"[11]

Zeppo was of the opinion that there wasn't a day in Chico's life that he didn't have a bet on something—a ball game, a card game, a horse race—and Zeppo knew what he was talking about. Besides being Chico's brother, he was a member of Hollywood's vast underground betting ring himself.

When asked late in life how much money he had lost gambling, Chico sheepishly replied, "Just see how much money Harpo has!"[12] Indeed, Harpo and Groucho lived out their days in refined comfort, while Chico survived on Social Security checks, often having to scrounge for money to pay the grocery bill, and owed the IRS $77,564.

Chico's predilection disgusted Harpo, but Groucho always took a conciliatory approach to his older brother's problem. At Chico's funeral, he wistfully recalled, "He's the only one of the Marx Brothers who didn't save his money. He died broke. But you know something? He enjoyed his life more than any of us."[13]

The Al Jolson Jive

What is it about movie stars that makes them crave acceptance to the point of obsession? Just as Chico Marx told everyone about his hot tip to be seen as a more likable fellow, Al Jolson's gambling problem reflected a deep desire to be seen as a winner. Perhaps that need for constant affirmation is something shared by all gamblers, but in Jolson's case, it manifested as pathetic self-deception.

The Lithuanian-born Jolson—a great vaudevillian and star of the first talkie, *The Jazz Singer* (in which he famously sings "Mammy" in blackface)—grew up in Washington, DC. That political enclave is surrounded on three sides by Maryland, the state whose horsey reputation is second only to Kentucky's. As a youngster, he would frequently skip school to sample the more entertaining temptations at racetracks in the area such as Bowie, Pimlico, and Havre de Grace.

"I lived from day to day on the dream of some time riding a horse to a surprise victory in a big race," he recalled, which sounds like the template for many of Hollywood's racing melodramas of the 1930s and 1940s. He got his chance to do just that in the 1925 Broadway musical *Big Boy,* in which he played a black stable hand, Gus, unjustly fired from his job and reduced to flipping burgers. Gus, however, has remained in the good graces of a prominent horse owner, who puts him aboard her prize three-year-old, Big Boy. After bamboozling a gang of race fixers, Gus rides Big Boy to victory in the Kentucky Derby. Throughout his life, Jolson always cited Gus his favorite stage role.[14] In 1930 Warner Bros. made *Big Boy* into a movie starring Jolson. After the story is over, he makes an appearance through stage curtains without his blackface makeup to confirm to the audience that he is really white. He offers to sing a song called "Sonny Boy" but then shyly demurs, slipping back through the curtains as the film ends.

Jolson bought his first horse in July 1921. The six-year-old gelding named Snapdragon II campaigned on the New York circuit (Belmont, Jamaica, Saratoga) but brought his owner little more than training and veterinarian bills. Jolson always had a marked preference for betting at the track. He was known to cancel a Broadway matinee so he could go out to Belmont and wager on a sure thing, often treating cast members to bets at his expense, so great was his desire to please. His booming voice could be heard throughout the vast Belmont grandstand cheering his horse home. Everyone knew when Jolson had a big bet on a horse.

Strangely, he never seemed to place a losing bet, if his noisy reaction was any indication. The horse he was cheering to victory almost always won, which begs the question: were all his bets really as successful as they seemed?

One August afternoon at Saratoga, Jolson was unable to conceal a particularly painful loss. A year earlier, the forty-two-year-old Jolson had wed nineteen-year-old singer-dancer Ruby Keeler. Running in the first race that day was a filly named Ruby Keeler, it being commonplace for racehorses to be named after show business personalities. Everyone at the track knew that Jolson must be betting on his young's wife's namesake, and bet he did; it is not known how many thousands of dollars he wagered. But Ruby Keeler the Thoroughbred turned out to be faithless and heartless. Jolson's disappointment at the loss was so great that he left the track almost as soon as the race was over.

With the advent of the talkie era in 1927, Jolson moved both his on- and off-track act to Hollywood. There was no racing in California at the time, so like everyone else in town, he sought entertainment down in Tijuana. In 1930 he bought a chunk of Agua Caliente, the new racing and gambling complex. Four years later, he was one of the first investors in Santa Anita, an act he would later repeat at Hollywood Park.

Tall stories were part of Jolson's social repertoire. One of the more improbable had him getting the best of racing scion Alfred Gwynne Vanderbilt, future owner of the great champions Discovery and Native Dancer. While socializing at Belmont one afternoon, they both liked the same horse in the day's feature race. To hear Jolson tell the story, Vanderbilt bet all of $7, while he himself wagered $4,000, and the horse cruised home at 40–1! This is the racing equivalent of the big fish story, and it stinks just as badly.

In fact, Jolson could never admit defeat, or even being wrong, in any endeavor, a characteristic he consistently displayed at the races. One particular incident throws light on Jolson's manic desire to be seen as a winner. Attending the races one day with his old Broadway buddy Georgie Jessel, Jolson asked him which horse he liked in the next race. When Jessel offered his opinion, Jolson pooh-poohed his friend's selection. "I got the winner right here!" he crowed, touting another horse whose credentials, he claimed, were impeccable. The two men placed their bets. As the race developed, their two horses hit the stretch dueling for the lead. Jessel began to cheer his horse home, but Jolson was unusually quiet. Finally, as Jessel's horse moved in front at the sixteenth pole, Jolson started cheering loudly for him. After the race, a puzzled Jessel said, "Al, I thought you backed the other horse," to which Jolson replied, "I changed my mind. I got the winner! Ha-ha! I told you so! I got the winner!"[15] How many of Jolson's lustily cheered "winners" over the years were really cover-ups for losing bets can never be known.

Jimmy "Schnozzola" Durante Laughs Himself to the Poorhouse

Whereas Al Jolson could not bear to be seen as a loser, Jimmy Durante flaunted his gambling losses as if they were a badge of honor, milking them for all the potential humor they were worth. Like Jolson, Durante lost a fortune at the betting windows. Unlike Jolson, he was able to laugh about it.

Like Chico Marx, Durante was born on Manhattan's Lower East Side, and like Marx and Jolson, he was attracted to gambling at an early age. A self-taught piano player, he had performed at dozens of bars and nightclubs in Chinatown, Harlem, and Coney Island before the end of World

War I, singing, telling jokes, and generally making fun of himself. It was an atmosphere permeated by gambling: backroom card games, floating craps games, and hot tips at nearby racetracks in Sheepshead Bay and Gravesend. A copy of the racing section of the *Morning Telegraph* was as big a part of his act as his trademark nose.

From the start, Durante—or "Schnozzola," as he self-effacingly titled himself—developed a surefire system for betting on the ponies. The problem was, that system consisted of betting on five or six horses in every race, so that even when he cashed a winning ticket, he still lost money. Whereas Jolson was terrified to be *seen* losing, Durante was just plain scared of losing. His system cost him a fortune, but he didn't seem to mind. There are famous photographs of him leaving Del Mar at the end of the day with his empty pants pockets turned inside out, a look of forlorn haplessness on his face.

A bartender at one of the Coney Island dives where Durante was working once played a cruel trick on him. Durante had been complaining that local bookies were paying off at less than track odds, so the barkeep gave him the phone number of someone who would "pay the limit." The "Schnozz" made a call and placed a number of bets, with instructions to deliver any winnings to the bar. Unbeknownst to Durante, the number he had dialed was the office of Brooklyn's antigambling district attorney Edward Swan. Every one of his bets was a loser, which was disappointing enough. Meanwhile, Swan sent a man to the bar to investigate. Durante, thinking he was the bookie's agent, paid the guy off for his losing bets and was promptly arrested for attempted bribery. Happily, Durante got off with a warning.

A success on Broadway and on radio, Durante split his time in the 1930s between the Great White Way and Hollywood, where he starred in *What! No Beer* with Buster Keaton, in *George White's Scandals* with Rudy Vallee, and in *Hollywood Party* with Laurel and Hardy. While on a tour of London and Paris, he had no trouble transferring his racetrack humor to the elegant surroundings of Ascot and Longchamp. But apparently, he had difficulty figuring out English money, which at the time was a bewildering system of guineas, sovereigns, crowns, pounds, shillings, pence, and farthings. That was no deterrent to the Schnozz. "So I puts five bob, whatever that is, on a horse named Durante and he wins . . . by a nose, of course, what did you expect?"[16]

Next, he crossed the English Channel to Paris for a fling at Longchamp, which, he said, "is what they call Jamaica over there. An American jockey

[Billy] Pearson [whose on-track greeting once cost John Huston a small fortune] is riding. He hems and haws, but finally he says there is one horse in the race he thinks can beat him. So I puts ten pounds on the horse he likes, but Pearson wins anyway."[17] It was a lesson well learned. Late in life, Durante provided this advice to all horseplayers: "Never take information from a man who doesn't have holes in his shoes."[18]

By the end of World War II, Durante had become an American institution and one of the country's most beloved entertainers. His audience consisted of a broad spectrum of America's filmgoing and radio-listening public. He played Carnegie Hall and the Metropolitan Opera, but he also beat electric guitar bashers Jimi Hendrix and Pete Townsend to the punch by thirty years when he took to smashing his piano to pieces onstage. In 1946 Del Mar's twin attractions of racing and beachcombing proved irresistible to him. Like couples Betty Grable and Harry James and Lucille Ball and Desi Arnaz, Durante bought a house on the Del Mar beach to be as close as possible to the racetrack.

"At Del Mar," he pointed out, "you study the ponies, stay out of the water, and establish supoib rapport with da fish." But his philosophizing didn't help him at the betting windows. According to *Los Angeles Herald-Examiner* sportswriter Mel Durslag, Durante developed a new betting system: instead of betting on five or six horses in each race, he bet on all the horses listed at 5–1 on the morning line. This proved no more successful than his old system, but he did hit the daily double one day and won $800. Informed that he would have to fill out a form to report his winnings to the IRS, Durante was irate. "It's an outrage," he fumed. "I'll take it to the appellate court. And if they don't listen, I'll take it to the Supreme Court. And if I don't get no satisfaction, I'll take it to a notary public!" In the end, the taxman still got 20 percent of Schnozzola's winnings, cutting even more deeply into his net losses. Poor Jimmy never learned. One day at Hollywood Park he bet on six of the nine horses in a single race to win. As the field turned into the stretch, he shouted, "C'mon everybody!"[19] Durante recognized the problem. "I don't play right," he lamented. "I play $2 here, $2 there and $2 here and $2 there." But most of the time, the bets were much larger than $2.[20]

Durante may have been losing his shirt, but he was winning the hearts of his fellow travelers at the track. He served as best man at the wedding of Oak Tree Racing Association founder and prominent California horseman Clement Hirsch Jr., who returned the favor by serving as best man at Durante's 1960 marriage to his second wife, Margie Little. A year later, someone left a three-week-old baby on the Durantes' front stoop on Christmas Eve. Jimmy and Margie took the little girl in, named her Cecilia, and adopted her.

Durante was at Del Mar so often, and he was so beloved by everyone there, that he became known as the "Mayor of Del Mar." The street in front of the track's main entrance is named Jimmy Durante Boulevard. Also bearing his name is the Del Mar turf course, where, since 2014, the Jimmy Durante Stakes—a Grade 3, one-mile turf race for two-year-old fillies— has been run. His longtime vaudeville partner Lou Clayton remembered Durante as a man who would give away everything he had to any unfortunate person he met, including, one must assume, all those underpaid Del Mar pari-mutuel clerks.

In 1969, at the age of seventy-six, Durante made a last confession of sorts about the ponies to the *Herald-Examiner*'s Gordon Jones: "I been playing 'em for 50 years and I still don't know anything about 'em." But he sure had a swell time trying to figure them out.[21]

John Huston the Hunter

If *The Career of John Huston* were a film, it might be depicted as a roller coaster ride: there were the heights of *The Maltese Falcon, The Treasure of the Sierra Madre,* and *Key Largo;* the depths of *Beat the Devil, The List of Adrian Messenger,* and *A Walk with Love and Death;* and then, at the tail end of his career, a return to the heights of *Prizzi's Honor* and *The Dead,* with stops in between at the middle ground of *The Unforgiven* and *The Kremlin Letter.*

Loquacious, literate, and charming, Huston was also a drunkard, a philanderer, and, according to his obituary in the *Guardian,* "a lifelong gambler. He went through millions and did not blame himself."[22] A contrarian to the point of perversity, he disdained Hollywood society, got away with murder at the age of twenty-seven, renounced his American citizenship in favor of Ireland, possessed perhaps the most beautiful male voice the world has ever heard, could act every bit as well as he could direct, and was an accomplished painter. An avowed liberal, he championed all leftist causes, including animal rights, yet he enjoyed nothing so much as the aristocratic sport of fox hunting. He breathily described the climax of the day's events—the hounds ripping the head off the cornered fox—as "Exhilaration, exaltation!" If he had been alive during the American and French Revolutions, he surely would have been a follower of Lafayette, a fighter for democracy in the New World, and a defender of royalty in the Old. His leading man and drinking buddy Humphrey Bogart not-so-jokingly called Huston "Double Ugly" and "The Monster." On the set of *The Barbarian and the Geisha* (one of his low points), he was coldcocked by John Wayne with a single well-placed punch to the chin. In short, John Huston was a human being with a capital *H* and *B*.

"My life is composed of random, tangential, disparate episodes," he wrote. "Five wives, many liaisons, some more memorable than the marriages. The hunting, the betting, the Thoroughbreds. . . ." Ah, yes, the betting and the Thoroughbreds. What percentage of the millions Huston lost can be attributed to the horses can never be determined, as he lost so very much during his riotously prolific life.[23]

Young John's first memories growing up in Nevada, Missouri, were of horseback riding, a sport he practiced most of his life, both socially and as a hunter, until drink and tobacco incapacitated him. His parents, Walter Huston and Rhea Gore, divorced when he was only six, and although he spent part of each summer traveling the vaudeville circuit with his actor father, he lived mostly with his sportswriter mother, who was particularly fond of horse racing. She brought John to racetracks on the Midwest circuit, inculcating him with a love of horses and paving his way to the pari-mutuel windows.

With the advent of talkies, Walter Huston parlayed his beautiful voice into starring roles in D. W. Griffith's *Abraham Lincoln* and Howard Hawks's *The Criminal Code*. This gave son John a leg up in the business, and he served as co-screenwriter on William Wyler's *A House Divided,* starring his father, and Robert Florey's *Murders in the Rue Morgue.* But one night in 1933, while driving down Sunset Boulevard, John plowed his car into young chorus girl Tosca Roulien, killing her instantly. Walter begged for help from Louis B. Mayer, who set his well-oiled fixing machine into motion. The ugly business was smoothed over, but John spent a year down and out in London, much of the "down" and a lot of the "out" the result of frequent trips to the city's many bookmaking shops. Given the chance to write a treatment for what turned out to be David Lean's first film, *It Happened in Paris,* he redeemed himself. Huston reappeared in Hollywood, where he scored screenwriting credits on Wyler's *Jezebel* and Raoul Walsh's *High Sierra,* an effort that led to his first directing job: *The Maltese Falcon.*

Huston's history of gambling, boozing, and womanizing is a familiar one. He suffered from the same disease as Chico Marx and Mickey

Rooney: too much money and too little self-discipline. Coupled with a weakness for the myriad charms and temptations of the racetrack, he fell prey at an early age and never recovered. He bought his first Thoroughbred at virtually no cost to himself from a generous Liz Whitney, the ex-wife of Jock Whitney and the proprietor of Llangollen Farm. The filly's name was, appropriately, Bargain Lass. Out of a mare by 1935 Triple Crown winner Omaha, she had the potential to be good but had repeatedly disappointed her previous owner. Bargain Lass was a bad "gate horse," so the ex–Mrs. Whitney unloaded her.

Jockey Billy Pearson (who had bamboozled Jimmy Durante at Longchamp a few years earlier) figured that he knew how to solve Bargain Lass's gate problems. At the start of a six-furlong allowance race at Santa Anita, a confident Huston watched as Pearson carefully placed Bargain Lass's tail over the back of the gate to keep her steady. The filly responded with a three-and-a-half-length victory. Huston not only cashed in a winning ticket but also found his regular rider and a lifelong friend. Huston eventually developed a small stable concentrating on fillies and mares that he bred to imported stallions, including Louis Mayer's Alibhai and Rex Ellsworth's Khaled. Although he never bred any major winners, he loved to watch his horses run.

Admitting his weakness for gambling, Huston wrote in his 1972 autobiography *An Open Book:* "I have, on various occasions, put down some fairly good bets. I don't think the rate of my pulse ever increased radically when I had a few thousands on a horse's nose, even when I could ill afford it. But to see babies of yours, born in your stable, entering the starting gate decked out in your colors is quite another matter. I never seem to be able to hold them in my binoculars. They have a way of jumping out of the picture with every heartbeat."[24]

There is nothing more frustrating for a horseplayer than failing to bet on a horse he really loves and then discovering that the horse has won. Those potential winnings always seem greater than the money actually lost.

In the spring of 1948 Huston was busy filming his third consecutive masterpiece, *Key Largo.* Lady Bruce, a filly he owned in partnership with actress Virginia Bruce, was entered in a six-furlong dash at Santa Anita. Billy Pearson assured the owners that Lady Bruce couldn't lose, pointing out that in her last race she had led for the first six furlongs before fading to finish a close fourth. Huston withdrew everything he had in the bank, borrowed $2,000 each from Anatole Litvak and William Wyler, and turned the money over to wife number three, Evelyn Keyes, with instructions to go to the track and invest it all on Lady Bruce. Huston was so confident of victory that he urged *Key Largo*'s cast and crew to follow suit, and that morning, the phones at the local bookies' shops must have been ringing off the hook. The horse to beat was a colt named Dry, a $20,000 Argentine import trained by Horatio Luro, a sly horseman and the future conditioner of the great Northern Dancer.

Listening to the race on the radio, everyone on the *Key Largo* set was overjoyed when Lady Bruce led throughout and defeated Dry, paying off at 12.40–1. Huston was over the moon. "This was the greatest news I'd ever received," he recalled. "I was rolling in dough!" He quickly put together a celebration dinner party at Chasen's, the famous West Hollywood eatery favored by everyone in show business.

Half an hour later, Huston's world came crashing down. Production assistant Art Fellows called him with the horrifying news that Evelyn had failed to wager his money on Lady Bruce. It seems that Senor Luro had invited her to watch the race from his box and managed to convince her that Dry would win the race. She had bet a mere $100 on Lady Bruce, so instead of some $85,000 in winnings, Huston's take amounted to just $1,240, barely enough to cover the cost of dinner and drinks. Such an act of unfaithfulness could drive a man to drink or, more to the point, to divorce. Fearful of John's reaction, Evelyn failed to show up at Chasen's, irritating Huston even more. He had a phone brought to the table and dialed her number. He listened patiently as she tried to explain, but the "monster" suddenly reared its ugly head, and he began to curse her out loudly enough for everyone in the restaurant to hear. It was the beginning of the end of their marriage, which was dissolved two years later.[25]

A 1951 visit to the old country warmed the Irish in Huston's blood, and a year later he purchased a Georgian manor house called St. Clerans in Craughell, County Galway, on Ireland's west coast. When he wasn't in Hollywood making a film, in London or Paris for a big race meeting, or in New York on business, he was in Ireland. By then, his family included Mrs. Huston IV, ballet dancer and *Life* cover girl Enrica Soma, and their two small children, Tony and Angelica. In Ireland, Huston led the life of a country squire. Named Master of Hounds of the Galway Blazers, his responsibilities included buying and caring for the Blazers' pack of dogs, as well as participating in the hunts themselves. And when he wasn't chasing the fox in Ireland, he might be chasing the tiger in India or filming Bogey and Katharine Hepburn in Uganda and the Belgian Congo in his next big hit, *The African Queen.*

Once one is bitten by the betting bug, one doesn't recover. Although Huston had limited time to spend at the track, he had the resources to assemble a team of trainers, agents, friends, and bookies through whom he could place bets anywhere in the world—Los Angeles, Chicago, New York, Dublin, London, or Paris—no matter where he was himself. In spite of his bad experience with Evelyn, Huston trusted these friends and agents, allowing them to place bets on his behalf without informing him beforehand. If the wager was successful, the money would be plowed back into the next bet. If it was unsuccessful, the friend might timidly remind Huston how much he owed in a carefully worded letter. In the long run, there were more of the latter than the former.

Warner Bros. executive Jean Thiroux was one of these friendly agents employed by Huston. On November 11, 1947, he wired Huston: "SAD NEWS STOP PLACED FIFTY ACROSS THE BOARD ON FIGHTING LEE TODAY STOP RAN OUT STOP RUSSO WORKED COLT SINCE RESHOD AND DOESN'T THINK LOOKS TOO GOOD AS FEELS NEEDS MORE EDUCATION BUT MAY RUN HIM MONDAY BARRING RAIN."[26]

The Russo referred to in the telegram was Joe Russo, Huston's trainer in San Francisco. After the fiasco of the unplaced wager, Lady Bruce was sent north to Bay Meadows for a minor stakes race. Billy Pearson was committed to ride at Santa Anita that day, so Russo gave a leg up to Harry Trent, his go-to man in the Bay Area. Lady Bruce failed to make the lead and finished out of the money, prompting an irate Huston to write to Russo. The letter, sent from the MGM studios in Culver City, where Huston was filming *Key Largo,* read:

April 14th, 1948
Mr. Joseph Russo
c/o Racing Secretary
Bay Meadows Racetrack
San Mateo, California
Dear Mr. Russo:
I was very disappointed in the ride Trent gave Lady Bruce last week. He acted completely against the instructions I heard you

give him in the paddock before the race, and I see no good reason for him having done so. In view of this it's my desire that you discontinue his services as a jockey.

I do not wish to imply that Trent behaved in bad faith or to cast any aspersion on his riding abilities. Twice before he gave the same mount praiseworthy rides and for that I am duly grateful. Very truly yours,

John Huston[27]

By April 30, *Key Largo* was in postproduction, and Huston was on holiday at the Hotel Nacionale in Havana. He received a cablegram from Thiroux containing more disappointing news: "Lady Bruce ran fourth. Led all the way until the home stretch. Will find out what happened. Preview [of *Key Largo*] was tonight. Mechanical difficulties ruined it as such. Sorry to report such sad news."[28]

The next day, the report from Thiroux was more encouraging: "Conejo Ranch called. You are proud owner of beautiful chestnut colt. He is well and strong. Will send full details after seeing him." On May 10 there was more good news from the breeding barn: "Just received following info: Aunt Lois foaled chestnut filly with blaze face and three white stockings on May Sixth. Foal perfectly normal and mare completed her delivery well. Conejo sent note saying Countess Bye bred to Niccolo on May Seventh. Preview *Key Largo* tomorrow."[29]

In this way, Huston was able to stay abreast of all matters cinematic and equine. Although none of these foals ever amounted to anything, *Key Largo* crossed the finish line twelfth in box office receipts in 1948, with $3,289,000, and Claire Trevor won an Oscar for best supporting actress. Huston's earlier 1948 film, *The Treasure of the Sierra Madre,* came in fifth at $4,307,000.

In 1950 Huston's first horse, Bargain Lass, was still in training as a five-year-old mare and doing well. In midyear at Hollywood Park she had a hot streak, as reported by Huston's devoted secretary at MGM, Jeanne. She cabled Huston at the Waldorf-Astoria in New York, where he was awaiting the world premiere of *The Asphalt Jungle:* "'Bargain' came in paid thirty-nine ninety (18.95–1) ten fifty and four ninety. Congratulations. Love, Jeanne."[30] A week later, Jeanne reported: "Bargain Lass won. Paid ten twenty (4.10–1). You're still better off collecting purses so don't be disappointed. Love, Jeanne." That message referred to the fact that no bet had been placed on the winner, but the prize money more than made up for the wagering loss.[31]

In the autumn of 1954 Ben Goetz, the brother of Louis Mayer's son-in-law Bill and the head of MGM's British branch, was staying at Claridge's in London. He had just returned from Paris, where he had attended Europe's most important late-season race, the Prix de l'Arc de Triomphe. Goetz wrote to Huston, who was at the Bay Hotel in Fishguard, Wales: "As you requested, I bet £5 [5,000 francs] for you on Sica Boy, my pick for the big race at Longchamps [sic], and it paid 51 francs for 10. You therefore win 25,500 francs. I assume you will prefer to have the winnings in Dollars, so I am enclosing my check for $57.40." These must have been hard times if the heavy-gambling Huston could afford only an $11 bet on one of the most important races in the world.[32]

During his frequent racing excursions to England, Huston had become friendly with one of its prominent owners, Jack Gerber. In 1955 Gerber was having a banner year with his sprinter Royal Palm, who would win the seven-furlong Challenge Stakes at Goodwood and what is arguably the best sprint race in Europe, York's five-furlong Nunthorpe Stakes, after earning blacktype as a two-year-old with victories in Epsom's Woodcote Stakes and Newbury's Horris Hill Stakes. Even before his three-year-old achievements, Royal Palm was being offered as a stallion prospect, and Gerber sent this thinly disguised sales pitch from his home in Hyde Park, London, to Huston at Courtown House in County Kildare:

30th May, 1955

My dear John,

Thank you both so much for putting us up for the Guineas.[33] It was awfully nice of you—it seems a shame that I cannot reciprocate h'ever much I try!

I enclose my cheque for your winnings of 35 pounds, being my approximate gin rummy losses.

Your winnings for this past week amount to only 205 pounds (because Nicholas lost) and this I will hold for you for betting purposes—as you (probably unwisely) suggested.

By Thunder! spread-eagled his field again in the valuable Winston Churchill Stakes at Hurst Park over 2 miles—there was the usual procession behind him stretching back about ¼ of a mile as he stormed home—he will run at Ascot in the Hardwicke

Stakes (against Narrator) and then in the King George VI and Queen Elisabeth [*sic*] Stakes.

Al Crown and Harold Mirish[34] [*sic*] came with me to see him run and they were most thrilled, and I made them back him (100 pounds each). They would like to go shares with me in my horses, which they would like me to send to America. If I ever decided to do this I think it would be much more fun with you and Greg [identity unknown].

Harold Mirisch let slip, (but quite emphatically) that something would have to be done to enable you to come back to England without financial loss to yourself. I did not flog the point but I am sure they would like you to be free to come here. . . . Even if it meant altering your schedule.

My good pal Jerome Whyte is putting on a special version of *Oklahoma* (at the U.S. President's [Dwight Eisenhower's] suggestion) in Paris on July 20th and you and I are specially invited— can you join me there (R.S.V.P.)?!! Jerry Whyte also fancies himself at gin rummy. . . .

Love to you all and the "brats,"
Yours ever,

Jack

50 pounds ROYAL PALM at 9/2 = 100 pounds BY THUNDER! at 4/5 = 80
100 pounds NICHOLAS NCKLEBY (the drains burst at Warwick and the course was a quagmire but he'll win for you on the 8th)[35]

This letter's fawning attitude suggests that Gerber was rather desperate to form a stallion syndicate for horses that were not quite as good as he made them out to be. A second letter less than a week later reveals that Gerber was in a state of gentlemanly panic over the matter:

6th June, 1955
Dear John,
This cutting might interest you. —Did you get my letter in which I asked you to let me know about Paris?
My news is not very exciting—I have not done much apart from a little racing at which I held my own.

My only runner this week is Nicholas Nickleby, who with a lot of luck might win on Wednesday. After that I have a lot of entries at Ascot where I love winning races as the punting is good and the prizes worthwhile.

By Thunder! would be favourite for the [Ascot] Gold Cup in which race I will probably not run him and it is more likely I will take on Narrator (rated the best middle distance horse in this country) in the Hardwicke Stakes at 1½ miles.

I think this is prudent policy because if we train By Thunder! for the Gold Cup (2½ miles) it will not be easy to bring him back to 1½ miles in the valuable King George VI and Queen Elizabeth Stakes, worth about 30 grand.

It is possible I will run Royal Palm in the St. James's Palace Stakes at level weights with Our Babu and Tamerlane in the hopes of beating them and thus proving Royal Palm to be the best miler over here (on sound going).

He will be a long price and I am by no means confident—but wouldn't it be lovely to prove Royal Palm and By Thunder! to be the best 3 and 4 year olds—because bred as they are they would have very high stallion values.

R.S.V.P. re Paris.

Love to all of you,

Jack[36]

In this letter, Gerber reveals himself to be a better handicapper than a salesman. Tamerlane won the St. James's Palace Stakes, with Our Babu third. Royal Palm failed to stay the mile at Royal Ascot and finished unplaced, as did By Thunder! in the Hardwicke. Huston had been wise to hold on to his dwindling supply of cash. Nicholas Nickleby won the Royal Hunt Cup; however, that handicap mile never fails to attract fewer than thirty-six runners, so it is not held in high esteem by breeders. Huston did not attend the *Oklahoma!* gala in Paris on July 20. He was much too busy chasing a certain white whale with his camera.

On September 2 Gerber changed his tack, touting one of his horses in a little race and trying to woo Huston with the promise of a nice betting payday: "I think Iron Horse will win at Sandown on Saturday week and I shall take the risk of investing 50 pounds for you. I also hope all is going well with *Moby Dick*."[37]

In fact, all was not going well with *Moby Dick,* and Huston didn't appreciate the reminder. "*Moby Dick* was the most difficult picture I ever made," he wrote. "I lost so many battles during it that I even began to suspect my assistant director (Jack Martin) was plotting against me. Then I realized that it was only God." When Iron Horse lost at Sandown, Huston was 50 pounds poorer and one step closer to the whale's belly.[38]

Huston finally responded to Gerber on November 9. Writing from Courtown House, he asked, "How are the horses? I'm all out of touch. I know I owe you some money on lost bets but I don't know how much . . . you might as well have it as Ladbrokes."[39]

After the Iron Horse incident, Gerber tried something new. Instead of writing directly to Huston, he sent his correspondence to Huston's secretary, Lorry Sherwood, as if he couldn't quite muster the courage to face Huston man-to-man, not even in the post. On November 24 he wrote, "Please show this letter to John and tell him that I am syndicating Royal Palm at £1500 per share and I am reserving 1 or 2 of same for John, and if possible I would like a yea or nay from him as soon as possible. Royal Palm is a lovely horse and is bred like a champion and I have had a number of large offers for him from America, and as I have read in the paper that John is going to breed in Galway (horses I mean), it would be nice and nearby to send his mares to Limerick."[40] This is an example of the "Buy now! Supplies running out!" technique, coupled with an overly familiar sense of humor. In reality, Huston had no money to spare on breeding shares, even if Royal Palm was fresh off his greatest victory in the Nunthorpe Stakes.

Gerber reached out again the following June, noting that he expected Nicholas Nickleby to earn a repeat victory in the Royal Hunt Cup. Huston responded quickly this time, writing to Gerber on June 11, 1956, from the Beverly Hills Hotel, where he was staying while in town for the premiere of *Moby Dick*. "Delighted with your hopes for Nicholas Nickleby," he wrote. "I wish you would put a hundred to win for me. I hope I will still be here. Thursday Tetread runs at Hollywood Park. Haven't seen him this trip but Greg says he is coming along." Nicholas Nickleby lost, so that was another 100 pounds down the drain.[41]

Another of Huston's trusted but unofficial racing agents was Tim Durant. A jack-of-all-trades, Durant made and lost a couple of fortunes as an investment banker before, during, and after the stock market crash in 1929. He settled in Beverly Hills, where he became a noted Hollywood socialite and Master of the Hunt of the West Hills Hunt Club, whose members chased coyotes out of Malibu. He was a serious amateur race rider, which he parlayed into a part-time career as an actor in cowboy movies. He was also a close friend of Charlie Chaplin, who gave him a part in *Limelight*. With racing and acting two of his chief interests, Durant could hardly avoid meeting John Huston, who cast him as a Union general in *The Red Badge of Courage* and, twelve years later, in an uncredited role in *The List of Adrian Messenger*. Durant was also keen on European racing, traveling to Ireland and England for many of the big jump-race meetings. While in Ireland in May 1954, he wrote to Huston, who was in Hollywood, and suggested that his friend bet on his horse Evian in a Galway maiden, which, Durant observed, "is not a bad idea if he stands up." He then added a footnote. "Do let me know what is happening with the picture. I know you will make a great one."[42] The picture in question was *Moby Dick,* then in the earliest stages of preproduction.

By this time, Durant was fifty-four years old, but his enthusiasm for riding remained unabated. Jim Murray perhaps let admiration override perception when he wrote: "No one ever sat on a horse better than Tim Durant—not John Wayne, Gary Cooper, Lady Godiva, 'Snapper' Garrison, Geronimo or Tom Mix." Durant was, indeed, an accomplished horseman, and after a few visits to Aintree for the Grand National Steeplechase, he got it into his head that he should ride in it—the world's most challenging jump race. By 1964, it had become an obsession. Durant hatched a plot not only to ride in the great race but also to make a documentary film about his experience.[43]

On March 11, just one month before that year's Grand National, he wrote to Huston, outlining his quixotic plans. "I am arranging to buy a horse that from most accounts seems to have a good chance to at least get around the course. I plan to come over [to England] the first of the week, have a ride on him, get him vetted and learn all I can in those few days as to the best way to ride the horse and get a few pounds off this already skinny frame." Then he got around to the real reason for the letter: "I need your moral support in this greatest of all adventures in the horse world. I also need your help to make this movie which I think would be very exciting and might get some of my dough back." He then asked for Huston's help in bringing the BBC on board, something that would have been impossible at that late date. In the end, it all came to nothing. Durant failed to find a ride in the race, so there was no film to be made.[44]

Durant, however, remained determined to ride in the Grand National, and in fact, he succeeded in three consecutive years, 1966 to 1968, when he rode three 100–1 no-hopers. The first was King Pin, who fell at the nineteenth of the thirty fences. The next was Aerial III, who lasted a little longer, falling at the twentieth. In 1968 he rode Highlandie, who deposited him on the far side of the treacherous Becher's Brook the first time around. Undaunted, Durant remounted and finished the race in fifteenth place, actually beating two other horses—no mean feat at the age of sixty-eight, when most men can't walk the 4½-mile course, let alone ride it.

John Huston continued to ride out in company with Durant from time to time during the 1970s. Huston also maintained accounts with numerous bookmakers in England and Ireland—big ones like Ladbrokes, and small ones like David Deyoung and Patrick Meehan. Most of the money went in the wrong direction.

Stricken with emphysema in 1978, Huston's last nine years were agony, but he still managed to make three very good films, remaining true to his literary inclinations in each case: *Wise Blood,* a deeply Catholic film based on the novel by Flannery O'Connor; *Prizzi's Honor,* from the novel by Richard Condon; and *The Dead,* set in his beloved Dublin and based on a story by James Joyce. Dying from lung disease, Huston remarked, "If I were a horse they'd stop racing me. Since I'm not a good mare and useful for stud, they'd have to put me down."[45]

7

Louis B. Mayer

King of Hollywood and King of the Turf

In the movies a man likes to develop stars. In racing it is very much the same way. You take a horse and train him and bring him along and watch him develop. You get a lot of satisfaction watching them blossom out.

Louis B. Mayer

Louis the Junkman

Louis B. Mayer was born Lazar Meir sometime in the late nineteenth century in Imperial Russia, in what is now Belarus or perhaps Lithuania. No one in his family could remember the exact date. His marriage certificate gives his year of birth as 1882. Later, when he became a US citizen, he had miraculously become three years younger. Whenever an actual birthday was required, he generally used the Fourth of July. It was easy to remember and reminded everyone that he was, indeed, an American.

His father was an unskilled laborer, his mother a peasant. Upon arriving in America in 1887, the family stayed briefly in New York and then settled in Rhode Island. Five years later, they moved to New Brunswick, Canada, where his father changed the family name to Mayer and Lazar became Louis—a name usually associated with royalty of the French persuasion. Finally, they made their way to Boston in 1904, by which time Louis had become a full-fledged junkman in his father's scrap-metal yard.

None of this was particularly unusual for an Orthodox Jew emigrating from eastern Europe at the time. What is extraordinary about Lazar Meir is that, after reinventing himself as Louis B. Mayer, he rose to the top of two of the most glittering and prestigious industries in mid-twentieth century America: the magical cinematic world of Hollywood and the exclusive world of Thoroughbred horse racing (also known as the sport of kings, a moniker that Mayer surely appreciated). That he held both crowns at the same time in the mid-1940s makes his ascent even more remarkable.

Louis didn't remain a junkman for long. By 1907, he was running a movie theater in Haverhill, Massachusetts, thirty-five miles north of Boston. In 1914 he purchased distribution rights for the screen's first blockbuster, D. W. Griffith's *The Birth of a Nation*, for $25,000 and tripled his investment. Two years later, he cofounded Metro Pictures Corporation; two years after that, he moved to Los Angeles and started Louis B. Mayer Pictures Corporation. There followed a series of small but successful films. Then, in 1924, New York–based distributor Marcus Loew bought and merged Mayer's Metro Pictures and Samuel Goldwyn's Goldwyn Pictures, creating Metro-Goldwyn, two-thirds of what would become the world's most famous film production company.

King Louis's Rise to Power

Mayer's early Hollywood hits included the Anita Stewart vehicles *Virtuous Wives* and *Human Desire*, along with the second of four film versions of Charles Dizney's venerable play *In Old Kentucky* (1919), which marked Mayer's initial interest in the horse racing genre. Loew had taken note of Mayer's early successes, among them the silent version of *Ben-Hur*, and promptly hired him to run Metro-Goldwyn. Ever keen to make the best of a good opportunity, Mayer got off to a fast start with Erich von Stroheim's film version of Theodore Dreiser's epic novel *Greed*. Within a year, he added his own name to the marquee, and Metro-Goldwyn became Metro-Goldwyn-Mayer, or MGM.

Combining an iron will, a keen eye for talent, and an ear for what would please the American public, Mayer oversaw the production of silent classics such as *The Big Parade, The Scarlet Letter,* and *The Wind*. With the advent of sound, he proceeded apace with *The Champ, Grand Hotel, The Thin Man, Naughty Marietta, Mutiny on the Bounty, A Night at the Opera, A Tale of Two Cities,* and *San Francisco*. MGM excelled in every category of film: melodramas, musicals, murder mysteries, screwball comedies, and adventures in exotic locales. Its stable of stars was second to none. The list of actors and actresses under contract to MGM in the 1930s is breathtaking: Greta Garbo, Clark Gable, Jean Harlow, John Barrymore, Norma Shearer, Wallace Beery, Spencer Tracy, Joan Crawford, Mickey Rooney, Judy Garland, Deanna Durbin, the Marx Brothers,

William Powell, and Myrna Loy. It is no wonder that MGM billed itself as having "more stars than there are in the heavens." It was almost true.

Most important, Mayer made MGM profitable. From 1931 through 1940 the profits of the eight leading Hollywood studios totaled $128.2 million, of which $93.2 million (72.7 percent) belonged to MGM. And Mayer was doing it with quality, as reflected in the number of Oscar nominations MGM's films collected. During the 1930s, approximately one-third of all best picture, best actor, and best actress nominees hailed from MGM.

In 1931 Mayer decided to make a talkie version of his successful racing silent *In Old Kentucky*. During preproduction, he telegraphed his chosen director, Lois Weber, and outlined his desires and expectations, which remained the same for every MGM production during his twenty-seven years at the helm: "Regarding my idea of leading man, it is the same as my ideas of the play and cast, namely the best. My unchanging policy will be great star, great director, great play, great cast. You are authorized to get those without stint or limit. Spare nothing, neither expense, time, nor effort. Results only are what I am after. Simply send me the bills and I will O.K. them."[1]

Self-confident, autocratic, yet unafraid to delegate responsibility, Mayer displayed all the qualities required of a winning corporate executive. As a result, MGM prospered, and so did its boss. In 1937 he earned a salary of $1.2 million, reputed to be the highest of any executive in the country. Mayer had money to burn. And what better place to do so than at the racetrack?

The opening of Santa Anita in December 1934 had whet the film world's appetite for horse racing, but Mayer showed no interest in watching horses run around in a circle. He enjoyed an occasional game of golf, but that sport was too time-consuming to play on a regular basis. A workaholic, Mayer needed to be at the studio, where as many as six movies might be shooting on any given day, with another eight or ten in the planning stages and two or three in new release. The pressures were so great that studio executives advised Mayer to find a hobby to relieve the tension. Yachting, one of Hollywood's favorite indulgences, bored him. Tennis was too strenuous. On a European holiday in 1937, Mayer consulted blood specialist Dr. Isidore Snapper in Amsterdam. The physician diagnosed the head of MGM as being run down and in need of rest and relaxation. A racegoer himself, Dr. Snapper recommended horse racing, observing that it served people like the Aga Khan very well. Mayer appreciated the allusion and made a mental note to check out Santa Anita and see what all the fuss was about upon his return to the States.

Back home, Mayer seemed to find a perfect playground at the racetrack. From some fans' point of view, it is a sedentary pastime, but for Mayer, a day at Santa Anita meant a healthy day out in the open air. There was a beautiful view of the San Gabriel Mountains from the grandstand, where he could socialize with his horse-loving Hollywood friends and colleagues.

Mayer enjoyed his racing excursions out to Arcadia, but like most of the leading Hollywood producers, he rankled at being denied access to the track's exclusive Turf Club, which denied membership to Jews. So when his cinematic rivals Jack and Harry Warner quietly drew up plans to build Hollywood Park, Mayer jumped on the bandwagon, becoming one of the first and most generous investors in the endeavor.

Mayer had been bitten by the racing bug. But a man of his means and prodigious ambition was not satisfied with merely betting on horses. He wanted to own them, and he wanted to own them in a big way, like the old-money eastern families the Whitneys and the Vanderbilts.

Mayer's Cast of Thoroughbreds

Mayer got off to a decidedly slow start with his first horse, a claimer aptly named Routine, who was a flop at Bay Meadows near San Francisco. Then he bought a horse from MGM producer Joe Schenck. An experienced horseman and notorious gambler, Schenck knew his way around a racecourse and a sales ring. In a sort of in-house MGM deal, he fobbed off a useless gelding named Marine Blue on Mayer, his boss, and was probably lucky not be fired. Or maybe luck had nothing to do with it: Joe Schenck was the brother of Mayer's boss, Nicholas Schenck, who ruled the MGM roost from Loews headquarters in New York.

In 1938, the year MGM released Oscar nominees *Boys Town, Test Pilot,* and *The Citadel,* newspapers began to report Mayer's growing interest in racing. "Louis B. Mayer Plans Classy Race Stable" blared the *Los Angeles Citizen-News* on June 25. The reports were true. In fact, Mayer was jumping feet first into the bigtime. He summoned Kentucky trainer and native Californian Don Cameron to his home in Beverly Hills for brainstorming sessions on the nature of the Thoroughbred business.

Mayer wanted to learn everything there was to know about running a major league stable—and not just the racing end of the game. He was astute enough to recognize that long-term success in the Thoroughbred world was achieved only by those who bred their own horses. Breeding quality racehorses requires money and patience, both of which Mayer possessed in abundance.

Mayer's daughter Irene, married to ex-MGM producer David O. Selznick, had a ringside seat on her father's new hobby. "My father . . . lost his head, not over women, but over horses," she wrote. "He threw himself into it as though he were creating a studio and used some of the same methods. He aimed for quality and looked for talent."[2]

Right off the bat, he went hunting for big game, and in America, there was no bigger game—or name—than Man o' War. A son of three-time champion North American sire Fair Play out of a mare by Epsom Derby winner Rock Sand, Man o' War won nineteen of his twenty races, including the classic Preakness and Belmont Stakes. He was the first truly great American racehorse and was responsible for elevating American Thoroughbred racing to an international footing. At stud, he was also a success, despite never covering more than twenty-five mares per season. His most notable son was Seabiscuit's archrival, Triple Crown winner War Admiral. As a broodmare sire, his influence is immortal.

Employing the same policy he used at MGM, Mayer went after the best. He offered Man o' War's owner, Sam Riddle, an astronomical $1 million (the equivalent of $17 million today) for his stallion but was rudely rebuffed. "Tell Mr. Mayer," Riddle said to his agent, "that Man o' War is not for sale at any price." Years later, Riddle joked that he was afraid Mayer wanted to use Man o' War in his movies. That was typical of the eastern racing elite's attitude toward the upstarts in California, many of whom had Hollywood connections. Mayer then offered Riddle $500,000 for War Admiral but was again turned down.[3]

Undeterred, Mayer soldiered on. He ordered his British agent Laudy Lawrence to buy the outstanding stallion Hyperion. Both Hyperion and his sire, Gainsborough, had won two classics: the Epsom Derby and the St. Leger Stakes. Hyperion would eventually become the six-time champion sire in Britain and Ireland. In 1938, however, when Hyperion's first foals were untested two-year-olds, no one could have predicted that he would be the single most important Thoroughbred stallion in the first half of the twentieth century. Mayer, however, sensed something. His eye for horseflesh was becoming as sharp as his eye for cinematic talent. Through Lawrence, he offered Hyperion's owner, Lord Derby, the same $1 million he had offered Riddle for Man o' War. Lord Derby was the great-great-great-grandson of the man for whom the Derby Stakes (known popularly as the Epsom Derby) was named; it was the most important horse race in the world at the time. He weighed the value of both Hyperion and the US dollar and came down decidedly in favor of the horse. "Though England be reduced to ashes," Lord Derby famously pronounced, "Hyperion will never leave these shores." And he never did.[4]

Mayer had probably bitten off more than he could chew in those early days. In the meantime, he was quizzing Cameron on every aspect of building a breeder-owner operation: the optimal size and location of a farm, the type of soil required, the best horse feed, the best trainers, and the most effective training methods. Most important, Mayer was keen to learn about Thoroughbred bloodlines. Cameron, who would achieve fame in 1943 as the trainer of Triple Crown winner Count Fleet, was a believer in importing European bloodstock to improve the American breed. Mayer was impressed and hired him as an adviser at the important Saratoga yearling sales later in the summer.

The day after the *Citizen-News* ran its story, the *Los Angeles Times* reported that Mayer was in the process of opening a major breeding and racing operation with "some high-class broodmares and first-rate stallions." Mayer got to work transforming his ranch near Malibu into a breeding farm and hired professional Kentucky horseman Frank Kelly to head the project. At Saratoga he spent $78,000 on six well-bred yearlings. The best of them was probably Sir Jeffrey, who finished a disappointing eighth in the 1940 Santa Anita Derby, California's major prep race for the Kentucky Derby. None of the others panned out in the long run. Mayer was so determined to get started in racing that he privately bought a handful of horses in training. Among them was a colt named Main Man, who would become his first stakes winner in the San Jose Handicap at Bay Meadows. But in his first year as a Thoroughbred owner, horses carrying Mayer's blue and pink colors won only three races and earned a total of $17,490—barely enough to cover Clark Gable's feed bill.

By the start of the 1939 spring season, Mayer had eighteen two-year-olds and a handful of older horses in training at Hollywood Park. Main Man was the budding stable star. Trained by Pinky Grimes, he was Mayer's hope in the opening-day Premiere Handicap, but Main Man came in fourth behind the Bing Crosby–owned Don Mike. Just four days later, Main Man returned to take the Los Angeles Handicap. Instead of rejoicing over his first stakes winner, Mayer promptly fired Grimes, apparently because the trainer had been receiving large kickbacks on the horses he bought for the MGM boss. As demanding in racing as he was in filmmaking, Mayer stunned the California racing community in July when he removed all his horses from Hollywood Park and sent them to Saratoga in New York and Rockingham Park in New Hampshire. He was unhappy with the hard ground at Hollywood Park and angry about the weights some of his horses were being assigned. Mayer's pique didn't last long. He liked to watch his horses run, and that wasn't always possible if they were all on the East Coast. Mayer's horses were back at Santa Anita for the 1940 winter-spring season.

By 1941, Mayer was winning races with a certain regularity on the Southern California circuit, testimony to his policy of stocking his stable with horses in training from around the world as well as with homebreds (horses he had bred himself). On successive Wednesdays in February at Santa Anita, he pulled off a feat that most owners only dream about. On February 19 he watched happily as three of his horses won. First up was his Argentine-bred import Beautiful II, who broke a five-race losing streak and survived an inquiry to win the Wilmington Stakes at 9.30–1. She was followed by a pair of victorious homebreds: Torch Lee at 7–1 and Queen Toke at 3.40–1. A week later, Mayer went one better with an incredible four winners: Singing Torch broke his maiden in the first race, Conscription completed the daily double in the second, and Sales Talk landed the fifth race, after which Flying Wild won the Santa Ynez Stakes.

Later that summer, Sir Jeffrey found his best form when he won the Inglewood Handicap at Hollywood Park, breaking the track record held by Mayer's own Beautiful II by three-fifths of a second. Mayer had found his stride and was looking to capitalize on his successes, and he certainly had the money to put his big plan into action. In 1940 his salary at MGM was $697,048, making him the highest-paid executive in the nation. His earnings topped those of Bethlehem Steel's Eugene G. Grace ($478,144) and American Tobacco's George W. Hill ($456,415) by wide margins. By 1943, Mayer's salary had skyrocketed to $1,138,992.

Mayer had money to spend and the support of some of Kentucky's leading bloodstock experts, among them Jockey Club chairman William Woodward. Mayer sent his agents around the world in search of

Thoroughbred talent for both breeding and racing purposes. If he couldn't get Hyperion, he would try to get the next best thing. In 1939 he privately purchased from the Aga Khan a yearling colt by Hyperion for a mere 3,200 guineas, or about $10,000 at the time. The colt's pedigree was impeccable. In addition to being a son of Hyperion, his dam, Teresina, had won the 2¼-mile Goodwood Cup, one of England's most prestigious staying races. Teresina, in turn, was a daughter of Tracery, who had won the classic St. Leger Stakes as well as the Champion Stakes, the most important race in England for older horses. Mayer had every reason to believe that he had bought a potential champion, but fate played him an unusual trick.

Named Alibhai, the apple of Mayer's eye began to burn up the track in morning workouts at Santa Anita in the early spring of his two-year-old season. One day he reportedly equaled the track record for a mile, an unheard-of feat for an unraced juvenile. Then, a few weeks later, while preparing for his racecourse debut, Alibhai suffered bowed tendons in both his front legs. The injuries were so severe that trainer Clyde Van Dusen had no choice but to retire Mayer's great equine hope—a devastating loss to his owner and to everyone else at the stable. With mixed feelings, Mayer assigned Alibhai to a stall at his state-of-the-art Mayer Stock Farm in Perris, California.

A year later, in 1942, the three-year-old Alibhai began stud duties, boasting a sterling pedigree but no racing record. In breeding circles, very few stallions that have never run in a race amount to anything. Louis Mayer, however, was a lucky man. Alibhai was a winner right out of the stud gate. His first crop included Cover Up, who would win the Hollywood Gold Cup for Mayer. His second crop included On Trust, who would land the 1947 Santa Anita Derby and finish third in the Kentucky Derby, but not for Mayer, who had generously given On Trust to his brother Jerry midway through the colt's two-year-old season. After five profitable years as California's leading sire, Alibhai moved on to even richer pastures in Kentucky when Mayer sold him to Leslie Combs II, owner of Spendthrift Farm, for a world record $500,000. With even better mares available to him in the Bluegrass State, Alibhai would go on to sire the likes of Your Host (the sire of five-time champion Kelso), 1951 Kentucky Derby winner Determine, the outstanding handicapper Traffic Judge, and the great broodmare Flower Bowl, whose offspring included the superb stallions Graustark and His Majesty.

A couple of years later Mayer set his sights on Australia. There was a stallion standing at St. Alban's Stud in Geelong, Victoria, named Beau

Pere, and Mayer went after him. A British-bred son of champion stayer Son-in-Law out of 1000 Guineas winner Cinna, Beau Pere (French for "father-in-law") had been an indifferent racehorse and a dud at stud, siring just five foals in two years for England's King George V. The king sold him to a buyer in faraway New Zealand, where Beau Pere blossomed as a two-time champion sire; then he was sent to Australia, where he became a champion sire three times. Mayer's agents reported that Beau Pere would be a perfect fit for the California breeding industry, so the MGM boss whipped out his checkbook. Mayer bought Beau Pere in 1942 for $100,000, a far cry from the 100 guineas ($350) the impatient King George had accepted to unload him, but it turned out to be a wise investment. He would provide Mayer with two of his best runners: Honeymoon and Stepfather. He would also sire Iron Reward, the dam of 1955 Kentucky Derby winner Swaps and a half-sister to 1957 Kentucky Derby winner Iron Liege. In just five seasons at Mayer Stock Farm, Beau Pere sired twenty-eight stakes winners.

Mayer was winning accolades from all quarters. Ben Lindheimer, owner of Chicago's Washington Park Racecourse and chairman of the board at Arlington Park (and father of future Hollywood Park president Marje Everett), was full of praise for Mayer's efforts in California. According to Lindheimer, the West Coast hadn't seen such an accomplished horseman since Lucky Baldwin, founder of the original Santa Anita. In his opinion, Mayer was producing the best California-breds ever. John Hertz, owner of 1928 Kentucky Derby winner Reigh Count and his son, 1943 Triple Crown winner Count Fleet, visited the Mayer Stock Farm and deemed it the best he'd ever seen. He promptly bought the adjacent property, where he intended to produce his own California-bred horses.

The exploits of Alibhai and Beau Pere vaulted Mayer into international prominence in the ultracompetitive Thoroughbred breeding market. Their progeny left a distinctive impression on the Thoroughbred breed—in California and throughout the world—for decades to come.

King of the California Turf

"Louis B. Mayer Credited with Owning Most Colorful Stable" read the Christmas Eve 1940 headline in the *Los Angeles Times*. The mercurial—one might even say quixotic—Mayer had relieved Don Cameron of his duties as trainer and replaced him with the more experienced Clyde Van Dusen, whose equine namesake, a gelded son of Man o' War, had won the 1929 Kentucky Derby. Always on the lookout for the main chance, Mayer had grown tired of what he considered the provincial surroundings of his ranch near Malibu and had packed his stallions and mares—more than fifty horses in all—off to Lexington, Kentucky, where they were boarded at A. B. Hancock's Claiborne Farm. Just a few were left behind at Barbara Stanwyck's Marwyck Stable. Not long afterward, he moved half of them back to California, to Deep Cliff Farm at Cupertino, near San Francisco. Less than a year later, he changed his mind completely and sent them all to his new Mayer Stock Farm, a 504-acre spread he had bought and developed in Perris, seventy-two miles east of Los Angeles.

His new breeding establishment was the equal of anything in Kentucky. It was equipped with a one-mile training track of the same dimensions as the racetrack at Santa Anita, and it was filled with the same topsoil used there. There were two thirty-six-stall training barns, two foaling barns, an isolation barn, and a stallion barn where Alibhai and Beau Pere resided. Mayer Stock Farm resembled a film studio lot. There were living quarters for the stable help, a commissary, and recreation areas. There was even a little bungalow for Mayer himself. He was spending more and more of his precious time at his farm and at the racetrack. Mayer's hobby was gradually becoming his preferred occupation.

Just as he liked to be involved in every aspect of film production, right down to controlling the lives (both professional and personal) of his young stars, Mayer took an active role in the development of his horses. He knew everyone employed at Mayer Stock Farm, from the grooms to the assistant trainers to the veterinarians. He knew what kind of feed was best for horses of a given age, when a foal should be weaned, and when a yearling could be saddled for the first time. He became an expert in the arcane subjects of Thoroughbred bloodlines and racing form, and like any good horseman, he had an opinion about everybody and everything at the track.

He was spending increasing amounts of time at the racetrack. At morning workouts at one of the three local tracks, he liked to pick the brains of trainers, jockeys, and exercise riders, asking them which horses were ready to win. He often hung around for the afternoon's races. The executives at MGM invented a secret code to cover for the boss's absences on race days, which seemed to increase with each passing month. If the

Table 2.   Louis B. Mayer's Thoroughbred Earnings and Film Productions, 1938–1957

Year	Racing				Breeding				MGM Releases under Mayer
	1st	2nd	3rd	Earnings	1st	2nd	3rd	Earnings	
1938	10	3	5	$17,490	—	—	—	—	Boys Town; The Citadel
1939	42	45	32	$77,835	—	—	—	—	The Wizard of Oz; Ninotchka
1940	61	50	38	$91,830	—	—	—	—	The Philadelphia Story; The Shop Around the Corner
1941	32	24	20	$113,340	—	—	—	—	Babes on Broadway; Dr. Jekyll and Mr. Hyde
1942	47	40	36	$113,440	—	—	—	—	Mrs. Miniver; Woman of the Year
1943	19	20	16	$140,300	43	46	54	$40,866	Lassie Come Home; Madame Curie
1944	26	20	18	$126,090	80	94	76	$139,307	Gaslight; National Velvet
1945	37	24	11	$533,150	108	91	60	$259,241	The Clock; Anchors Aweigh
1946	41	33	22	$449,195	192	174	131	$788,729	The Postman Always Rings Twice; The Yearling
1947	13	8	9	$60,575	200	2699	186	$1,277,377	It Happened in Brooklyn; The Sea of Grass
1948	—	—	—	—	169	193	177	$1,105,901	Easter Parade; The Three Musketeers
1949	—	—	—	—	209	204	161	$1,257,342	Little Women; Madame Bovary
1950	—	—	—	—	222	217	201	$1,081,342	Annie Get Your Gun; The Asphalt Jungle
1951	0	1	0	$6,000	212	180	174	$1,134,253	The Red Badge of Courage; Royal Wedding
1952	20	18	14	$113,670	186	150	149	$559,461	—
1953	17	18	15	$103,850	114	138	116	$383,463	—
1954	9	1	10	$31,825	88	82	68	$220,996	—
1955	17	136	12	$237,910		NA			—
1956	9	14	16	$91,790	39	32	40	$132,999	—
1957	12	11	5	$86,419		NA			—

NA: not available.

boss was on Lot 14, that meant he was at Santa Anita; if he was on Lot 15, he was at Hollywood Park.

All the time, effort, and money Mayer put into the sport eventually began to pay off at the track. In each of the four years from 1941 through 1944, his horses earned more than $100,000 (equivalent to $1.5 million today). But he struck it rich in 1945, when he had thirty-seven winners and accumulated earnings of $533,150 ($7 million today), most of it courtesy of the great filly Busher.

And the Winner Is . . . Busher!

Given Mayer's lifelong philosophy of seeking the best—be it a director, an actor, a screenplay, a stud prospect, a well-bred yearling, or a horse in training—he left no stone unturned in his never-ending search for excellence. In his purchase of Busher, he combined an ability to identify prospective talent with a nose for being in the right place at the right time with the right offer.

Bred and owned by Colonel Edward R. Bradley, Busher was born in 1942 at Idle Hour Farm, just outside of Lexington—the Kentucky equivalent of Buckingham Palace. By then, Idle Hour had produced four Kentucky Derby winners, two Preakness Stakes winners, and two Belmont Stakes winners, including Blue Larkspur, the 1929 Horse of the Year. The mares at Idle Hour included the outstanding French-bred producer La Troienne. Busher herself was the product of a mating between Triple Crown winner War Admiral and La Troienne's daughter Baby League. As a two-year-old, she won five of seven races for Bradley, including the Adirondack Stakes and Matron Stakes at Belmont Park and the Selima Stakes at Laurel Park, earning the two-year-old filly championship in 1944.

When war forced the cancellation of racing throughout America from January 3 through mid-May 1945, the aging Colonel Bradley decided to sell much of his racing stock, and Louis B. Mayer was waiting with his checkbook. The asking price for Busher was $50,000, and Mayer did not demur. On March 15 Busher arrived at the Santa Anita stable of George Odom, the latest in the ever-changing cast of trainers hired by Mayer. He immediately put her into light training in anticipation of the war's end and the resumption of racing.

Santa Anita reopened on May 15, and on May 26 Busher lined up for a six-furlong allowance event with new rider Johnny Longden in the saddle.

The result was a handy five-length victory against opponents of her own age and sex. A week later, on June 2, she overpowered similar rivals by seven lengths, giving weight all around in the seven-furlong Santa Susana Handicap, a race that would eventually become the Santa Anita Oaks.

American racehorses were tougher animals in those days, and Busher had just another week off before making her first start against colts in the one-mile San Vicente Stakes. So impressive were her first two outings as a three-year-old that she was sent off as the 7–5 favorite and emerged victorious, despite being hampered by a riderless horse, Quick Reward.

Her next assignment came against colts her own age in the Santa Anita Derby on June 23. Designed to be the key California prep race for the Kentucky Derby, that year's race actually took place two weeks after the Churchill Downs classic, owing to the entire racing calendar being pushed back because of the four-month wartime postponement. With Mayer looking on from his private box near the finish line, Busher started as the prohibitive 1–2 favorite and took the early lead under Longden, opening up three lengths on the field entering the stretch. But this was not to be her day. She was reeled in near the finish line by the patriotically named Bymeabond (who, ironically, had been sold by Busher's former owner, Colonel Bradley, to J. Kel Houssels).

It was just eleven days until Busher's next race on the Fourth of July in the Santa Margarita Handicap, her first start against older fillies and mares. Giving weight all around, she prevailed by one and a half lengths, finishing the 1¹⁄₁₆ miles in 1:43 flat, the fastest winning time in the ten runnings of that race at that distance.

It was now clear to everyone that Busher wasn't just another good horse; she was, in fact, something very special, perhaps the equine equivalent of MGM superstar Greta Garbo. A brief hiatus allowed Odom to ship Busher east to Chicago for a summer campaign. Mayer—realizing that the farther east you went, the better the competition became—wanted to test Busher against the very best. Racing in Chicago was, in those days, considerably better than it has been in recent times, yet Busher's presence added luster to the local talent. Her first Midwest outing on July 25 was actually a step down in class. The Cleopatra Handicap at the now defunct Washington Park was easy pickings for her. She led from start to finish, defeating a field of outclassed three-year-old fillies by four and a half lengths.

Just ten days later she was back again, this time against sterner competition in the Arlington Handicap at Washington Park. It would be her first start against older males, coming at the midway point in her three-year-old season. It would also be her first race at 1¼ miles. It is always difficult for a horse to adapt to new conditions, and in this case, expecting Busher to overcome both older males and a longer distance seemed to be asking too much. Any anxious prerace moments Mayer and Odom might have had, however, were quickly dissipated as Longden broke Busher on top, guiding her to a wire-to-wire, four-and-a-half-length victory while giving weight to most of her male opponents.

Given her impressive resumé, Busher was assigned 129 pounds for her next start in the Beverly Handicap against older fillies and mares. That impost proved too much for her. Busher finished third in the 1⅛-mile contest in which she spotted the victorious Durazna 12 pounds and the second-place Letmenow 27 pounds. There was no disgrace in this defeat, but Mayer and Odom wanted a rematch, and so did the racing public, which had taken Busher to heart.

Washington Park officials obliged and arranged a one-mile match race at equal weights between Busher and Durazna, who was owned by Kentucky blueblood Brownell Combs. Busher had the rail and took a narrow lead early on, only to have Durazna gain a neck advantage on the far turn. Longden soon had Busher back in front, and she maintained her advantage to the finish line, winning by three-quarters of a length. She had taken her revenge on Durazna, a trait that would ultimately become her trademark.

On September 3 Busher would face the toughest test of her career when she went up against older colts in the Washington Park Handicap, which would soon become one of the most important races in the nation for three-year-olds and up. Mayer knew exactly what this race was all about; his own Thumbs Up had dead-heated for the victory two years earlier. Among Busher's rivals in the 1¼-mile contest were the four-year-old Armed, color-bearer for the mighty Calumet Farm; the great weight-carrying champion Stymie, fresh from victory in Belmont Park's Suburban Handicap; the Preakness Stakes winner Polynesian; and the three-year-old filly Gallorette, a three-time stakes winner on the East Coast.

Faced with such competition, Longden had to be more cautious. Instead of letting Busher take the lead, as he had in the Cleopatra and Arlington Handicaps, he had her tracking the pace in third place, where he could keep an eye on the front-runners. Shortly after entering the stretch, less than two furlongs from home, Busher took control of the race, eventually holding off Armed, the older male who was carrying

4 pounds less than her. In victory, she set a new track record of 2:01⅖. This was a truly outstanding performance. Mayer's heart swelled with pride, and rightfully so, for Busher had beaten four subsequent champions in the Washington Park Handicap, a race that Armed would win each of the next two years, once Busher was out of his way.

With the onset of autumn, Odom shipped Busher back to California for the Hollywood Park season, which had been moved from the late spring and early summer to the fall. The one-mile Will Rogers Handicap against other three-year-olds figured to be a stepping-stone to bigger things, but Busher was stymied by the heavy weights her previous accomplishments were imposing on her. In tight quarters for much of the race, she closed like a shot, only to lose by a short head to the colt Quick Reward (spotting him 11 pounds)—the same horse that had tossed his rider and almost cost her the San Vicente Stakes earlier in the spring.

Two weeks later she was sent off as the 3–5 favorite before an adoring crowd of 42,159 in the 1⅛-mile Hollywood Derby. Despite starting from the highly disadvantageous number 12 post in a field of thirteen, Busher overcame a rough trip and took her revenge on both Quick Reward and her Santa Anita Derby conqueror Bymeabond. Jockey Longden was ecstatic. "When I called on Busher she really responded," he said. "I think she could have run four miles today and nobody would have beaten her."[5]

She ended her three-year-old season with a handy two-length score over older fillies and mares in the 1⅟₁₆-mile Vanity Handicap. That brought her lifetime earnings to $334,035, making her the richest distaff Thoroughbred in history at the time. More important, she laid claim to a "triple crown" of her own making, as she was named champion three-year-old filly, champion handicap filly or mare, and Horse of the Year. For Mayer, this was like having one of his actresses win three Academy Awards in a single year.

Mayer was even happier when the New York Turf Writers' Association named him Breeder of the Year. He had beaten Calumet Farm, the Whitneys, and the Vanderbilts at their own game, and he had done it in less than eight years, with no previous experience, in one of the most competitive and cutthroat games in the world.[6]

Storm Warnings

Mark October 16, 1945, as the day when Mayer's fortunes—racing and otherwise—began to unravel. That morning, trainer George Odom saddled Busher for a seven-furlong workout at Hollywood Park. It would prove to be a turning point in Mayer's fortunes. The work wasn't intended to be anything special, just a pipe opener, but Busher returned to the barn limping, her left foreleg swelling. The injury, a badly bowed tendon, was devastating. She would be sidelined for more than fifteen months.

But Busher wasn't the only successful performer in Mayer's star-studded 1945 stable. His six-year-old homebred Thumbs Up had equaled the track record for 1¼ miles in winning the all-important "Hundred Grander," the Santa Anita Handicap. On December 30, opening day at Santa Anita, Mayer capped his championship season before a crowd of 48,000 with an astonishing one-two-three finish in the California Breeders' Championship Stakes for California-bred juveniles. In first place was his very promising filly, the 2–5 favorite Honeymoon; second was Moneybags; and third was Charivari. All three were sired by Beau Pere, and all three were bred by Mayer. "It's a great race," Mayer crowed, "and a grand day for Beau Pere."[7] Unfortunately, the crowd didn't agree. Some bettors had grown weary of Mayer's parade of short-priced winners, and taking the top three places in a stakes race was the last straw. When Joe Hernandez announced the official order of finish, the crowd booed. Mayer was visibly hurt by the reaction. He couldn't understand why people didn't share in his joy.

Meanwhile, there were ominous signs appearing in the sun and the stars. On August 10, 1946, Busher and Thumbs Up were barely saved from a barn fire at Hollywood Park that burned 400 tons of hay. More to the point, Mayer was facing both personal and professional problems. In 1944 he had been forced to take a $560,000 pay cut, reducing his salary to a mere $568,000. In 1946 MGM's profits slipped to $18 million—a seemingly vigorous figure, but one that was well behind the profits posted by Paramount ($39 million), 20th Century Fox ($25 million), and Warner Bros. ($22 million). Back in New York, Nicholas Schenck, who was in charge of Loews, MGM's parent company and the distributor of MGM's films, was growing antsy about all the time Mayer was spending at the track and at his breeding farm and away from the studio.

The *Los Angeles Times* did him no favors when, on December 21, it ran the headline: "Mayer Bucks Studio to Watch Horses Drill." MGM's biggest hit of the year, *The Yearling* (a film about a deer, not a horse), had been released just three days earlier. But Mayer, the newspaper reported, had taken a day off to watch Busher work out at Santa Anita in preparation for her highly anticipated return to the races. It went well, as she traveled seven furlongs in 1:25⅘ after running an opening quarter mile in 46⅘ seconds.

On the personal front, things were even worse. Mayer had become bored with his wife Margaret. Although twenty years his junior, she preferred the quiet life of a homebody, while her husband was more interested in movie stars, fancy dinners, wild parties, and racetrack outings. He was candidly critical of her in public, telling friends that he wasn't the sort of man to "stay home and sit in front of the fire in a smoking jacket and carpet slippers, the way my wife wants me to do." Beginning in 1944, Louis and Margaret were rarely seen together in public, and they were rarely together in private either.[8]

Mayer used horse racing to buffet the growing storm. He was the leading Thoroughbred owner in California in 1945 and 1946. His total earnings nationwide over the five-year period from 1942 to 1946 ranked him second behind only the mighty forces of Calumet Farm. Mayer had setbacks, but he was resourceful and had reinforcements aplenty. If Greta Garbo retired, he could replace her with Greer Garson. If Jean Harlow died, he could turn Lana Turner into a star. Similarly, if Busher was sidelined, Honeymoon could pursue many of the same prizes his champion filly had captured a year earlier.

Honeymoon would win seven stakes races as a three-year-old, among them a repeat of Busher's victory against colts in the Hollywood Derby, plus the Hollywood Oaks, the Cinema Handicap, and the Santa Maria Handicap. Just short of championship caliber, Honeymoon was proof positive that Mayer was making extraordinary improvements in the quality of the California breeding program. They would never be the equal of Kentucky-breds, but California-breds could compete with the best horses in the world, thanks largely to Mayer's unstinting efforts. Another Mayer-owned filly, Be Faithful, repeated Busher's victory in the Vanity Handicap and also took the Beverly Handicap in Chicago, making up for Busher's unlucky loss to Durazna the year before. Be Faithful would set three track records during her career.

Despite these bright spots, Mayer's unfaithfulness to his wife Margaret was threatening to result in an expensive divorce; the studio heads were demanding that he pay more attention to their film products; and new tax laws were taking a bigger chunk out of his earnings. Mayer realized that he had painted himself into a corner, and there was only one way out. When a wealthy man is in financial difficulty, the first thing he does is sell his racehorses, and Mayer was no exception. Much to his regret, he announced a series of dispersal sales, the first and most prominent of them scheduled for February 27, 1947, at Santa Anita. Mayer declared that his horse business was getting too big and was interfering with his movie business, although people on the racing side of the fence might have seen things differently.

Fall from Grace

After a long and patient struggle, trainer George Odom had rehabilitated Busher back to racing fitness, and she was entered in a six-furlong allowance race worth $7,500 at Santa Anita on January 2, 1947. Mayer watched anxiously as the gates opened and Busher took her place near the back of the pack, where she remained throughout, finishing a dull fifth in a six-horse race won by Miss Doreen, a filly from the stable of Charles Howard, Seabiscuit's owner. The injury to her foreleg and the long layoff had taken the fight out of Busher. Odom conferred with Mayer, and they made the sad decision to retire the great filly.

The loss of his beloved Busher had a profound effect on Mayer. The Associated Press reported, "Close observers declared that Mayer's heart went out of racing when Busher failed to come back."[9] She would be the number-one prize offered at the dispersal sale, for which Mayer issued 7,000 private invitations. A special sales ring was built in front of the Santa Anita clubhouse stand. Fasig-Tipton, the leading Kentucky Thoroughbred sales company, was hired to conduct the business. The most important figures in American racing and breeding were there: Jock Whitney of Greentree Stables; J. S. Phipps, brother of Wheatley Stable owner Ogden Phipps; Ivor Balding, manager of C. V. Whitney's stable; and William Du Pont Jr., owner of Foxcatcher Farm. They mingled with filmdom's Harry Warner, Mervyn LeRoy, Cary Grant, Barbara Stanwyck, and Betty Grable. Looking decidedly morose, Mayer sat with automobile manufacturer Henry Ford, a neutral figure who was not involved in either racing or filmmaking.

"Anybody who amounted to anything in Southern California's racetrack and cinema industries (an almost indistinguishable cast of characters) was there," wrote *Time* magazine.[10] In fact, the Mayer dispersal sale might have been the first recorded media circus. Newspaper reporters, newsreel cameras, and radio broadcasters were there in force. Searchlights scanned the evening skies, turning a horse sale into something resembling a Hollywood premiere. But it was almost more like a funeral. The great Louis B. Mayer—respected more than loved, feared as much as he was hated—was admitting defeat on the Thoroughbred level at least. A lot of people in the Santa Anita grandstand that night were experiencing a delightfully warm sensation of schadenfreude.

The sale was top-loaded with all the most famous horses early in the evening, so the national radio broadcast would reach the East Coast at a reasonable hour. Stepfather, a promising homebred son of Beau Pere, had crossed the finish line first in the San Vicente Stakes eleven days earlier, only to be disqualified for interference; he was considered a strong Kentucky Derby candidate. Mayer's archrival Harry Warner bought Stepfather for a sale-topping $220,000; he also made off with Honeymoon for $135,000. Then the multiple-stakes-winning filly Be Faithful sold for $100,000 to Elmer Shaffer of Coldstream Stud. When Busher was led into the ring, Mayer teared up. He could hardly watch as the hammer came down at $135,000 in favor of Mayer's attorney and adviser Neil McCarthy, who almost immediately received an offer of $50,000 for her forthcoming Man o' War foal. By night's end, sixty horses had passed through the ring, bringing a gross turnover of $1,553,500, or an average of $25,891 per horse—the highest average of any Thoroughbred sale in history. Afterward, Fasig-Tipton president Humphrey Finney asked Mayer if he was satisfied with the proceedings. "Satisfied, yes; pleased, no!" came the curt reply.[11]

From then on, it was one setback after another for Mayer. On March 26 Margaret sued him for divorce, claiming that he had deserted her in May 1944. The case wrapped up on April 28, with Margaret winning a settlement of $3.25 million.

Mayer was keeping the wolf away from the door by disposing of his racing stock, but he had no intention of selling his breeding stock. Mayer Stock Farm continued to function—for the time being. However, Mayer sold his next two two-year-old crops in Fasig-Tipton–run sales at Hollywood Park. The first of these in January 1948 brought $1,025,000 for forty-two juveniles, the sale-topper being Honeymoon's half-sister, Graphic, at $42,500. The following January, Mayer sold fifty-one of his 1949 two-year-olds for $635,000, with Honeymoon's full sister, Honey's Sister, bringing $57,200.

A month before that second two-year-old sale, Mayer unloaded his Stock Farm in Perris for $600,000 to the Church of Latter-Day Saints. The Mormons later sold the property for $1.8 million to William G. Helis, owner of Tanforan Racetrack near San Francisco, Garden State Park in New Jersey, and the Fair Grounds in New Orleans. Mayer continued to breed Thoroughbreds, sending his remaining mares to stallions in California and Kentucky. He was determined to maintain his position as one of the leading breeders in the country. Just a few weeks before his first dispersal sale, he bought the outstanding Australian stallion Bernborough for $310,000, a maneuver that appalled every horseman and racing fan Down Under. Bernborough would go on to sire Bersoon, who would set a new Santa Anita track record for six furlongs; Parading Lady, winner of the Acorn and Vosburgh Stakes at Belmont; and Whitney Stakes winner First Aid. Seemingly in spite of himself, Mayer ranked among the leading breeders in the nation each year from 1947 to 1951.

After a power struggle with Nicholas Schenck at Loews headquarters in New York and Dore Schary, MGM's head of production (whom Mayer himself had hired), Mayer was ousted from MGM in 1951. Unable to restart himself as an independent producer, the essentially unemployed Mayer turned to running a racetrack instead. An opportunity arose when Joe Schenck (Nicholas's brother) announced that he was quitting as president of Del Mar Racecourse. "I have always enjoyed my association with racing but do not feel that I can continue to be active in track operations because of my primary interest in motion pictures," the president of United Artists explained. Quick to seize his chance, Mayer threw his hat into the ring. "Mayer Heads 4-Man Group Buying Del Mar," exclaimed the *Los Angeles Citizen-News* on September 27, 1951. Four months later, on January 28, 1952, he was elected Del Mar's chairman of the board.

Locked out of film production, Mayer's itch for horses took hold again. On February 11 he spent $300,000 and bought twenty horses from his brother-in-law Bill Goetz, the head of Universal-International Pictures. After a four-year hiatus, Mayer was back in the game as an owner, albeit on a much more modest scale. He had a small stable that he maintained for the rest of his life. His legacy as a breeder, however, continues to the present day.

One of the best horses he ever bred was Clem. By the Australian stallion Shannon out of the Mayer-owned mare Impulsive, Clem was a member of the extraordinary 1954 foal crop that included Bold Ruler, Iron Liege, Gallant Man, and Round Table. As a four-year-old in September 1958, the Adele Rand–owned Clem went on a tear, defeating Round Table three times: first in the Washington Park Handicap; then in the United Nations Handicap at Atlantic City, setting track records on turf in both those races; and finally in the Woodward Stakes at Belmont Park on dirt. One of the last horses Mayer bred was a 1956 foal by Royal Charger out of his Nearco mare Admirals Belle. Named Royal Orbit, he would win the 1959 Preakness Stakes, the second jewel of the Triple Crown.

Mayer had an influence in jump racing as well. The three-time (1955, 1957, 1958) American steeplechase champion Neji was a son of Mayer's British-bred import Hunters Moon IV. Jay Trump, whose damsire was Bernborough, won the Maryland Hunt Cup three times (1963, 1964, 1966) and England's Grand National Steeplechase in 1965. More recently, California Chrome—2014 Kentucky Derby and Preakness winner, 2016 Dubai World Cup winner, and two-time Horse of the Year—can be traced back to the Mayer-bred daughter of Beau Pere, Iron Reward. Fittingly, California Chrome won the last stakes race run at Hollywood Park, the King Glorious Stakes, on December 22, 2013.

Mayer's last winner carrying his own colors was Prize Host, who won a modest event at Garden State two weeks before his owner's death on October 29, 1957. Widely regarded today as a monstrous genius who bent his employees to his iron will, Mayer combined cinematic and racing accomplishments that remain unparalleled today. It is extraordinary for someone to be successful in two completely different professions in a single lifetime. Johnny Weissmuller and Buster Crabbe were both Olympic gold medalists in swimming who later became popular movie stars. Ronald Reagan is an even better example—a successful actor who became president of the United States. But Mayer achieved preeminence in the film world and the racing world at the same time. It would be lovely if geniuses were nice people, but that is rarely the case. He may have been a louse in private, but in public, Louis B. Mayer was a great man.

Perhaps he wrote his own epitaph when he said near the end of his life, "The sign of a clever auteur is to achieve the illusion that there is a sole individual responsible for magnificent creations that require thousands of people to accomplish."[12] But then there is the point of view expressed by Luise Rainer, who won Academy Awards for best actress in MGM's *The Great Ziegfeld* and *The Good Earth*: "I was one of the horses in the Louis B. Mayer stable."[13]

Eadweard Muybridge's photographic study of the horse in motion, proving conclusively that horses raise all four hooves off the ground in a full gallop. (Library of Congress)

Bing Crosby (left) greets the first guest through the turnstile on opening day at Del Mar, July 3, 1937.

Del Mar cofounders Pat O'Brien (left) and Bing Crosby address the crowd, 1937.

Bing Crosby–owned High Strike wins the first race ever run at Del Mar, July 3, 1937.

Bing Crosby (center) doing his NBC radio show at Del Mar with Oliver Hardy (right).

Bing Crosby making the rounds on horseback at Del Mar, 1938.

George Raft (in the black hat) and Bing Crosby celebrate a winner at Del Mar, 1938.

Seabiscuit (A), ridden by George Woolf, defeats Bing Crosby's Ligaroti (B), ridden by "Spec" Richardson, in a match race at Del Mar, August 12, 1938.

Mickey Rooney at Del Mar, 1940. That year, he flew his Piper Cub from Los Angeles to the track every day to attend the races.

From left to right: Georgie Jessel, Harry James, and Betty Grable watching a race at Del Mar, early 1950s.

Jimmy Durante (second from left) and Eddie Cantor (second from right) enjoy a day at Del Mar with friends.

From left to right: Jimmy Durante, Jayne Mansfield, and Hoagy Carmichael at Del Mar, 1958.

Barbara Stanwyck and Robert Taylor steal the show at Del Mar.

Barbara Stanwyck with one of her homebreds at Marwyck Ranch in Northridge, California. (Paramount Pictures publicity still)

Joan Blondell and hubby Dick Powell survey the Del Mar scene.

Dorothy Lamour graces the Del Mar winner's enclosure, 1937.

Gloria Swanson swamped by Del Mar autograph hounds, 1937.

W. C. Fields dining at Del Mar, 1938.

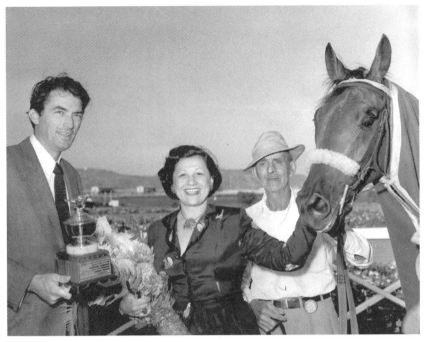

Gregory Peck (left) makes the trophy presentation in the Del Mar winner's circle.

Chico (left) bilks Groucho in a scene from *A Day at the Races*. (Stronach Group)

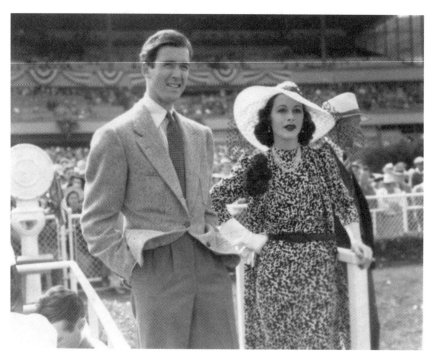

Jimmy Stewart and Hedy Lamarr light up Hollywood Park. (Stronach Group)

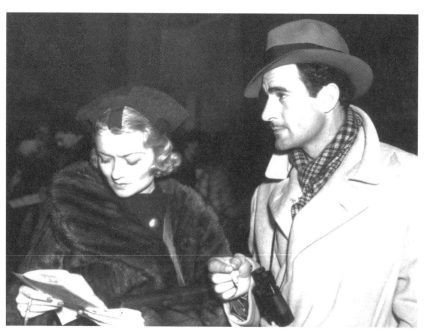

Constance Bennett and Errol Flynn at Santa Anita. (Stronach Group)

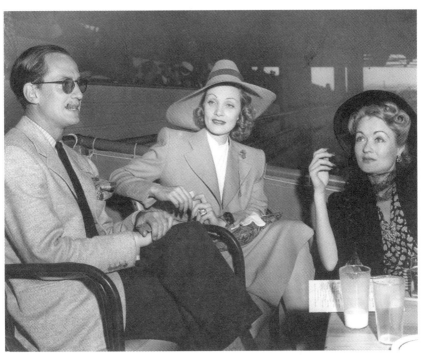

Marlene Dietrich (center), Constance Bennett (right), and a friend at Santa Anita. (Stronach Group)

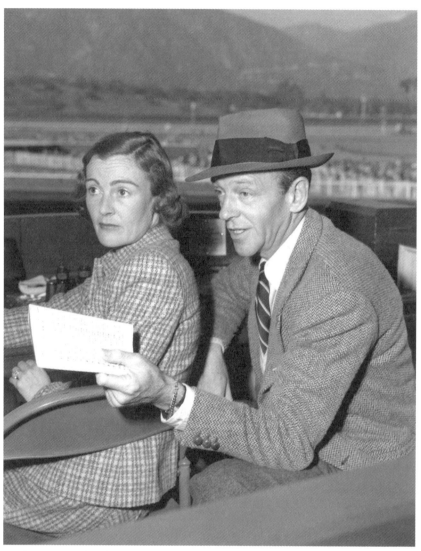

Fred Astaire and wife Phyllis at Santa Anita, 1951. (Stronach Group)

8

Hollywood Horsemen and Horsewomen

Fred Astaire, Betty Grable, and the Further Adventures of Bing Crosby

I train just like a race horse.

Fred Astaire

Fred Astaire's Dancing Hooves

Fred Astaire's analogy of the Thoroughbred racehorse and the professional dancer is apt. Both are sleekly elegant and well-muscled creatures, and both require long and strenuous periods of repetitive training before their finely tuned bodies can be revealed to the public in all their glory on the track or on the stage. Astaire would have appreciated the accomplishments of 1964 Kentucky Derby winner Northern Dancer, who became the most important stallion in the second half of the twentieth century and sired champions with the balletic names Nureyev, Lyphard, and Nijinsky, one of whose best sons was named Fred Astaire!

Astaire's interest in horse racing predated Hollywood's late 1930s craze for the sport. He first discovered the Thoroughbred world in 1924, while headlining the Gershwin musical *Lady Be Good* in London. He was enthralled by the British passion for racing and wanted to get involved. When he heard that Sidney Beer, a leading British owner, had a horse for sale, he made inquiries. Beer owned the era's best sprinter, Diomedes, who in 1925 won all three of England's most important sprint races: the King's Stand Stakes, the July Cup, and the Nunthorpe Stakes. Beer sold Astaire a colt named Dolomite for 500 pounds ($1,500), and even though Dolomite never won a race, Astaire was able to sell him for twice the purchase price. With that money he bought himself four eventual winners: High Hat, Mavis, Rainbow Tie, and The Greek. They were all in training at Newmarket, the headquarters of British racing, but these horses were really nothing to write home about, winning small maidens and handicaps on an irregular basis. Astaire was only dabbling in those days, in the game merely for the pleasure of ownership.

His first real winner in England (or anywhere else) was Social Evening, whom he co-owned with Sidney Beer. That prompted an observation by Astaire that captures the thrill of victory from a racehorse owner's point of view: "There's nothing like a winner of your own to give you that certain feeling."[1]

Living in London among show business people in the 1920s was an easy way to get hooked on horse racing. Astaire took to writing the names of horses he fancied in the next day's races on his dressing room mirror. Most stories about Astaire imply that he rarely went to the betting windows or approached a bookie, but that isn't true. Whether he was in London, New York, or Hollywood, Fred Astaire knew exactly what was going on at the local tracks, and he learned his lessons well. "I soon discovered that there is no profit in horse racing—that the only money in racing was my money."[2]

In England he was on a first-name basis with all the best jockeys: Gordon Richards, Steve Donoghue, Charlie Smirke, and Fred Winter. He had accounts with at least five bookmaking firms, including Ladbroke's. "I enjoyed my wagers immensely," he recalled wistfully, "and so did they."[3]

Two of his early Broadway shows, *Funny Face* and *Lady Be Good,* were backed by Jock Whitney of Greentree Stables. Whitney's colt Twenty Grand won Horse of the Year honors in 1931, the year *Lady Be Good* opened. Astaire and Whitney became fast friends, further inclining the dancer toward equine pursuits.

With the advent of sound pictures, Astaire was inevitably drawn to Hollywood. Talking onscreen was one thing, but singing and dancing onscreen opened a whole new world of entertainment possibilities. Yet Astaire's first foray in Hollywood was a bust. A 1930 screen test with Fred and his sister Adele for *Funny Face* failed to impress the executives at Paramount. Astaire headed back to Broadway, but Tinseltown couldn't ignore him for long. His cinematic partnerships with Ginger Rogers, Rita Hayworth, Judy Garland, and Cyd Charisse are the stuff of legend, but only once did he approach that exalted level at the racetrack.

His involvement with films during the 1930s precluded any serious ventures into racehorse ownership, and World War II forced the cancellation of racing in Southern California for nearly three years. Before the end of the war, however, Astaire wanted to get back into the game. In February 1944 he telegraphed his old friend and prominent New York trainer Clyde Phillips: DEAR CLYDE HERE'S THAT WIRE I TALKED ABOUT FIFTEEN YEARS AGO— BUY ME TWO YOUNG ONES POSSIBLY AS HIGH AS TEN THOUSAND APIECE IF NECESSARY AND I HOPE YOU ARE AVAILABLE TO TRAIN FOR ME.[4]

Phillips informed him that prominent Kentucky owner Colonel Edward Bradley of Idle Hour Farm was thinking of selling a promising two-year-old filly that would soon be ready to race. Bradley had promised Phillips right of first refusal on the daughter of Triple Crown winner War Admiral, who might be available for $5,000. But Bradley changed his mind and decided to keep the filly for himself. She turned out to be none other than Busher, the champion filly Louis B. Mayer bought a year later for $50,000.

He couldn't have known it at the time, but Astaire had narrowly missed out on racing immortality. Like everything else in life, he took the temporary setback in stride and plunked down $6,000 for a three-year-old colt in training. Triplicate was by 1928 a Kentucky Derby winner and Horse of the Year Reigh Count, the sire of 1940 Triple Crown winner Count Fleet. Phillips thought he might be able to do something with him, but meanwhile, he convinced Astaire to fork over $5,000 for a sore-legged nag named Fag (British slang for cigarette). He would finish third in his first start wearing Astaire's colors—dark blue, with a yellow belt and red cap—before winning a claiming race and being claimed for $4,000. Fag thus turned a small profit during the brief time he spent in Astaire's budding stable.

Despite his mediocre race record, Triplicate was turning the heads of clockers during his morning workouts at Jamaica Park in New York. Phillips entered him in an allowance race in September, and he won by five lengths, but Astaire wasn't there to see it, as he had shipped out a few weeks earlier to do a USO tour for the troops in Europe. In his second start for Astaire and Phillips, Triplicate surprised even his trainer when he beat a field of older horses in an overnight handicap by four lengths. Astaire missed that race too, but he was present when Triplicate ran fourth at Belmont, at which point it was decided to send the horse to California, where his owner could watch him run more often. On June 7, 1945, Astaire finally saw Triplicate win; it was only a minor stakes event, but the effort was good enough to earn him a place in the Santa Anita Handicap.

As the day of the Hundred Grander approached, Astaire was in Aiken, South Carolina, visiting family, but he hustled back to California for the big race. Triplicate was fourth early, then moved into a challenging third on the turn, but he could not sustain his rally and faded back to fourth. The winner was Mayer's Thumbs Up, who equaled the track record of 2:01⅖ set two years earlier by Seabiscuit. Still, this was Triplicate's best performance to date, and trainer Phillips was optimistic. "There's no tellin' just how good this horse might be," he told its owner.[5]

Triplicate—or "Trip," as Astaire affectionately called him—continued to progress, albeit without winning any races of note. He won his prep race for the March 9 Santa Anita Handicap but then had the misfortune of drawing the number 22 post in that star-studded twenty-three-horse field. Five of the horses had Hollywood connections. The longshot War Knight was owned by Ethel Hill, a screenwriter who had penned the scripts for Shirley Temple's *The Little Princess* and Walter Brennan's racing film *Maryland*. Harry Warner and Mervyn LeRoy were co-owners of Paperboy. Director Howard Hawks was the owner of War Valor, and Louis B. Mayer was seeking a second straight Hundred Grander with his brilliant filly Be Faithful.

As the huge field passed the stands the first time, a cloud of dust obscured the tote board. War Knight was tracking the leader, with Triplicate wide in midpack, while Johnny Longden was trapped on the rail with the favorite, First Fiddle. Entering the stretch, War Knight took the lead and held off the cavalry charge to win from First Fiddle. The unlucky Triplicate, wide all the way around, closed to take sixth place, beaten by only two lengths. Ethel Hill, who had spent $1,500—her life savings—on War Knight, had beaten the Hollywood and Kentucky elites with a seven-year-old that had missed his entire six-year-old season with an injury. A year later, she sold a screenplay about War Knight's exploits for $100,000 to Liberty Films, a newly founded production company headed by Frank Capra, George Stevens, and William Wyler, but it was never produced.

Fred Astaire was not unhappy with the Big 'Cap result. His jockey, J. D. Jessop, the nation's leading rider in 1945, said that Trip would have won but for a rough trip, and he urged owner and trainer to enter him in the 1½-mile San Juan Capistrano Handicap, held just one week later. Racing so soon after a tough outing like the Santa Anita Handicap was asking a lot, but Jessop's judgment proved correct. Triplicate stormed to a five-length victory over Hawks's War Valor in the San Juan Capistrano, setting a track record of 2:28⅖. Next up was a move down the road to Hollywood Park for its signature event: the $100,000 Hollywood Gold Cup.

Astaire described Triplicate as "a somewhat moody sort, sometimes disappointing."[6] Indeed, he had won just six of his previous fifty-two starts, but that spring and summer he hit a purple patch, as in-and-out horses sometimes do. He was training brilliantly in the run-up to the Gold Cup, a 1¼-mile race that suited him perfectly. But when jockey Jessop was hit with a suspension that would sideline him on Gold Cup day, Phillips and Astaire scrambled to find a replacement. All the other top riders at Hollywood Park were already engaged for the Gold Cup. They tried to get Eddie Arcaro to fly in from New York, but he wasn't interested. They finally decided on Basil James—a good choice. James had led the nation in victories in 1936 (at age sixteen) and in earnings in 1939. The problem was that James, like Arcaro, was based in New York, where stormy weather had caused the cancellation of many coast-to-coast flights.

Howard Hughes came to their rescue. The producer of *Two Arabian Nights, Hell's Angels, The Front Page,* and *Scarface* had met Astaire in 1940, when Hughes was courting Ginger Rogers. The record-setting aviator arranged for James to fly on one of his private planes, and the jockey arrived at Hollywood Park for the Gold Cup in the nick of time. A crowd of 50,451 had gathered, among them cowboy star Randolph Scott, who was seated in Astaire's private box. The Gold Cup field included Mayer's ace fillies Honeymoon and Be Faithful, who were sent off as the favored coupled entry. Be Faithful led for more than a mile, but then Honeymoon took the lead a furlong out. She seemed headed for victory until James and Triplicate made a late outside run to snatch the race by a neck. The 7–1 Triplicate rewarded Astaire with $81,000 in first-place prize money plus the $6,000 he won at the betting window.

Bad luck was stalking Triplicate, however. Trainer Clyde Phillips, who had been suffering from lung problems for years, died on December 17 at the age of fifty-three. His assistant Lloyd Campion took over the stable, and Triplicate soon reverted to his in-and-out form—mostly out. Trip would win only one more major event in his last three years of racing. That was the $75,000 Golden Gate Handicap at Golden Gate Fields, across the bay from San Francisco, in October 1947. Triplicate defeated Busher's old rival Bymeabond, going 1¼ miles on a muddy track and providing Johnny Longden with his fourth win of the day before a crowd of

33,039. Two years later, Trip ended his racing days with a healthy bankroll of $245,000—not bad for a horse that had been a questionable purchase at $6,000.

Astaire sent his star to stand at stud in Kentucky in 1950, but Triplicate could not even duplicate himself in the breeding barn and eventually wound up in Japan. Astaire would remain an active owner for decades to come, racing the fillies Sharp Curve and To Glory. In 1950 he bought a farm in the San Fernando Valley that he called Blue Valley Ranch, where he raised a small string of homebreds. "Horses are my favorite topic," the most popular dancer-singer-actor in the history of Hollywood said. "Mention horses and I'm off and running." From 1948 on, a portrait of Triplicate hung above the fireplace at his Beverly Hills home.[7]

During his many sojourns to England, both professional and personal, Astaire formed a friendship with the Queen Mother, an important figure in British jump racing throughout her long life. He was a frequent visitor at Royal Ascot, where he was sure to be invited into the Royal Box for a glass of Pimm's, a dish of strawberries and cream, and a chat about the day's races. He even owned a horse in Australia. When he traveled Down Under in 1959 to make the nuclear disaster film *On the Beach* with Gregory Peck and Ava Gardner, one of the first things he did was head to Flemington, Melbourne's leading racecourse. Well aware of the American exploits of Australian-breds Phar Lap and Beau Pere, he made inquiries among local trainers and soon found himself in possession of a colt named Anything, who, unfortunately, turned out to be nothing.

Despite his lifelong attraction to the Thoroughbred world, Astaire never became sentimental about horses. In his autobiography *Steps in Time* he writes, "I've learned never to fall in love with a horse. When it becomes economically unsound to keep one, it must go." That dictum, however, didn't apply to jockeys, especially those of the female variety.[8]

When Fred Astaire's wife, Phyllis, died on September 13, 1954, leaving him with two teenaged children, he embarked on a lengthy bachelorhood that would last twenty-six years. He had first spotted Phyllis in the Belmont Park clubhouse but didn't formally meet her until they were introduced at a golf luncheon thrown by Mrs. Graham Fair Vanderbilt out on Long Island. He wooed her for two years before their July 12, 1933, wedding, after which they spent a one-night honeymoon on Payne Whitney's yacht, *Captiva,* and then hightailed it out to Hollywood, where

Fred had a supporting role in his first movie, *Dancing Lady,* with Joan Crawford. He and Phyllis were deeply devoted to each other, and although she supported his racing endeavors, she was not particularly keen on the sport. When they went to the track together, she was likely to spend the day knitting in their private box. After Triplicate scored his greatest victory in the Hollywood Gold Cup, the retiring Phyllis remained in their box while Fred accepted the winner's trophy. One day in July 1953 at Belmont Park, Phyllis felt ill and asked to return to her parents' house out on Long Island, where they were spending the summer. At first it appeared to be nothing more than a dizzy spell, but there was a recurrence at Santa Anita the following winter and a quick trip home to Blue Valley. It turned out to be lung cancer. After two surgeries, both deemed "successful," Phyllis died, leaving Fred bereft and alone.

His long bachelorhood might be attributed to both his age at the time of Phyllis's death (fifty-five) and the niche she would always occupy in his heart. He made an adjustment to his public persona, adding serious dramas such as *On the Beach* and *The Towering Inferno* (for which he received an Oscar nomination for best supporting actor) to his repertoire, while continuing his song-and-dance routine with musicals such as *Funny Face* (costarring Audrey Hepburn), *Silk Stockings* (Cyd Charisse), and *Finian's Rainbow* (Petula Clark). But the romance of the racetrack was never far from his heart.

In 1973 Astaire was ringing in the New Year at Santa Anita with Alfred Gwynne Vanderbilt, who had a filly named Exciting Divorcee running in a little allowance race. She would be ridden by Robyn Smith, a young woman who was causing a sensation and no little upset as the first genuinely prominent female jockey in the country. Vanderbilt introduced Fred and Robyn in the paddock, where she advised him not to bet on Exciting Divorcee, who was a hopeless longshot with little chance against the 3–5 favorite ridden by Bill Shoemaker. Fred smiled and promptly placed a big bet on Robyn's mount. When she got Exciting Divorcee up on the line to beat Shoemaker's horse by a nose, Fred was richly rewarded with either $5,000 or $10,000, according to conflicting reports from the jockey herself. Together, they spent some of that money on dinner at Chasen's, the venerable West Hollywood eatery beloved by movie stars since 1936.

Shortly thereafter Robyn returned to New York, where she became the first woman to ride the winner of a stakes race when she booted home Vanderbilt's North Sea in the Paumanok Handicap at Aqueduct on March 1. The New York circuit—Aqueduct, Belmont, and Saratoga— was Robyn's regular stomping grounds in those days, and she didn't run into Fred again until five years later, when she was in Los Angeles to film a television commercial for Shasta soft drinks. She called him up and invited him to dinner, and apparently, love bloomed. Robyn moved her tack back to the Santa Anita–Hollywood Park–Del Mar circuit to be closer to Fred, and the couple became an item.

On March 5, 1980, the *Los Angeles Herald-Examiner* announced that the Astaire-Smith partnership might soon be formalized. "Looks like they're about to make their stable a permanent one," it reported. "We're thinking about it," Robyn demurely replied, but Fred was more explicit. "We've become very, very, very good friends," he said. One more "very" and he would have exposed himself completely. The news of impending nuptials between eighty-one-year-old Fred and thirty-six-year-old Robyn raised eyebrows from Santa Anita to Aqueduct and from Hollywood to Broadway.[9]

Robyn felt that she was still capable of achieving greatness as a jockey, but her hopes had consistently been dashed in both California and New York. She claimed that male owners refused to let her ride their good horses because she was a woman, despite evidence that she was just as talented as her male counterparts. During the winter of 1972, she won more races at Aqueduct than any rider except for the great Angel Cordero. Throughout that year, Smith rode a higher percentage of winners on the New York racing circuit than anyone except Cordero. She continually complained to owners, trainers, and the press that even though her mounts won 18 to 20 percent of the time, all the good horses were going to male jockeys with lower winning rates. She could take some consolation, however, when she appeared on the cover of the July 31 edition of *Sports Illustrated*.

Robyn had started her career as a professional jockey at a very late age. She rode in her first race at Golden Gate Fields in late 1969, when she was twenty-five years old. Her childhood had been a troubled one: her father absent, her mother indifferent and mean-spirited. She spent most of her early years in a succession of California foster homes. Somehow she found herself at a Columbia Pictures acting workshop, but nothing came of it. In 1968 she began to ride morning workouts at tracks in the San Francisco area and finally obtained a license to ride professionally in the autumn of 1969. But even her rapid progress through the ranks failed to result in many choice rides. Jockey Eddie Arcaro summed up her plight. "The better Robyn gets," he said, "the more jealous others get."[10]

She went a long way toward proving her critics wrong on October 3, 1975, when she rode three winners in successive races at Belmont Park. The first two, both owned by the ever-faithful Alfred Vanderbilt, were Lead Line (3.20–1) and Slink (5.10–1), followed by the 29.20–1 longshot Togs Drone. "It only proves what can be done when a rider gets good horses," she pointed out, and of course, she was right.[11] It is a measure of her frustration that her three rides that day brought her monthly total for the Belmont fall meeting to just twenty-five—an average of barely one ride per day.

Finding herself in Fred Astaire's loving arms must have been like a soothing balm to her sore heart. Later in life, she said that he was the only person who ever loved her, and she was probably right. Despite her athletic ability and undeniable good looks, Robyn Smith was a charmless woman with a short temper and an abrasive personality, traits that surely impeded her racing career. When she and Fred tied the knot in a quiet ceremony at his Beverly Hills home on June 24, 1980, the groom's sister, Adele, and his daughter, Ava, were conspicuous by their absence. "It's a woman thing," Robyn pooh-poohed, as she pointed out the friendship she had developed with her new stepson, Fred Jr. The honeymoon was a short one. The day after the wedding, Robyn was back in action at Hollywood Park, her happy husband proudly looking on from the grandstand.[12]

The racing and film communities, as well as the public at large, thought that Fred had gotten himself a youthful and attractive trophy wife, and if their marriage had been a film, its title might have been *Gold Diggers of 1980*. The newlyweds ignored the criticism. Flush with new-found fame, Robyn took off on a worldwide tour, riding in Argentina, England, Italy, and West Germany; her name was still listed in programs as R. C. Smith. Fred headed east to Vermont to star in the horror film *Ghost Story*. Almost immediately, the press opened fire. Before the summer was over, rumors were circulating that the marriage was on the rocks. The fact that Robyn was riding more frequently in New York than in California added fuel to the fire being fanned by gossip columnists on both coasts, who predicted that the coupled entry of Astaire and Smith was about to be scratched.

Both parties pleasantly denied that they were breaking up, and when Robyn announced in August that she was retiring from the saddle, everything appeared to be hunky-dory. "Fred thinks that riding horses is dangerous," she explained. "It isn't, but he is my No. 1 priority. I like to keep him happy."[13] And that appeared to be the scenario for the rest of their seven years together, although in a candid moment, Fred revealed, "She can be quick tempered," and Robyn admitted, "I'm moody." On December 12, 1980, they put in an appearance at Frank Sinatra's sixty-fifth birthday party in Palm Springs. Seven days later, they were at the Hollywood Park Christmas party thrown in Fred's honor at the Paramount commissary, where the guest list included Hollywood Park CEO Vernon O. Underwood and racetrack board members Mervyn LeRoy and Cary Grant.[14]

But as Fred aged, their public appearances waned. Robyn tended to shun the spotlight and was basically antisocial. She didn't even enjoy entertaining at home and would sit glumly when Fred had friends like Randolph Scott over for dinner. Racing was no longer a part of their lives; Robyn even gave up riding socially. Mrs. Lester Holt, wife of Fred's long-time trainer, said, "Fred and Robyn never came racing after they were married." In declining health, eighty-eight-year-old Fred caught a cold that quickly developed into pneumonia. He died in Robyn's arms on June 22, 1987. "I had him for seven years" she recalled, and "buried him on our anniversary. That alone is unique, special and awful."[15]

Robyn Smith's life since the death of her famous husband has been that of a recluse. She is fiercely protective of the Fred Astaire legacy and has filed numerous lawsuits against people who have used his name or image without her consent. Yet she allowed a clip of one of Fred's cinematic dance numbers to be reedited for strictly commercial purposes, so that he appears to be dancing with a vacuum cleaner! Surely she went too far when she refused to allow film clips of Fred dancing with Ginger Rogers to be shown when Rogers was honored by the Kennedy Center in 1993. As a result, Astaire was effectively airbrushed out of cinematic history, at least on that occasion.

Astaire's legacy is not in any danger of disappearing, however. He remains one of the brightest stars in the Hollywood firmament, but it should not be forgotten: Fred Astaire's offscreen heart belonged to horse racing, and his marriage to Robyn Smith was a reflection of his devotion to the sport.

Betty Grable's Million-Dollar Legs

Thoroughbred racehorses that have sold for $1 million or more are commonplace and are often grossly overpriced. In 1982 Sheikh Mohammed bin Rashid al-Maktoum set a new world record for foolishness when he parted with $10.2 million at Keeneland for a Northern Dancer yearling; the horse, eventually named Snaafi Dancer, never made it to the races. In 2006 John Magnier of Coolmore Stud saved Sheikh Mohammed from further embarrassment when he outbid the ruler of Dubai at Calder, laying claim to an unraced two-year-old for $16 million. The horse, named The Green Monkey, subsequently failed to win in three lifetime starts.

Put in perspective, the $1 million 20th Century Fox allegedly paid Lloyd's of London to insure Betty Grable's legs looks like a bargain, until you figure that's the equivalent of $14.2 million today. That made Betty even more valuable than The Green Monkey or Snaafi Dancer, because she had just two legs. That comes to $7.1 million per leg, compared with the $4 million per leg Magnier paid for The Green Monkey. In actuality, however, the studio insured Grable's legs for a mere $250,000. The extra $750,000 was added for the public-relations effect.

At the height of her considerable fame in 1945, Betty proudly proclaimed, "I have got two reasons for my success and I'm standing on both of them."[16] The popularity of her teasingly famous pinup pose, coupled with a string of box office smashes, made her the highest-paid actress in the land in 1943 and 1945. She was in the top ten among all actors nine times during the 1940s, but her career during the previous decade had been touch and go. A string of uncredited bit parts was followed by a small dancing role in *The Gay Divorcee* (1933) with Fred Astaire and Ginger Rogers. She had a singing part three years later in *Follow the Fleet.* Grable sang and danced alongside Judy Garland in *Pigskin Parade* (1936) but didn't get top billing until 1938 in George Archainbaud's *Campus Confessions.*

Paramount gave her a second starring role in a quasi–horse racing picture called *Million Dollar Legs,* in which a group of college students bets on a 20–1 longshot to raise money to buy a new boat for the rowing team. In retrospect, one might assume that the film was named for Betty's legs, but in fact, it refers to the horse's legs. In any case, the movie flopped, and Paramount failed to renew Betty's contract. After a one-film stopover at RKO for a second racing movie, *The Day the Bookies Wept,* she latched on to 20th Century Fox, where producer Darryl F. Zanuck spared no expense in her first A film, *Down Argentine Way.*

Hollywood seemed to be telling Betty Grable something: she set a record of sorts by appearing in three consecutive horse racing films— *Million Dollar Legs, The Day the Bookies Wept,* and *Down Argentine Way.*

The last was a lavish Technicolor tale about a young American equestrienne who travels to Argentina in search of a new horse for the Olympics and gets involved in a race-fixing scam. Alongside Don Ameche (a noted Thoroughbred owner in real life), she sang and danced her way into America's heart. "I never saw anything as gorgeous as Betty in Technicolor," exclaimed Mack Gordon, lyricist for the film's Oscar-nominated title song.[17]

Maybe all that dialogue about racing whet Betty's appetite for the real thing. During her much-publicized affair with George Raft, she was frequently seen at racetracks from coast to coast. After dumping Raft, she hooked up with trumpeter Harry James, who had been dabbling in racehorse ownership. Shortly after their marriage on July 5, 1943, they began to invest in Thoroughbreds. At a sale in San Mateo, they spent $75,000 on seven horses, but they didn't have a winner until Deviled Egg turned a 63–1 trick at Santa Anita on January 18, 1946. At that point, Harry and Betty decided that this was the game for them. They bought a sixty-two-acre farm in Calabasas, thirty miles west of Los Angeles, and named it the Baby-J Ranch. When they took possession in July, they already had a dozen Thoroughbreds on the ranch and a few more in training at Santa Anita. With their combined salaries and love of racing, they built one of the most formidable stables in the racing-mad Hollywood film community.

By 1948, the Grable-James tandem was in full swing. That winter, they had seven winners at Santa Anita. One day while filming *That Lady in Ermine*, Betty bragged that her filly Colette had just won a race at Bay Meadows. The next day she passed around a brief item in the *Los Angeles Times* reporting the victory, as proud as if she were announcing the birth of her daughter. That summer, they had eight broodmares, five foals, three yearlings, and five two-year-olds on the farm at Calabasas.

Betty could be loquacious about her horses. Like Louis Mayer, she understood that breeding was the foundation of any Thoroughbred operation worth its salt, as she explained in a lengthy 1949 interview with Louella Parsons:

> One of the biggest thrills I've ever had in my life came when a colt was born on our ranch. He turned out to be a great racing horse. We called him Sociability and he won his first three races out. We bought some of our horses at auction and others we claimed at the races and while we love them, we don't have the same feeling

as we have for the ones born on the farm. Of course, it's expensive to start with but our horses have pretty well paid for their keep. I can't truthfully say we have made any money yet, but that doesn't worry us. Harry has a good job and so have I.[18]

Those good jobs were the key to the whole business. In 1947 Betty Grable was the highest-paid woman in America, with a salary of $320,000. Harry James generally made about $100,000 a year. Some rather well-off people can afford to own a few racehorses. Middle-class and even working-class people can probably afford to be part of a syndicate that owns a horse or two. But in order to have sustained success at the top level of racing, one must be rich with a capital *R*. The most successful Thoroughbred owners from the cinematic world during Hollywood's Golden Age—Louis B. Mayer, Bing Crosby, and Betty Grable—were all among Tinseltown's highest-paid employees. Not that money is the sole factor in running a first-class racing stable. Harry Warner and Mervyn LeRoy poured millions into their Thoroughbred operation but never had a major winner.

"That's where the money is—in the Thoroughbred breeding business," Betty held. To that end, she attended one of Louis Mayer's late 1940s dispersal sales and bought a broodmare named Merry Soul for $35,000. She was by King Cole, a winner of the Withers Stakes and runner-up to Whirlaway in the 1941 Preakness Stakes. Betty and Harry were serious about building a major racing and breeding stable.[19]

"I like it," Betty said of the racing game. "I couldn't do without it and I am lucky that I can afford it."[20] Betty's racing career progressed as far as her cinematic legs would take her, and they took her pretty far. Once, they even brought her to the brink of glory. Betty and Harry's first success was their homebred son of Khaled (the future sire of Swaps). They named him Big Noise, after Harry's trumpet, and he turned out to be the first stakes winner Khaled produced in America, winning the Del Mar Futurity and the California Breeders' Champion Stakes in 1951. Betty was excited by this horse. "When Big Noise is working I leap out of bed at 5:30 to watch him," she said. "When I'm making a picture, it's all I can do to drag myself onto the set at 6:30 for a make-up call."[21]

But Big Noise was a troublesome individual. He was hard to handle on the track and failed to fulfill his two-year-old promise. At three, his only victory was in the Berkeley Handicap up at Golden Gate Fields. Big Noise stood stud duty in California for a few years, without much success, but Betty never lost faith. "Big Noise's legs are nearly as valuable as mine. We insured them for $125,000. Mine are insured for a million," she fibbed, "but I don't think they're worth that," she admitted.[22] That was the way Betty Grable was: honest and self-effacing. "There are thousands of women with legs prettier than mine," she said. "I can't sing. Dance? I just get by. And yet I'm a terrific success. All this amazes me." When the *Harvard Lampoon* rudely named her "The World's Worst Actress," she wired right back: "YOU'RE SO RIGHT!"[23]

Big Noise retired with a healthy $135,000 in the bank, so Harry and Betty bred his full brother, Laughin' Louie, named for Harry's idol Louis Armstrong. But the equine Louie was not in the same league as either his older brother or his namesake.

Betty and Harry had better luck with Blue Trumpeter, a colt that James named in honor of Tiny Naylor, the six-foot-four, 300-pound owner of a hot-spot diner on the corner of Sunset Boulevard and La Brea favored by jazz musicians. Blue Trumpeter won four races in a row at one point, but he fell just short of being a genuine stakes race performer.

A bigger and better opportunity arose in 1953 in the shape of James Session, named for Harry's jazz connections. James Session won Hollywood Park's five-furlong Haggin Stakes in June of his juvenile season, then followed up with a victory in the six-furlong Salinas Handicap. He also finished second in the two races Big Noise had won two years earlier: the Del Mar Futurity and the California Breeders' Championship Stakes. James Session blossomed at age three when he landed Santa Anita's important Derby prep race, the San Vicente Stakes. He ran the six furlongs in 1:09⅖, the fastest time recorded in the five runnings of the race at that distance. Betty had this to say about James Session as she watched Eddie Arcaro working him in preparation for the Santa Anita Derby. "He's a hell of a fine horse. He has won over $100,000 in fourteen starts. He is the best horse we own."[24]

The problem was that James Session couldn't stay much further than a mile. Even though he faded tamely in the 1⅛-mile Santa Anita Derby, Betty and Harry decided to send him to Churchill Downs for the Kentucky Derby. On the face of it, this looked like a celebrity vanity project, but James Session had beaten the highly regarded Determine in both the San Vicente and the Salinas, so they took their chance.

Tote-board watchers could have told them that James Session was in trouble when he went off at a discouraging 71–1. Determine, the

4–1 second choice, won by a length and a half, while James Session was outrun throughout and finished eighth. Neither Harry nor Betty was there to see it. Betty was working on the musical *Three for the Show* with Jack Lemmon, and Harry had a concert date in Billings, Montana, where he watched the race at a television appliance store.

In addition to concert dates, Harry had plenty of the other kind as well. His philandering and drinking caused problems throughout their turbulent marriage. It might have been their shared interest in racing—and, of course, their two children—that kept them together for twenty years. Harry also like the wagering side of racing and, like most gamblers, exaggerated his skill: "I can read a Form and turn around and remember the post position and where he (the horse) ran and the trouble he had and everything else," he bragged. "It's just something I'm so interested in and have been for a long time. My mind's adjusted to it."[25]

But their marriage had become maladjusted. Harry's gambling losses added to declining revenue from racing, which led to the sale of the Baby-J Ranch and all forty horses in 1961. It was the beginning of the end. With less and less to bind them together, they divorced on October 7, 1965, Betty citing extreme cruelty and mental cruelty. She did not request alimony, and they remained friends. "You're better off betting on a horse than betting on a man," Betty lamented. "A horse may not be able to hold you tight, but he doesn't wanna wander from the stable at night."[26]

Betty Grable died on July 2, 1973, at the age of fifty-six. Harry received news of her death while playing a gig at Disneyland. She is commemorated each November at her favorite racetrack, Del Mar, with the Betty Grable Stakes, a seven-furlong event for fillies and mares.

Rochester in Louisville

Betty Grable wasn't the only Hollywood luminary to have a runner in the Kentucky Derby. Eddie "Rochester" Anderson, famous as Jack Benny's jack-of-all-trades and the first African American to have a starring role on a national radio program, entered Burnt Cork in the 1943 edition of the Run for the Roses. The drolly named colt (burnt cork was what white performers used to blacken their faces in the early days of vaudeville) was considered a no-hoper. Anderson took a lot of heat for entering the horse—seemingly for publicity purposes—but by any rational account, Burnt Cork deserved his place in the Derby field. As a stakes winner, he had been ranked the twentieth best two-year-old of 1942 in the *Daily Racing Form*'s Experimental Free Handicap. Burnt Cork started at odds of 21–1 (part of a two-horse mutuel field with the aptly named Bankrupt) and proved the critics right. After tracking the pace early on, he weakened badly to finish dead last, thirty-eight lengths behind the redoubtable Count Fleet.

On his radio program a week before the race, Jack Benny jokingly lamented that he had sold Burnt Cork to Anderson for $4, and now he was running in a race for $50,000. After Burnt Cork's flop, Benny had a good laugh at Rochester's expense. When told that Rochester was so broke after Burnt Cork's loss that he would have to ride the horse back to Los Angeles, Benny suggested that they'd make better time if the horse rode Rochester.

Don Ameche Invents the Telephone

Don Ameche never had a runner in the Kentucky Derby, but his love of racing lasted as long as his storied film career. The dapper native of Kenosha, Wisconsin, was born Dominic Amici, and he was as friendly as his name implied. During his sixty-year career in show business, he remained one of the most popular stars in Hollywood.

Early on, he was cast as turn-of-the-century types in films like *In Old Chicago* and *Alexander's Ragtime Band,* but he hit a purple patch in 1939 when he played D'Artagnan in *The Three Musketeers,* starred in the hilarious comedy *Midnight* with Claudette Colbert, and portrayed the man who invented the telephone in *The Story of Alexander Graham Bell.* His performance as Bell made such an impression that "Ameche" became synonymous with "telephone," as in, "Get off the Ameche already!" In fact, some people actually thought the actor had invented the telephone. One day at Beverly Hills High School, an institution of midlevel learning attended by the offspring of many Hollywood stars, the question was posed: "Who wrote 'My Old Kentucky Home'?" To which one wag answered, "Don Ameche!" "No!" another budding scholar responded. "Stephen Foster wrote that. Don Ameche invented the telephone!"

In 1938 Ameche narrowly missed out on the opportunity to star in a major Technicolor production that dripped with "My Old Kentucky Home" sentiment. He had been penciled in by 20th Century Fox to play opposite Loretta Young in *Kentucky,* a historically accurate account of how the Bluegrass State became the center of America's Thoroughbred industry. But a bad case of tonsillitis necessitated a tonsillectomy, so he lost the role to Englishman Richard Greene. Two years later, Ameche got a chance to act in a racing film when he costarred with Betty Grable in *Down Argentine Way.*

Down Argentine Way was intended to curry favor with the people and government of Argentina, but it did exactly the opposite. It was part of Franklin Roosevelt's Good Neighbor policy, an attempt to woo South American countries away from the influence of Nazi Germany. Unfortunately, 20th Century Fox and director Irving Cummings failed to do their home-work. The film's three main musical elements—a number by Brazilian dancer Carmen Miranda, a lilting Mexican ballad from the Flores Brothers, and a tap routine by the magnificent Nicholas Brothers—have absolutely nothing to do with Argentine culture. Even more offensive was the film's portrayal of a race-fixing scam concocted by Argentine gangsters. Fox seemed to be unaware that membership in the Argentine Jockey Club was a rite of passage for those hoping to attain the upper reaches of society and government and that such shenanigans would never be tolerated (at least not publicly). Shortly after its release in Buenos Aires as *Serenata Argentina,* the film was banned throughout the country, and the government of President Roberto Maria Ortiz lodged an official protest with Washington.

Viewed decades later, far removed from the heated political climate of 1940, *Down Argentine Way* comes across as a lush and lively musical comedy with a cliched plot. Ameche defended the film from an American point of view in the *Los Angeles Times:* "It wouldn't, couldn't and didn't offend anyone—it entertained them. It was still the depths of the Depression, and anything that could distance people from the brutality of the times was desperately welcome. The euphoria that a film like 'Argentina' could produce wouldn't last just during the picture itself, it would be there when you left the theater and it might last as long as two weeks."[27] The Academy of Motion Picture Arts and Sciences agreed with him, nominating the film for three Oscars. In 2014 the Library of Congress deemed the film cultur-ally, historically, or aesthetically significant. It was certainly culturally and historically significant, but for all the wrong reasons.

After the Argentine dust settled, Ameche was bitten by the racing bug that had hit Hollywood like the plague. In 1944 he played the same card as Louis B. Mayer and purchased a pair of two-year-old colts—Sir Bim and Son of Chance—from Colonel Edward Bradley at Idle Hour Farm in

Lexington, Kentucky. By Preakness and Belmont Stakes winner Bimelech out of a mare by Kentucky Derby winner Bubbling Over, Sir Bim had the makings of a good one. A second-place finish as a two-year-old in the Arlington Futurity earned him a nomination to the Kentucky Derby, and when he trotted up to win Santa Anita's San Felipe Stakes by three lengths with Johnny Longden aboard, Ameche could be forgiven for setting his sights on Louisville on the first Saturday in May. Alas, his hopes were dashed by subsequent failures in the San Vicente Stakes and the Santa Anita Derby. Sir Bim, however, remained a useful inmate at Ameche's barn until a decline in cinematic fortunes forced Ameche to sell all his horses in January 1947. By that time, Sir Bim had won nine of thirty-nine starts in three seasons, earning $54,275.

That spring, reduced from getting star billing at Fox to struggling for roles at the poverty-row studios, Ameche joined forces with another big name who suddenly found himself out in the cold. At Republic, he collaborated with Frank Borzage (director of the Oscar-winning *Seventh Heaven,* as well as *A Farewell to Arms* and *History Is Made at Night*) to make the modest racing film *That's My Man,* in which he plays an inveterate gambler whose horse, Gallant Man (no relation to the 1957 Belmont Stakes winner of the same name), wins the big race. Ameche and Borzage had to make a living, after all.

In the 1950s Ameche opened a small Thoroughbred farm he called L'Aquila Ltd. He always had at least two or three horses in training and usually named them after towns and cities in Italy.

Ameche's film career enjoyed a revival in the 1980s, highlighted by his Oscar-winning performance as a break-dancing septuagenarian in the Ron Howard–directed *Cocoon.* These late-in-life successes enriched his bank account to the point where he could afford to buy a promising Capote yearling he named Ferrara, after the Renaissance town near Bologna. Third-place finishes in a pair of Grade 2 races, the Norfolk Stakes and the Del Mar Futurity, had Ameche thinking Kentucky Derby again. However, Ferrara's ninth-place finish behind Brocco (owned by Cubby Broccoli, producer of sixteen James Bond films) in America's premiere event for two-year-olds, the Breeders' Cup Juvenile, all but dashed those hopes.

Ameche died on December 6, 1993, at his son's home in Scottsdale, Arizona. Tom, who had overseen operations at L'Aquila for many years, summed up his father's passion for Thoroughbreds: "He lived for horses.

L'Aquila was his company. Making money was not his primary concern. He would've liked to have had stakes winners, but only had two early on, Sir Bim and Son of Chance."[28]

Although Don Ameche never reached Olympian heights as an owner, he helped make racing history in 1955. That was the year the California-based Swaps won the first leg of the Triple Crown, the Kentucky Derby, beating the New York–based Nashua. Nashua then won the second and third jewels of the Triple Crown, the Preakness and Belmont Stakes, while Swaps skipped those two races to return to California, where he defeated the 1954 Kentucky Derby winner, Determine, in the Californian Stakes at Santa Anita.

That Swaps and Nashua were two of the greatest racehorses in history has long been gospel among horsemen of every stripe in every part of the country. In 1955 the question of which was the better horse became the nation's most hotly debated sporting subject. Everyone from coast to coast wanted to see them clash again, except perhaps their owners and trainers. The Swaps team—owner Rex Ellsworth and trainer Mesh Tenney—were quite content to keep their California-bred son of Khaled at home in sunny California. Their horse had beaten the Kentucky-bred son of Nasrullah fair and square in the East. If Nashua wanted to try Swaps again, he could come to the West Coast. Nashua's people—owner William Woodward Jr. and trainer "Sunny" Jim Fitzsimmons—felt the same way. All the best races were run on the East Coast, and if Swaps wanted a part of Nashua again, he should come to New York.

Enter Don Ameche. He was a close friend and racing buddy of Ben Lindheimer, owner of Washington Park Racetrack in Chicago. In fact, the affable and charming Ameche was a close friend of almost everybody who was anybody in the racing world. His Kenosha, Wisconsin, roots brought him back to the Midwest with a certain frequency. In 1950 Ameche had further endeared himself to Lindheimer when he hosted an NBC racing show called *The Blue Ribbon Sport of Kings,* Blue Ribbon being the best-selling beer produced by Pabst in Milwaukee. The program centered on Chicago's two leading tracks, Arlington and Washington Park—both owned by Lindheimer—and featured interviews with Gloria Swanson and Harry Daniels, among others (Daniels was the trainer of the Louis Mayer–bred Your Host, owned by Mayer's son-in-law, producer Bill Goetz). One night over dinner, Ameche and Lindheimer reasoned that

Washington Park, though not exactly halfway between Belmont and Santa Anita, was at least neutral ground for the East Coast and West Coast champions. Ameche was dispatched to convince both the Swaps and the Nashua teams of the efficacy of a match race, preferably for sometime in August.

He was the perfect man for the job. The 1950s were relatively lean years for him. Almost all his appearances were on the small screen in TV movies or one-time guest shots in dramatic specials. After a six-week run on Broadway in the Cole Porter musical *Silk Stockings,* during which time he made frequent forays to Aqueduct and Jamaica, Ameche found himself unemployed. Back at Santa Anita, he called Rex Ellsworth and pitched the idea for the Chicago rematch. Then it was back to New York and a meeting with Bill Woodward. Ellsworth was amenable, at first; Woodward less so.

But there was a feeling of inevitability about the match. Both horses would be in Chicago that summer. Swaps won the Arlington Classic against older horses on turf, while Nashua took the Arlington Derby on dirt. Then Woodward withdrew his support for the match race. One night while Woodward was dining at Sardi's in New York, who should arrive with a perfectly timed run but Don Ameche. He ambled over to Woodward's table and soon had Nashua's owner back in the fold.[29]

The Match Race of the Century, as it was dubbed, would take place on August 31 at Washington Park. The distance would be 1¼ miles, and both horses would carry 126 pounds, the same weight they had carried in the Derby, when Swaps had prevailed by one and a half lengths. Lindheimer insisted that the race be run on a Wednesday afternoon, claiming that a Saturday crowd for such a ballyhooed event would be too large to handle, but in fact, he just wanted to create two big paydays for himself in a single week. An astonishing crowd of 35,262 filed through the Washington Park turnstiles that day, an unheard of number of people for a midweek meeting, even in those halcyon days. The entire city of Chicago—and much of the nation—stopped what it was doing to watch on TV or listen on the radio.

The Swaps versus Nashua match was more than just a horse race. It was a sporting contest of the highest order, and the meager betting handle that day proved it. People came to the track to see two great equine athletes duke it out, and betting on the winner was of secondary importance. Just $175,000 was wagered on the big race. Spectators bet more on every other race on the card that day except for the opener, and that was likely because, owing to traffic jams in the neighborhood, many Chicagoans had not yet arrived at the track. In any event, Swaps was sent off as the 3–10 favorite, with Nashua at 6–5.

The icing on this rich cake was the jockeys. Eddie Arcaro (Nashua) and Bill Shoemaker (Swaps) are arguably the two greatest riders in the history of American racing. Arcaro, already known as "The Master," would win a total of five Kentucky Derbies, six Preakness Stakes, and six Belmont Stakes—a record seventeen American classics. He is also the only rider to win two Triple Crowns, aboard Whirlaway in 1941 and Citation in 1948. Shoemaker, though still in the early stages of his hallowed career, would retire in 1990 with a world-record 8,033 winning rides, earning him the racetrack nickname "God."

Nashua drew the rail in the match, but it had been decided beforehand that the rail horse would break from post 2, and the other horse would break from post 4. This was intended to prevent any rough stuff out of the gate, something Arcaro was well known for. In 1942 at Aqueduct, he had deliberately veered into a rival while dueling in the stretch, knocking both horse and rider through the rail and into the infield. That incident resulted in a suspension that lasted a full year, and it was well deserved. Arcaro admitted to the stewards, "I was trying to kill the bastard!"[30]

It was Arcaro's will to win that led to Nashua's victory in the match race. Rain earlier in the week produced a rather deep racing surface that was officially termed "good," but Arcaro determined that it was heavier out where Swaps was breaking from post 4. Nashua was a good gate horse: he had broken on top in the Derby and led for about 100 yards before being beaten to the turn by Swaps. Swaps, however, possessed greater pure speed. And in a match race, speed is everything. A large majority of match races throughout history have been won by the horse that gets the lead out of the gate, among them Seabiscuit in his famous 1938 match with War Admiral. In the run-up to the race, Arcaro could be seen mentally preparing to bust Nashua out of the gate on top, working his arms as if imagining how it would be on Wednesday.

When the gates opened on race day, Arcaro let out a war whoop that could be heard above the clanging of the bell. He whipped Nashua furiously for the first 150 yards, succeeding in gaining a one-length lead. He also angled Nashua out slightly, ensuring that Swaps would be running in the heaviest part of the track. Swaps recovered somewhat to move within a neck of the leader as they entered the backstretch, setting a fast pace. Arcaro was still pumping away on Nashua, who always required strong handling. With half a mile to go, Nashua opened a two-and-a-half-length lead, but then Shoemaker got to work on his mount. Halfway around the final turn, Swaps moved to within half a length of Nashua, but almost as quickly, Nashua regained a clear lead. Midway through the stretch, it was all over. Swaps wavered, drifting into the rail, as Nashua, with Arcaro still driving for all he was worth, crossed the finish line six and a half lengths in front.

The East Coast elites prevailed over the West Coast upstarts—at least this time—earning Nashua Horse of the Year honors. Years later, however, it was revealed that Swaps had suffered a foot bruise the day before the race. Art Sherman, Swaps's exercise rider at the time (and, more recently, trainer of two-time Horse of the Year California Chrome), has always maintained that Swaps never should have run against Nashua that day—and that Swaps was always the better horse.

The 1955 Thoroughbred championship had been decided, but the debate over which was the better match race, Swaps versus Nashua or Seabiscuit versus War Admiral, remained. In its definitive 1999 ranking of the top 100 American racehorses of the twentieth century, *Blood-Horse* magazine rated Swaps number 20, Nashua number 24, War Admiral number 13, and Seabiscuit number 25. That would seem to give War Admiral and Seabiscuit an inconclusive edge, and the popularity of Gary Ross's 2003 film *Seabiscuit* no doubt tilted the argument in favor of the 1938 race. However, a deeper investigation produces a different verdict. The quality of American horse racing improved greatly between 1938 and 1955, thanks largely to the importation of European stallions Alibhai, Khaled, Nasrullah, and Princequillo, and Australian Beau Pere. Swaps was a son of Khaled out of a mare sired by the Louis Mayer import Beau Pere, while Nashua was a son of Nasrullah out of a highly regarded French female family. The importation of European stallions and mares to America between the world wars enabled the United States to become the preeminent racing nation in the world by the 1950s, a position it held for thirty years. Throughout their storied careers, Swaps and Nashua ran against horses that were superior to the competition faced by War Admiral and Seabiscuit. Thus, the Swaps-Nashua match race was the better of the two, thanks to successful American efforts to improve the breed.

Bing Crosby Rides Again

After selling his interest in Del Mar Racecourse and Binglin Stable, Bing Crosby was largely absent from the racing stage throughout the 1950s. However, his role in *Riding High* enabled Bing to switch from real-life racehorse owner to cinematic racehorse trainer.

After directing one his most enduring films, *It's a Wonderful Life,* in 1946, three-time Oscar winner Frank Capra hit a wall. He moved to MGM in 1948 to make *State of the Union,* but even the talents of Spencer Tracy and Katharine Hepburn failed to light a fire under that stodgy political satire. At a crossroads, Capra moved to Paramount, where he found himself in an office just around the corner from Crosby's.

Moviegoers in America were no longer interested in the homespun warmth that had been Capra's hallmark. The war had toughened them, to a certain extent, and they wanted pictures that more closely reflected reality, such as *Key Largo, The Snake Pit,* and *All the King's Men.* So Capra decided to lay off the kind of pious social messages that had carried *Meet John Doe* and *Mr. Smith Goes to Washington* and settled on a remake of his 1934 racing picture *Broadway Bill*—part comedy, part morality tale, and, in this version, part musical.

Capra had been disappointed with the original *Broadway Bill* because its star, Warner Baxter, was petrified of horses, so the director had to eliminate a number of tender scenes between horse and trainer. But when he cast Crosby in the role, Capra got a horse lover who understood every aspect of the racing game. Retitled *Riding High,* the film enabled Bing to warble "Let's Bake a Sunshine Cake," "Camptown Races," and the infectious limerick–cum–drinking song "The Horse Told Me," whose Johnny Burke lyrics went like this:

The owner told Clarence the clocker
The clocker told jockey McGee
The jockey, of course
Passed it on to the horse
And the horse told me.

Crosby insisted that his horseplaying friends Oliver Hardy and Joe Frisco be given minor roles, for which they were grateful, as both men were in the twilight of their careers.

Released in 1950, *Riding High* elicited a warm response from most critics. Writing in the *New York Times*, the frequently acerbic Bosley Crowther stated: "Mr. Crosby has not been so fortunate in a role since *Going My Way*. *Riding High* is his feedbox full of barley. Bing has a stakes winner in Broadway Bill."[31] *Time* magazine was even more effusive, calling it "the most shrewdly effective show ever put together about horse racing."[32]

Although *Riding High* failed to recharge Capra's flagging career, the director enjoyed working with a box office magnet like Crosby and cast him in his next picture, too: *Here Comes the Groom*. Bing was nominated for a Golden Globe Award as best actor in a musical or comedy for his portrayal of easygoing newspaperman Pete Garvey, but *Groom* is best remembered for the Hoagy Carmichael–Johnny Mercer number "In the Cool, Cool, Cool of the Evening." Bing performed it as a duet with Jane Wyman, and it won the Oscar for best song. But despite Bing's contribution, *Here Comes the Groom* did nothing for Capra. He wouldn't make another film until 1959.

It is the dream of every Thoroughbred owner to win a Derby, be it in Kentucky, England, Argentina, or elsewhere. That dream had eluded Crosby, but in 1947 he won a Derby of a different color.

Bing had long been one of Hollywood's most coveted commercial endorsers. Attach the name "Bing Crosby" to a product, and a company was halfway to heaven. Wearing his entrepreneur's cap, Jock Whitney had helped Crosby get started in the purely commercial aspect of the market when he staked him to a share in Minute Maid, maker of the first orange juice concentrate. Although Bing was a silent partner in that moneymaker, his name and face were very much in evidence in newspaper and magazine ads for Royal Crown cola, Chesterfield cigarettes, and Stetson hats; these ads almost always included racehorses or scenes of Del Mar in the background.

In 1947, a year after he sold his interest in Del Mar, Bing lent his name to a horse racing board game called Crosby Derby. This was the age when home entertainment was limited to radio and phonograph records, and Crosby was a master of both. While listening to lilting ballads like "White Christmas," which Bing had introduced in the 1942 film *Holiday Inn*, families could buckle down to a hard-nosed game of Monopoly. Crosby Derby never managed to slide Monopoly off the dining room table, but not for a lack of trying. Bing's grinning portrait appeared in the middle of the orange game board as the advertising copy blared: "Closest thing to a real horse race! Packed with hours of fun and excitement! Everybody plays!"

But in horse racing, the most pertinent question is: does everybody win? Bing's Del Mar anthem "Where the Turf Meets the Surf" promised "a winner in each race"—and there is, but it's a horse. With a 15 percent pari-mutuel takeout on every bet placed, every player, on average, leaves the track at the end of the day 15 percent lighter than when he or she arrived. And as tough as it is for a $2 bettor to turn a profit, making money as an owner is an even dodgier proposition. Factoring in the price of a horse, training and veterinary expenses, entry fees, plus travel fees when a horse is shipped from track to track, it is a mystery how any Thoroughbred owner ever winds up in the black.

Crosby crashed head-on into exactly that problem when Dixie Lee, his wife of twenty-two years, died on November 1, 1952, of ovarian cancer, just three days short of her forty-first birthday. Dixie, who had borne Bing four sons, had also been a partner in many of his business ventures. As a result, the inheritance taxes were so great that Bing had no choice but to sell his horses—all of them—once again proving the maxim that when a rich man is in dire need of money, the first thing he does is sell his racehorses.

A year after Dixie's death, Bing was out of racing entirely, except as an occasional fan. This gave him more time to devote to his career. In 1954 he starred in what many critics consider his best film: *The Country Girl*. He portrays to perfection an aging, alcoholic singer married to a modest young woman who props him up at every turn, despite his failings. Grace Kelly won the best actress Oscar for her performance in the title role. Crosby, who must have recognized how much his character's situation paralleled his own life, lost the best actor Oscar to Marlon Brando in *On the Waterfront*.

But Bing's newfound maturity did not slow him down entirely. The fifty-one-year-old lothario engaged in a much-publicized affair with the twenty-four-year-old Kelly during production, but they were about as compatible as the characters they played in the film. Bing was later involved with neophyte Swedish American actress Inger Stevens, but he finally found a soulmate in second wife Kathryn Grant. Thirty years his junior, she married Bing in 1957, when she was twenty-four.

The late 1950s brought the rise of rock 'n' roll and the decline of Bing Crosby as a major force in the recording industry. By 1960, the Tin Pan

Alley market Crosby had dominated for thirty years was drying up fast in America. It was, however, still going strong in England, where Bing had always been popular, and where Beatlemania was still at least three years away. So he started to spend more time concertizing across the pond. In England as well as in his ancestral home of Ireland, horse racing has always been an integral part of the social fabric—much more so than in America. As a result of his transatlantic travels, Bing soon felt the itch to get back into the sport he had largely abandoned a decade earlier.

Crosby had long been a friend of California-based jockey Johnny Longden, who in 1956 at Del Mar set a world record for number of races won: 4,871. Born in England, Longden had immigrated to Canada in 1913 at age five, after narrowly escaping tragedy on the *Titanic*. He and his mother were supposed to be aboard the ill-fated liner, but their train to Southampton arrived late, and they missed the boat. Longden would later establish himself as the leading rider on the West Coast, riding many winners on the Southern California circuit for Canadian horseman Max Bell, who owned Golden West Farms in Alberta in partnership with Frank McMahon.

Longden introduced Crosby to Bell, and the two became lifelong friends. In the early 1960s Bell began to invest in European bloodstock, and he struck it rich in 1963 when he bought a British-bred yearling colt by Court Harwell. Named Meadow Court, the horse had all the right connections, including being trained by Paddy Prendergast, proprietor of a stable at Erindale in Ireland's County Kildare. As a trainer, Prendergast was ranked second only to the peerless Vincent O'Brien. A late-blooming three-year-old, Meadow Court got his chance to run in the classic Epsom Derby in 1965, when Prendergast's three best British-based three-year-olds were sidelined by a virus. Lester Piggott, arguably the twentieth century's greatest jockey, would be in the saddle.

Meadow Court was a very good horse, but he had the misfortune to be born in the same year as the great Sea-Bird, who beat him at Epsom by an easy two lengths, without ever coming off the bridle. Undeterred, Prendergast sent his English Derby runner-up to the Curragh for the Irish Derby three weeks later, on June 27. That day, Sea-Bird would be otherwise engaged in France, running in the Grand Prix de Saint-Cloud.

A few days before the Irish classic, Bell sold Crosby a share in Meadow Court. Bing may have been attracted by Meadow Court's female family. His second dam was the Argentine-bred Miss Grillo, who had won the

Argentine Oaks and beaten colts in the Argentine Derby. She was then sold and raced in America, where she won eight stakes races. Bing had not forgotten the exploits of his own Argentine-breds Ligaroti and Don Bingo, and he hoped Meadow Court's Argentine blood would stand him in good stead.

Sent off as the 11–10 favorite, Meadow Court fulfilled everyone's hopes with an emphatic two-length victory in the Irish Derby. Bing was so happy that he treated the crowd at the Curragh to a rendition of "When Irish Eyes Are Smiling" during the trophy presentation. "Wait 'til Hope finds out," he remarked, chuckling at the thought of his comedic foil's reaction upon learning that he had finally won a Derby.

Prendergast had even bigger plans for Meadow Court. A tilt against older horses in Ascot's King George VI and Queen Elizabeth Diamond Stakes, England's most important weight-for-age event, was next. The ease with which Meadow Court won that race prompted the normally phlegmatic Piggott to predict that Meadow Court would beat Sea-Bird the next time they met. But that optimism hit a snag in the St. Leger Stakes, which at 1¾ miles, 132 yards, is the longest classic race in the world. It was also more than a quarter of a mile longer than the 1½-mile distance over which Meadow Court had won the Irish Derby and the King George. Even worse, the ground at Doncaster Racecourse that September 12 afternoon was very heavy, and Meadow Court, the 4–11 favorite, just couldn't handle it. He finished second, ten lengths behind the 28–1 longshot Provoke.

Meadow Court would get a second shot at Sea-Bird on October 3 at Longchamp in Europe's championship race, the 1½-mile Prix de l'Arc de Triomphe. With Piggott aboard and Crosby watching anxiously from the grandstand, the 8–1 Meadow Court was soon seventh in the seventeen-runner field, but the 6–5 favorite Sea-Bird was traveling easily just in front of him. When Sea-Bird's rider, Etienne Pollet, asked for a winning move entering the stretch, the horse's response was immediate and irresistible. Sea-Bird crossed the line a handy four lengths in front, as Meadow Court faded to finish ninth, twenty-four and three-quarters lengths behind the great champion. Some observers still believe that Sea-Bird is the best Thoroughbred to set foot on a racetrack since World War II.

Crosby's Pittsburgh Pirate buddy John Galbreath was in Paris that day, keeping a close eye on his future property. After the Epsom Derby, Galbreath had cannily cut a deal with Sea-Bird's French owner, Jean

Ternynck, to lease him for stud duty at Galbreath's Darby Dan Farm in Ohio. During his time in the United States, Sea-Bird sired an Arc winner himself, the filly Allez France; he also sired champion hurdler Sea Pigeon and Preakness and Belmont Stakes winner Little Current, owned by Galbreath.

Conversely, Meadow Court—who was, by any measure, the best horse Bing Crosby ever owned—was a dud at stud. After suffering fertility problems at Sandley Stud in Dorset, England, he was brought back into training as an eight-year-old but failed to regain his old sparkle. He was sent to stud again but never sired anything of value.

Crosby had high hopes for a second Irish Derby victory in 1967 with Dominion Day, a horse he owned in partnership with Bell and McMahon. But a few days before the big race, trainer Prendergast pronounced that the colt was "not himself," and he was withdrawn. Dominion Day would redeem himself to a certain extent by winning the Blandford Stakes at the Curragh in September. Bell then sent him to Canada, where he won three more stakes races at Woodbine. A Grade 3 race named for Dominion Day is run at Woodbine every July.

Dominion Day would be the last of Bing's notable horses. As his singing and film careers wound down in the late 1960s and 1970s, he spent more and more time hunting, fishing, and playing golf. He made the occasional trip to Royal Ascot in June to visit Queen Elizabeth in the Royal Enclosure. Crosby's two-week run at the London Palladium ended triumphantly on October 6, 1977. Four days later, he opened the Brighton Centre before 5,000 adoring fans. The next morning, he taped a dozen songs for the BBC. They would be his last recordings.

That night at dinner, he announced to Kathryn that he was leaving the next morning for a golfing and hunting holiday in Spain. On October 14 he played a round of golf as part of a foursome that included a pair of Spanish professionals at the Club de Golf La Moraleja in Madrid. Seventy-four-year-old Crosby shot an 85, a score that some very good pros fail to make from time to time. As he walked off the eighteenth green, he chirped, "That was a great game of golf, fellas," upon which he collapsed and died of a massive heart attack.

"At least he had died as he had wished," his widow wrote in her memoir *My Life with Bing*. Kathryn called Madrid that night to get details about her husband's death and asked his last golfing partner, Cesar Zulueta, "How well did he play? Did he win?"

"Why yes, Senora," Zulueta replied. "He won all the bets. It was a very good round."[33]

It had been a very good life, and Bing Crosby had gone out a winner.

Bing made a nostalgic farewell visit to Del Mar on July 31, 1977, just three months before his death, to witness the race that bears his name, the Bing Crosby Handicap. It was the first time he had been back to his old racetrack in more than thirty years, and it must have pleased him to see that the place was prospering. A new attendance record of 16,532 per day was set that year, and the daily handle topped the $2 million mark for the first time.

Today, Del Mar is one of the few bright spots on an American racing scene that has deteriorated alarmingly over the last twenty-five years. While most tracks struggle to attract both people and good horses, Del Mar averages 17,000 racegoers who plunk down $2.2 million per day in wagers, enabling it to live up to its reputation as the "Saratoga of the West." In fact, some Californians consider Saratoga the "Del Mar of the East."

Opening day at Del Mar might be the closest thing on the West Coast racing calendar to a day at Royal Ascot. The local ladies bedeck themselves in the latest summer fashions, and the Fabulous Hat Contest recalls the 1930s and 1940s, when wearing a chapeau to the track was de rigueur for both women and men. These events help attract more than 40,000 people to Del Mar's season opener each year. A single-day attendance record was set on opening day in 2011, when 46,588 took part in the festivities. In addition to the Bing Crosby Stakes, Pat O'Brien has a race named for him at Del Mar. The Pat O'Brien Stakes serves as a key prep race for the Breeders' Cup Sprint.

The attractions of the modern grandstand, renovated in 1992–1993 in the same Spanish Mission style as the 1937 original, include the Bing Crosby Grill. Dozens of blown-up photographs of Golden Age movie stars line the grandstand walls. There is an impish Mickey Rooney searching for a last-race winner to get him out of the hole. Red Skelton looks bewildered, wondering where he can reclaim his lost shirt, while Lucy and Desi study the *Racing Form*. Dorothy Lamour shows some leg in a vain effort, perhaps, to entice Crosby and Hope into letting her get a word in edgewise in their next "Road" picture.

A blend of old and new—racy, colorful, and sometimes just a little bit dangerous—Del Mar is a fitting tribute to Bing Crosby's enduring legacy as a sportsman and a showman.

9

Jock Whitney

David O. Selznick's Banker

[Jock] gave pleasure and affection and fulfillment to David's dreams.
Irene Mayer Selznick

Stage-Door Johnny

Born into the upper reaches of American aristocracy, John Hay Whitney could have cruised his way through life at half-speed, living off his inherited wealth and daydreaming, like so many of his friends and relatives on the Upper East Side–Long Island–Saratoga–Lexington social circuit, about his close relationship to those intrepid souls who had come over on the *Mayflower*. But Jock, as he was popularly known, was never content with what he had been given or born into. He risked his name and his wealth on a wide range of business ventures, including investment banking, art collecting, horse racing, the stage, cinema, espionage, diplomacy, and publishing. "Money has three purposes," he said: "to be invested wisely, to do good with, and to live well off." A skeptic might see this as a rich man's way of saying, "If you've got it, flaunt it," but Whitney always kept a low profile, preferring the background to the foreground, the wings to the footlights.[1]

Born in Maine in 1904, Jock Whitney was a direct descendant of 1620 *Mayflower* passenger William Bradford, the first governor of Massachusetts, as well as John Whitney, that Johnny-come-lately who arrived in Massachusetts fifteen years later. His paternal grandfather was William Collins Whitney, Grover Cleveland's secretary of the navy; his maternal grandfather was John Milton Hay, who, in his twenties, had been a private secretary to Abraham Lincoln before serving as secretary of state under both William McKinley and Theodore Roosevelt. His father, Payne Whitney, founded the fabulously successful Greentree Stables in 1914 and soon had breeding and training farms in Manhasset, Long Island; Saratoga

Springs, New York; Aiken, South Carolina; and Lexington, Kentucky. Payne once dropped $250,000 on the first five races at Saratoga before bouncing back to leave the track $16,000 richer than when he had arrived. Jock's mother, Helen Hay Whitney, became known as the "First Lady of the American Turf."

As a little boy, Jock saw horses wherever he went and could ride almost before he could walk. As a teenager, however, he seemed more interested in movies than in horses. He went to the local cinema in Manhasset up to six nights a week with his sister Joan. The experience served as his out-of-school education, as he absorbed the early silent classics of D. W. Griffith (*Hearts of the World, Broken Blossoms, Way Down East*), Douglas Fairbanks (*The Mark of Zorro, The Three Musketeers*), Mary Pickford (*Amarilly of Clothes-Line Alley*), Rudolph Valentino (*The Sheikh*), and Erich von Stroheim (*Blind Husbands*). His nights at the little movie house on Long Island's North Shore had a profound and lasting effect.

As a young man at Yale, Jock preferred girls—specifically, showgirls—to both movies and horses. It was a short ride from New Haven down to Manhattan, where Times Square's bright lights announced that thrilling new stage spectacle: the Broadway musical. Whitney was stricken with a peculiarly American strain of red-and-gold fever. Hardly a weekend went by that he didn't go backstage and pick up a chorine, and he didn't have to work very hard: the girls knew exactly who he was, and his boyish good looks made his job that much easier.

As he got older, Jock worked his way up through the cast. Soon he was dating the stars. He had a brief fling with Bette Davis in 1929, after backing her Broadway debut, *Broken Dishes*. That was when he met Fred Astaire, who was dancing and singing his way to fame in Jerome Kern's *The Bunch and Judy* and the Gershwins' *Lady Be Good*. With a shared love for the stage and the track, they became lifelong friends. Fred served as an usher at Jock's 1930 wedding to Mary Elizabeth Altemus; Adele Astaire, Fred's sister and dancing partner, was one of the bridesmaids, and humorist Robert Benchley was best man. At the same time, Jock took up the cudgels on Fred's behalf, backing him in *The Band Wagon* (1930) and *Gay Divorcee* (1932).

Jock's presence on Broadway did not go unnoticed in Hollywood. Although he didn't coin the term "stage-door Johnny," it suited him from his top hat down to his patent leather shoes. His real name was John, after all, and he had become very successful at his hobby: chorus girls literally swooned at the sight of him. In 1930 MGM latched on to Jock's Broadway persona in the Irving Thalberg–produced, Harry Beaumont–directed Oscar winner *The Broadway Melody*. It tells the tale of two midwestern sisters who bring their vaudeville routine to the Great White Way. The younger, more impressionable one is quickly seduced by a suave character named Jacques Warriner—his first name pronounced with a hard *J*. At one point in the film, Warriner even signs his name "Jock." In 1947, long after Whitney had made a name for himself in Hollywood, Cornel Wilde was cast in H. Bruce Humberstone's racing film *The Homestretch* as a jet-setting playboy-horseman by the name of Jock Wallace. In spite of these characters' negative personalities, Jock Whitney turned the other cheek, refusing to be provoked.[2]

Twenty Grand and Easter Hero

After graduating from Yale, Jock attended graduate school at Oxford. Much to his delight, he discovered that the venerable and ancient university town is even closer to London than New Haven is to New York, allowing him to continue his theater "studies." Oxford is also in the vicinity of Cheltenham, the site of England's most important jump-racing course. A keen amateur rider, Whitney rode in point-to-pointers—informal hurdle races for nonprofessionals—at Oxford in between his studies at school and his extracurricular activities in the West End, which included frequent meetings with Fred Astaire, who was appearing in *Lady Be Good.*

Whitney seemed to be everywhere and to have a hand in myriad endeavors. One day he walked into a New Haven barbershop and asked for a "Hindenburg," that ultrashort, bristly haircut favored by the German general and all other Prussian men of arms. As the stroke on the Yale crew, perhaps he was looking for a way to cut down on wind resistance for the upcoming race against Harvard. But it was 1925, just seven years since the end of World War I, and things German were not very popular (except for Babe Ruth and Lou Gehrig). The barber suggested a new name—crewcut—and so Jock Whitney became part of tonsorial history.

In 1927 Jock's father died, leaving his widow an estate valued at $178,893,655, including the sprawling Greentree racing empire. It was mainly Jock, however, who ran the operation, with help from his sister Joan (who would later win a place in the hearts of baseball fans as the first owner of the hapless New York Mets). Both father and son were enamored of British bloodstock and were convinced that introducing better strains of British Thoroughbred blood would have nothing but positive effects on the American breed. In 1925 Payne had purchased a young British-bred stallion prospect named St. Germans from Lord Astor. Second in the 1924 Epsom Derby, St. Germans improved at age four to win the Coronation Cup at 1½ miles and the Doncaster Cup at 2⅛ miles. In 1928, to prove the Whitney theory, Jock arranged for St. Germans to be mated with a Greentree mare named Bonus. She was a daughter of a stakes-placed British-bred colt named All Gold, whose sire and grandsire were two of the greatest horses in British racing history: Persimmon and St. Simon. The result was Twenty Grand, who, as a three-year-old, won the Kentucky Derby, Belmont Stakes, Travers Stakes, and Jockey Club Gold Cup—an extraordinary grand slam that earned him Horse of the Year honors in 1931.

But Jock wasn't content with American victories. He was lured by the beauty of British jump racing, and two races in particular caught his attention: the Cheltenham Gold Cup and the Grand National Steeplechase. In 1929 he purchased the promising chaser Easter Hero from the estate of Belgian businessman Alfred Loewenstein. Loewenstein had died under mysterious circumstances, apparently falling out of his private plane over the English Channel. There was speculation that he had faked his own death or perhaps had been pushed, the victim of a drug deal gone bad with Arnold Rothstein, the man behind the 1919 Chicago Black Sox World Series scandal. In any case, Loewenstein was dead, and Jock was in possession of Easter Hero.

Easter Hero's first attempt in the Grand National had been in 1928. Well out in front, he landed squarely on top of the Canal Turn the first time around, slipping awkwardly back into the open ditch and causing a massive pileup. Only two of the forty-two starters finished the race, with 100–1 shot Tipperary Tim distancing the American champion Billy Barton.

But Jock Whitney must have seen something in Easter Hero that day. The horse had been outpacing the field and jumping brilliantly until the mishap. When Loewenstein's horses came up for sale, Jock pounced, getting Easter Hero for 20,000 pounds ($60,000). His first major objective was the Cheltenham Gold Cup, which is actually more highly rated among racing professionals than the Grand National. Easter Hero duly obliged, giving nothing else a chance in the 3¼-mile contest and winning by twenty lengths. He was, however, penalized for this impressive win when he was assigned the top weight in the Grand National: 175 pounds! Whitney could take some consolation in the fact that the open ditch in front of the Canal Turn had been removed, making the obstacle Easter Hero had botched a year earlier much easier.

Starting as the 9–1 favorite in a grossly oversized field of sixty-six—the largest in Grand National history—Easter Hero led after the fourth fence. Twice he handled the Canal Turn with aplomb and appeared to be headed for a handy victory when disaster struck. After jumping Valentine's Brook safely the second time around, Easter Hero spread a plate (cracked a shoe) just five fences from home. His big lead evaporated as he shortened his stride. He was overtaken between the last two fences and finished second, beaten by six lengths. Ironically, the winner was his half-brother, Gregalach, a 100–1 shot who was carrying 20 pounds less than Easter Hero.

Easter Hero repeated his twenty-length triumph the next year in a watered-down four-runner Cheltenham Gold Cup, but he missed the 1930 Grand National with an injury. Jock replaced him in that race with the 100–7 third choice Sir Lindsay, who jumped the last fence vying for the lead but faded to finish third, beaten by one and three-quarters lengths by the 100–8 second choice Shaun Goilin. The following year, at age eleven, Easter Hero was denied a chance at a third consecutive Gold Cup title when the three-day Cheltenham meeting was canceled due to frost. At the Grand National, Easter Hero started as the 5–1 favorite, despite carrying 175 pounds again. Summer-like temperatures on March 27 attracted a crowd of more than 200,000 to Aintree, where they saw Easter Hero fall victim to the worst possible luck: he was brought down after Becher's Brook in a collision with a riderless horse. Whitney would finish third in both 1934 and 1935 with Thomond II and eighth with Double Crossed in 1936, but Grand National glory would forever elude him. As small consolation, he could take familial pride in Golden Miller, the winner of an incredible five consecutive Cheltenham Gold Cups from 1932 through 1936, who was owned by his cousin, Dorothy Paget.

Recalling Easter Hero in 1979, Whitney said: "I realized even way back in 1929 that I would never see his like again. Easter Hero was the kind of horse that really got your emotions involved. He had such a terrific personality. It was a great sight to see him doing anything—even exercising. The mere sight of him floating over the water jump in the Grand National would produce a roar from the crowd and from me." After his retirement,

Easter Hero was stationed in Virginia, where Whitney rode him in hunts. He was eventually moved to Greentree's farm in Kentucky, where he lived out his days with Twenty Grand and American jump-racing champ Jolly Roger, part of a group of retired Whitney horses known as the Gashouse Gang. Jock's astute application of his wealth toward the building of the Greentree racing empire prompted his friend, University of Kentucky football star "Shipwreck" Kelly, to dub him the Aga John. It was a well-deserved tag. Jock's devotion to racing—and his family connections—led to membership in the Jockey Club at age twenty-eight—the youngest person ever elected.[3]

Dreaming in Technicolor

Jock Whitney's love of cinema, not to mention his understanding of its potential to generate wealth, continued to exert a strong influence. One summer season at Saratoga, he met Herbert Kalmus, a man who had started experimenting with color film technology as early as 1914 with fellow researchers at MIT. Kalmus was a horseplayer of some renown and, like Whitney, couldn't resist the charms of Saratoga Springs in August. Whitney and Kalmus were introduced at the track one afternoon, and the talk turned from horses to movies. One thing led to another, and Whitney, recognizing an opportunity that so many in the black-and-white film industry had ignored, invested $300,000 in Kalmus's Technicolor Motion Pictures Corporation, making him a 15 percent shareholder.

Ask the average filmgoer what the first color film was, and most will answer *The Wizard of Oz*—or at least the second half of it. In fact, the Technicolor process was first used in 1917 in *The Gulf Between,* produced by Kalmus's company. *The Toll of the Sea* followed in 1921, with Kalmus's name appearing in the credits as producer. But it took a long time to process color film, and the colors displayed were inferior. Known as two-color processing, early Technicolor pictures could not reproduce blue, so filmmakers tended to avoid sky, water, blue eyes, and blue costumes in those early days.

Whitney, however, immediately recognized Technicolor's potential. Warner Bros., quicker on the draw than most studios (it had produced the first feature film with sound, *The Jazz Singer,* in 1927), made the first all-talking, all-color film: *On with the Show,* in 1929. This was soon followed by Roy del Ruth's *Gold Diggers of Broadway.* These fully realized color productions seemed to be the way of the future. Jock Whitney developed a burning desire to produce color films, so, with cousin C. V. Whitney, he started a production company called Rainbow Pictures, which quickly became the Spectrum Corporation.

Walt Disney soon picked up on the Technicolor craze, which was particularly well suited to cartoons. In 1932 he used three-strip Technicolor (incorporating the color blue in all its glory) in his Silly Symphonies, most notably in his runaway hit *The Three Little Pigs.* In 1933 he was developing plans to make a combination live-action–animated Technicolor version of *Alice in Wonderland* starring Mary Pickford. Kalmus showed Pickford's Technicolor screen test to Whitney and Merion C. Cooper, coproducer and codirector of the immortal *King Kong,* and they were both impressed. Whitney had made a small investment in *King Kong,* and the two men were on the same wavelength when it came to color films, so they put their heads together. Whitney invited Cooper to become head of production at Spectrum, which was renamed Pioneer Pictures—the stated intent being to make movies in Technicolor. As for Disney's *Alice,* it foundered after Paramount announced its own all live-action version. That was probably for the best, as the forty-two-year-old Pickford was old enough to be Alice's mother.

Pioneer's first film was a twenty-minute musical short called *La Cucaracha,* the first live-action film of any length to employ three-strip Technicolor. Released on August 31, 1934, by RKO Radio, the film won the Academy Award for best short subject (comedy). Jock Whitney had busted out of the cinematic gate with a winner. There were plans to make *The Last Days of Pompeii, Joan of Arc* (with Katharine Hepburn), and *Hamlet* (with John Barrymore), but they all fell through; *Pompeii* wound up as a black-and-white RKO production. Instead, Pioneer turned to William Makepeace Thackeray's 1848 novel of English social manners, *Vanity Fair,* as dramatized on Broadway in Langdon Mitchell's adaptation *Becky Sharp.* Released in 1935, the Rouben Mamoulian–directed film version became the first feature-length movie produced in full three-strip Technicolor.

Becky Sharp was named the best color film at the Venice Film Festival, and no less an authority than Graham Greene proclaimed it "a delight to the eye."[4] Whitney was riding the crest of a wave. Recognizing his love of art and film, the Museum of Modern Art (MoMA) named him president of its newly created Film Library in 1935. Among his contributions to

MoMA was the rescue of numerous early D. W. Griffith shorts that were about to be thrown into the bonfire. Along with Iris Barry, he helped preserve William Hart westerns and many of Douglas Fairbanks's early comedies. His stewardship at MoMA even took a political turn in 1944 when he invited Spanish filmmaker Luis Bunuel to New York to analyze Nazi newsreels.

Meanwhile, Pioneer's next production, *The Dancing Pirate,* was a dud, proof that bright colors alone do not make a successful motion picture. Pioneer's fortunes were flagging, but there were bigger things awaiting Whitney just around the corner—much bigger things.

Whitney's March to Atlanta

The crisis at Pioneer more or less coincided with David O. Selznick's final farewell from his father-in-law's operation at MGM. Selznick and Louis B. Mayer had never really gotten along. Shortly after David married Louis's daughter Irene, Mayer had offered to buy the newlyweds a house, and David took umbrage. "We'll buy our own house," the groom grumbled. A few weeks later, Mayer sent Irene an expensive diamond bracelet, which David promptly returned, along with a note informing his father-in-law that if anyone was going to buy his wife expensive presents, it would be him.

After brief stints at MGM and Paramount during the silent era, Selznick was appointed head of production at RKO Radio in 1931, where he oversaw *A Bill of Divorcement, What Price Hollywood,* and *King Kong.* In 1933 his father-in-law hired him back at MGM, where he rivaled the prodigious Irving Thalberg in producing titles such as *Dinner at Eight, Anna Karenina,* and a pair of Charles Dickens adaptations, *David Copperfield* and *A Tale of Two Cities.* In the process, he cemented MGM's reputation for quality literary productions.

But despite his success, Selznick was the odd man out at MGM. He was socially ostracized by his fellow producers, perhaps because of jealousy, perhaps because of his family connection to the boss, or perhaps because he was simply difficult to get along with. In any case, Selznick wanted out of MGM. He yearned to be his own man, with no one to answer to, especially his father-in-law. After *A Tale of Two Cities* in 1935, he decided to strike out on his own.

Seed money was hard to come by in those Depression years, even in Hollywood. Selznick could expect no help from Mayer, who had predicted his son-in-law's failure when he left MGM. So Selznick looked east to New York, the ways-and-means capital of the capitalist world and the home of movie-mad Jock Whitney and his cousin C. V. Whitney. Together, they formed Selznick International Pictures. Selznick put up 42 percent of the capital, the Whitney cousins contributed the same percentage, with the final 16 percent was supplied by assorted investors, among them a secretive Irving Thalberg, who registered his shares in the name of his wife, Norma Shearer.

Named chairman of the board, Jock threw himself headfirst into the venture from the start. "[He] had complete charge of the New York selling and financing end of the operation," Selznick said. "He was inordinately active for the chairman of the board. He handled bookings and the advertising and the foreign distribution, and, equally with me, the acquisition of stray properties and major casting decisions." Selznick was so pleased with Whitney—both professionally and personally—that Jock stood as godfather to both of David and Irene's sons, Daniel and Jeffrey.[5]

Selznick International was quick out of the gate with *Little Lord Fauntleroy,* for which Louis Mayer generously lent his son-in-law the British child star Freddie Bartholomew for the title role. The soppy, homey tale of an aristocratic English kid dumped into a Brooklyn slum, *Fauntleroy* has not aged well, but at the time, the American public loved it. This encouraged Selznick to risk its $447,000 profit on a pet project: *The Garden of Allah.*

Both Selznick and Whitney were in their element—Selznick as the boss, Whitney in a position to "do good" with his money. But all their energy and good intentions couldn't prevent Selznick International's second film from being a flop. *The Garden of Allah,* based on an old-fashioned 1905 novel about a monk who is unsure of his vocation, failed to resound with either critics or the public, despite an international all-star cast featuring Charles Boyer, Marlene Dietrich, and Basil Rathbone. Still, the picture managed to win a special Oscar for color cinematography, and Dietrich, who called the script "trash," rated it the most beautiful color film ever made, proving once again that pretty does not necessarily mean successful.[6]

A Star Is Born (1937) would turn out to be much more than a pretty picture. An exposé of Hollywood's inner workings, it was a critical and popular success, not least because it reflected the career of its leading lady Janet Gaynor, whose own star had been on the wane since winning an

Oscar for her collective work on *Seventh Heaven, Sunrise,* and *Street Angel* ten years earlier. Selznick had scored a coup at MGM's expense in getting a disgruntled William Wellman to direct the film, which was saddled with the confusing working title *The Stars Beneath.* It was Jock Whitney's idea to call it *A Star Is Born,* evidence that he was more than just Selznick's moneyman. The picture won two Oscars: one for the original story by Wellman and Robert Carson, and a second for W. Howard Green's color cinematography.

There followed the mildly successful swashbuckler *The Prisoner of Zenda* and the color screwball flop *Nothing Sacred,* the latter a victim of too many cooks spoiling the broth. Squabbling scriptwriters Ben Hecht, Budd Schulberg, Ring Lardner, Dorothy Parker, Moss Hart, and George S. Kaufman made a hash of it, costing the producers a cool $400,000.

The 1938 productions of *The Adventures of Tom Sawyer, The Young in Heart,* and *Made for Each Other* were all nice films of no particular distinction, but Selznick had bigger plans in mind. He had his eye on two of Europe's biggest cinematic personae: Ingrid Bergman and Alfred Hitchcock. More important, he had already set in motion the high-powered mechanism for what would become the most famous and most profitable film in history.

On June 30, 1936, midway between the releases of *Little Lord Fauntleroy* and *The Garden of Allah,* Macmillan published Margaret Mitchell's page-turning Civil War saga, *Gone with the Wind.* Six weeks earlier, Selznick's ace New York–based scout Kay Brown had wangled galley proofs of the book from the publisher. She read the proofs and sent them to Selznick with a strong recommendation that he buy the rights as soon as possible, before any other film companies got the bright idea. Selznick, who was used to turning fat Victorian novels into films, was not inclined to agree, having read only a synopsis. Mitchell was a first-time author; at 1,037 pages, the book was too long to make into a movie; and nobody cared about the Civil War anymore, he whined. Undeterred, Brown showed the galleys to Jock Whitney, who read the novel on a train from New York to Los Angeles. Upon arriving in Hollywood, Jock strongly urged Selznick to buy the rights. Selznick was still skeptical, but when Jock said that he would buy the rights himself and sell David an option, Selznick relented.

"Why did I decide to buy the book?" Whitney asked. "It was easy. I read it." By December, just six months after it was published, *Gone with the Wind* had been read by 1 million people. Poor Margaret Mitchell. If she had waited just a few weeks before signing with Selznick International, she could have named her price. Instead, she got only $50,000.[7]

With connections to the Fifth Avenue publishing world, Whitney got wind that the one millionth copy of *Gone with the Wind* was about to roll off the presses on December 15. He arranged to have that copy delivered to him and then presented it to the author, asking her to sign it for him. Miss Mitchell responded with a firm "No!" In fact, she never signed a single copy of her world-famous novel.[8]

Whitney showed more faith in the movie version's potential than he did in Mitchell's capricious public-relations quirks. "It'll be the best picture ever made," he predicted. He was so full of optimism that he named two of his Greentree juveniles Tara and Scarlett O'Hara, although they both turned out to be as hopeless as the Confederate cause. In the meantime, Selznick was overseeing a pair of beauty contests to determine the lead roles in the film.[9]

Mitchell herself had firm ideas as to who should play Rhett Butler, and she listed her preferences, in order, in a memo to Selznick: (1) Basil Rathbone, (2) Fredric March, (3) Ronald Colman. Selznick had other ideas: he wanted Clark Gable. Always the eccentric, Mitchell was opposed to Gable because she thought he wasn't southern enough. But if so, what were the South African Rathbone and the English Colman doing on her list? The problem was, Gable was under contract to MGM. So Selznick went after Gary Cooper at Goldwyn Pictures and Errol Flynn at Warner Bros., but both deals fell through. Forced to deal with his father-in-law, Selznick actually considered selling *Gone with the Wind* lock, stock, and barrel to MGM. Well known for his lengthy memos, Selznick sent one of his most important to Whitney on May 27, 1938. Typed entirely in capital letters for emphasis, it asked for Whitney's opinion on selling the rights to MGM. Mayer had made an offer that included a rider allowing Selznick to produce the film for MGM. Such a move, David explained, would ease Selznick International's financial woes, and he could still spend a few hours a day at their own studio. What did Jock think? Jock thought it was a bad idea and voted nay. He forked over additional money to support the production, and in the end, Selznick got Clark Gable and $1.25 million from MGM in return for half the film's profits.

The battle over who would play the film's heroine, Scarlett O'Hara, was more interesting. Jean Arthur, who had had a fling with Selznick a few years earlier, was tested. So was Gable's ex-wife Joan Crawford.

Warner Bros. offered Bette Davis in a package deal with Gary Cooper, but that was turned down. Joan Fontaine disdained the role of Scarlett as well as that of Melanie Wilkes, which eventually went to her sister, Olivia de Havilland. The Selznicks' good friend Paulette Goddard lost the part because she couldn't produce a marriage license for her wedding to Charlie Chaplin, and Selznick was skittish about such things. Miriam Hopkins, who might have done wonders with the role, was passed over, despite being born and raised in Savannah, Georgia. Katharine Hepburn proclaimed, "I am Scarlett O'Hara!" but lost the part anyway. Norma Shearer was disinclined, and Lana Turner was deemed too young, too inexperienced, and not famous enough—yet.

Jock Whitney had a soft spot for Tallulah Bankhead. Although she spoke with an English accent after spending years on the West End stage, she had been born in Alabama and could have easily rediscovered her southern drawl. Jock and Tallulah had been a backstage item in London, and he spared no effort in trying to convince Selznick that she was right for the part. To keep his personal life on an even keel, Jock even arranged a screen test for his wife, Liz, who (no surprise) failed to make the cut.

Meanwhile, Selznick had decided on Vivien Leigh, an Englishwoman who, as everyone now agrees, was the perfect Scarlett O'Hara. Even Whitney concurred. When he saw her screen test in New York, he wept tears of joy—and relief. In fact, he was so happy that he named one of his yearlings that year, a filly out of a mare called Gay Vixen, Scarlett O'Hara.

Whitney made two other important contributions to *Gone with the Wind*. When the Hays Office protested the strong language used by Rhett Butler in the film's closing scene, Whitney calmly and rationally explained to Hays himself that the word "damn" was perfectly respectable; indeed, it was biblical. And so Clark Gable was allowed to speak the immortal words, "Frankly, my dear, I don't give a damn." Years later, Selznick revealed that "every major decision [on *GWTW*] was made jointly with him [Jock Whitney]."[10]

After a private Los Angeles preview three days before the world premiere, Whitney also convinced Selznick to trim the film from 285 minutes to 238 minutes, including intermission. Some critics still thought the film was too long; a few even suggested that the curtain should have rung down for good at intermission. None of that mattered on December 15, 1939, when 300,000 people jammed downtown Atlanta to see the South rise again, if only for a few hours.[11]

Whitney, who sat next to Margaret Mitchell at Loews' Grand Theatre (the film was being distributed by MGM), fell victim to a faux pas committed by Selznick at the grand postscreening gala. Selznick went up to the dais and proposed a toast to the one person without whom the film could not have been made. Everyone held their breath in anticipation of a standing ovation for Mitchell but were aghast when Selznick announced, "Ladies and gentlemen, Jock Whitney!" Jock was probably the most embarrassed man in the room, especially since he tended to shun the spotlight. He could have received screen credit as executive producer or associate producer or assistant producer on all the films made at Selznick International Pictures, but not once did his name appear onscreen. That was the way he wanted it.

All the blood, sweat, and tears put into *Gone with the Wind* paid off. The film grossed $56.6 million in the domestic market alone, miles ahead of the 1939 runner-up, *The Wizard of Oz,* which made $9.8 million.

Almost immediately after the film's release, Selznick began badgering Mitchell to write a sequel, but she could not be moved. Whitney, sensitive to her artistic inclinations, backed her up. Mitchell never published another story for the rest of her life. She apparently understood that she had only one book in her and left it at that, content with her lot in life. Selznick would spend the rest of his life searching the world over for a smash follow-up to *Gone with the Wind* but never found one. He did, however, show some sympathy for the author, sending Mitchell a check for $50,000 as the picture was breaking all box office records and giving her the Oscar *Gone with the Wind* won for best motion picture.

Reconstruction

During all the brouhaha surrounding *Gone with the Wind,* Selznick and Whitney were also involved with two of their company's most successful films: *Intermezzo* and *Rebecca.* After seeing the naturally beautiful Ingrid Bergman in Gustav Molander's 1936 Swedish production of *Intermezzo*— about a doomed love affair between a married violinist and a young pianist—Selznick decided that he wanted to remake the film himself. He dispatched Jock Whitney and Kay Brown to Stockholm with orders to obtain the rights from Svensk Filmindustri, and they succeeded. Ten days later, Selznick decided that he wanted Ingrid Bergman to reprise her role as the pianist in his production. Kay returned to Stockholm and, after sensitive negotiations with the actress and her husband, Petter Lindstrom, escorted her back to America. Ingrid spent two weeks resting at Jock's Greentree mansion on Long Island, during which time she affectionately took to calling him "Boss," just like one of his stable hands.

Intermezzo, subtitled *A Love Story*, was released three months before *Gone with the Wind*. Meanwhile, Selznick had already begun production on Daphne du Maurier's modern Gothic romance *Rebecca*, with his prize British catch Alfred Hitchcock at the helm. With Vivien Leigh's husband Laurence Olivier starring opposite Olivia de Havilland's sister Joan Fontaine (the only American in the cast), *Rebecca* would earn just $2 million in the domestic market but would garner a second successive best picture Oscar for Selznick International. This time, David kept the statuette for himself.

By 1941, *Gone with the Wind* had grossed $32 million worldwide ($540 million in today's money), but David Selznick was an unhappy man. For one thing, he had to share half of those immense profits with his hated rivals at MGM. He was also dissatisfied with United Artists' distribution of *Rebecca*. And, he was tired. The rigors of making *Intermezzo*, *Gone with the Wind*, and *Rebecca* in quick succession, coupled with an addiction to amphetamines that fueled his notorious predilection for penning long and garrulous memos, had taken a toll. Selznick wanted out, so he quietly removed himself from the movie business. In 1941 he sold what remained of Selznick International's *Gone with the Wind* distribution rights to Jock and his sister Joan for just $500,000. To David's horror, they subsequently sold those rights to MGM's parent company, Loews, for a $28 million taxless capital gain. Selznick International was effectively broken up, and Selznick himself was retired—at least for the time being.

Whitney joined his former partner on the cinematic sidelines, dropping out of Hollywood altogether. After having dinner with Louis B. Mayer of MGM and Nicholas Schenck of Loews, he wrote to a friend of his "total loss of interest in this industry, this business and the once fond hope I held of the possibilities of its medium. It's the mountainous inflexibility of their closed little minds which makes negotiation impossible and exhausts my patience." He was also weary of the endless arguments with Selznick. Whitney was basically a frugal man, whereas Selznick was a veritable spendthrift. He once asked Jock to spend $50,000 to buy a useless hulk of a shipwreck, the USS *Leviathan*, with the idea of making a movie about the sinking of the *Lusitania*. Jock wisely declined, and the project was dropped.

Jock Whitney had invested more than $2 million in films, and by 1948, he would show a cinematic profit of $1.5 million, $1.1 million of that from *Gone with the Wind*. However, his workaholic personality and concentration on moviemaking had led to a certain neglect of Greentree Stables, which had no classic winners during his tenure at Selznick International. But in 1942 Whitney was back on track when his Equipoise colt Shut Out won the Kentucky Derby, the Belmont Stakes, and the Travers Stakes.

Once the United States entered World War II, the patriotic *Mayflower* descendant signed up for duty, a move that Mayer called "screwy." Jock found himself a position as a colonel in the Office of Strategic Services (OSS), but it was no cushy office job. Stationed in Morocco, he was sent on a mission to France in late 1944 to meet with French resistance fighters. On August 21, 1944, while traveling in a weapons carrier to Aix-en-Provence to deliver a pair of French resistance fighters to a meeting with members of the Soviet-allied Maquis, he was captured by retreating German forces. Two weeks later in Dijon, Whitney was loaded into a boxcar bound for a prisoner of war camp in Germany. Somehow, he managed to escape when the train was attacked by Allied forces, and he was led to safety by the Maquis. How ironic that one of the world's wealthiest capitalists was rescued from the Nazis by communist guerrillas.

Safely home at Greentree Stables, Jock was back in his element as a horseman. His horse Capot won both the Preakness and the Belmont Stakes and was named 1949 Horse of the Year. This must have been especially pleasing to Jock, as Capot's damsire was his father's British import St. Germans, the sire of Twenty Grand. A year later, he bought a yearling for $20,000 that would prove to be the best horse he ever owned. Tom Fool, like Capot, was a son of the Pharamond stallion Menow. Trained by John Gaver and ridden by Ted Atkinson in all thirty of his career starts, Tom Fool was named American two-year-old champion in 1951 and recorded one of the greatest seasons in the history of the turf as a four-year-old, when he had a ten-for-ten record at distances ranging from 5½ furlongs to 1¼ miles. He won the 1-mile Metropolitan Handicap; the 1¼-mile Suburban Handicap; the 7-furlong Carter Handicap, in which he equaled the Aqueduct track record set a year earlier by his Greentree stablemate Northern Star; the 1¼-mile Brooklyn Handicap, while spotting his rivals 26 to 31 pounds; and the 1¼-mile Whitney Handicap at Saratoga, a race named for Jock's illustrious family.

So overpowering was Tom Fool during his championship season that his last four victories in 1953 (the Wilson, Whitney, Sysonby, and Pimlico Special) came in nonbetting contests that attracted only one or two fearful rivals. Racetrack officials were equally fearful of large minus pools should the horse succeed at painfully low odds. Tom Fool's feats earned him a trio of championships that year as best sprinter, best handicap horse, and Horse of the Year. In its 1999 poll of the leading American Thoroughbreds of the twentieth century, the *Blood-Horse* ranked Tom Fool number 11, behind Spectacular Bid and ahead of Affirmed. He was a rousing success at stud for Greentree as well. His best son, Buckpasser, was the 1966 champion three-year-old, champion handicapper, and Horse of the Year; he ranked three places behind his sire in the *Blood-Horse* poll, in fourteenth place.

But Whitney wasn't merely a horseman and a movie man. An avid and generous supporter of Dwight Eisenhower's successful 1952 and 1956 campaigns for the presidency, Whitney was rewarded with the ambassadorship to Great Britain in 1957. He held that post for four years, during which time he wielded considerable influence in smoothing the relationship between the two nations, which had become frayed after Eisenhower put a stop to Britain's adventure in the 1956 Suez crisis. Whitney also served as the last publisher of the *New York Herald-Tribune,* where one of his employees was sportswriter Red Smith. A man with broad experience in many sports, Smith held that more stories could be found on the racetrack than in any other sport, an accurate surmise that is sadly lost on today's sporting media. An idealist, Jock Whitney was just as worried about the path horse racing was taking as he was about Hollywood's "closed little minds."

On October 17, 1963, he appeared as the guest of honor at the annual dinner of the Thoroughbred Club of America in Lexington, Kentucky, where he took the opportunity to warn his fellow horsemen about the future of the game in the United States. Admitting the necessity of commercializing the sport through betting—especially what would become known as "exotic wagering," or bets on combinations of horses as opposed to simple win wagers—he cautioned that the promotion of such wagers "increase[s] the temptation to treat horse racing as a giant lottery rather than as a sport." He expressed even greater concern about the type of people who were running American racetracks. "The spirit of racing is in jeopardy wherever and whenever sportsmen lose control. Nearly all of our tracks are now owned, operated and controlled by businessmen, in racing as a business. We find state governments greedy for ever more and more track revenue—not to advance the interests of racing, but simply to fatten the state treasury. . . . Quantity, not quality, is the watchword. In order to increase racing profits, we find racing seasons lengthened into northern winters, night racing inaugurated; now a ninth race, sometimes even followed by a tenth." In more recent years, the daily card has added an eleventh, twelfth, thirteenth, or even fourteenth race, all of them designed to bleed horseplayers dry in the misguided belief that they are being provided with additional opportunities for wagering entertainment.

A lifelong veteran of racing in America and England, Whitney concluded his speech with a comparison of the sport in those two countries, and his observations are even more valid today than in 1963: "Compared to ours, English racing is what the country corner store is to the supermarket. On a big day at Newmarket, 10,000 is a big crowd. And very few of these get to sit down. But sitting or standing, they appreciate the horse. Not merely as a gambling device that happens to breathe, but as a horse—as a creature of flesh and blood and heart and spirit. What they have, and what we seem to be losing, is personal interest in the animal. And this concern for the horse is central to the spirit of racing. Lose this spirit, and there will be no racing—only races."[12]

Since 1963, the almost universal failure of American racing to heed the wise words of John Hay Whitney has led to the deterioration of the sport. Today, it has disappeared not merely from our sporting calendar but also from our collective cultural consciousness. That decline, and the concurrent decline of American film culture, is addressed in the concluding chapter.

In 1978 and 1979 Whitney had a pair of halcyon seasons at Greentree, when his pink and black colors were carried to victory by his last two champions. His four-time Grade 1 winner Late Bloomer was named champion older mare in 1978, and Bowl Game was declared the 1979 champion turf horse with victories in the Washington, DC, International, the Turf Classic Invitational, and the Man o' War Stakes. But back in 1968, the exploits of his Belmont Stakes winner must have touched his heart even more intimately. A son of Prince John out of a mare called Peroxide Blonde, the colt was named, self-effacingly enough, Stage Door Johnny, in memory of the rich, cheeky college kid who had charmed the skirts off so many chorus girls.

10

La Princesse Aly Khan
Rita Hayworth at Longchamp

She was marrying the most promiscuous man in Europe, just the worst marriage that ever could have happened.

Orson Welles

Dancing with Daddy

When thirteen-year-old Margarita Cansino first stepped onto the stage at the Agua Caliente nightclub in 1931, partnered with her overbearing father in a red-hot dance number, she had no idea that one day she would be Rita Hayworth—cinema's reigning sex symbol—much less a jet-setting princess with untold millions at her disposal.

Shy by nature, Rita seemingly achieved success in spite of herself. Forced to play public lover to her father onstage, she was forbidden to even intimate that they were father and daughter, for if that were known, it might spoil the sexual frisson of their act. At her first screen test in 1933 she was so withdrawn that Warner Bros. didn't bother to take a second look. So she returned to the Spanish dance routine with daddy, who didn't seem to mind her early cinematic failure. With age and a certain hesitant maturity, Rita eventually relaxed in front of the camera and reached a peak of popularity rarely achieved, even in Hollywood. But if one looks very closely, one can detect something forced about her onscreen performances, especially when she is asked to purr like a sex kitten (which she never really was). Only when she is dancing does she seem to be relaxed onscreen, especially with Fred Astaire in *You'll Never Get Rich* and *You Were Never Lovelier*. Astaire called her his favorite partner (take that, Ginger!). Admitting an inherent reticence in a 1941 interview with *Picturegoer*, Rita revealed, "I am naturally very shy, and I suffer from an inferiority complex."[1]

She also admitted to a penchant for marrying "mean personalities" (like her father?). She had five husbands, all of whom wound up on the divorce heap. Perhaps the meanest was husband number three, His Highness Crown Prince Aly Khan. He was also the richest, the handsomest, and the most popular, as well as being a leading member of one of the most successful Thoroughbred racing dynasties the world has ever seen.

The Reluctant Racegoer

The story of how the queen of Hollywood nearly became the queen of the French turf has never been made into a movie, perhaps because it outglitters anything a Hollywood screenwriter could come up with. Throughout the 1940s Rita Hayworth commanded America's attention. The flame-haired star of *Gilda, The Lady from Shanghai,* and *Cover Girl* was every GI's perfect pinup pipe dream. The world was her oyster.

In catching the eye of most of the planet's sighted male population, Rita could not fail to be noticed by the world's sharpest-eyed man-about-town. Aly Khan—son of the Aga Khan, European racing's leading Thoroughbred breeder-owner—was the original A-list jet-setter with a stable full of horses, cars, and women, all of them fast. At every big social event—a race at Ascot, a party in Paris, a dinner in New York, a weekend in St. Moritz, a yearling sale at Newmarket, a premiere in Hollywood—Aly would be there, oozing charm and a wealth of banknotes in the currency of his country of the moment. Women fell at his feet, seduced by his dark, dreamy eyes and his fat wallet. If a woman was beautiful and famous, Aly would find her. Rita Hayworth was beautiful and famous, and find her he did.

The occasion was a July 1948 dinner party thrown in the Côte d'Azur resort of Cannes—home of the famous film festival—by gossip columnist Elsa Maxwell. If it wasn't actually love at first sight, it was surely seduction. Rita was on sabbatical from Hollywood, and Aly, who was always on sabbatical, seized the opportunity. That they were both married—she to Hollywood wunderkind Orson Welles, he to English socialite Joan Barbara Guinness (mother of the current Aga Khan)—didn't seem to matter to either of them. In fact, they could hardly take their eyes—or hands—off each other. A whirlwind courtship followed, with stops in Biarritz, Los Angeles (where Rita joined the Del Mar Thoroughbred Club and replenished her touring ensemble), Mexico City, Acapulco, Havana, Paris, London, and Geneva. Rita then took up official residence in Reno, Nevada, so she could qualify for a quickie divorce from an irate Welles, whose huge ego had been punctured in full public view. Explaining her reason for divorcing Welles, the director and star of *Citizen Kane,* Rita quipped, "I got tired of his genius."[2]

Much of the Western world was shocked at the idea of one of their favorite Hollywood stars marrying a Muslim prince. A headline in the British daily *The People* screamed, "THIS AFFAIR IS AN AFFRONT TO ALL DECENT WOMEN," and it referred to Aly Khan as "a colored prince." A prince he certainly was, but "colored" he certainly was not. He returned the volley by saying, "They call me a bloody nigger, so I pay them out by winning all their desirable women."[3]

Married in the Cannes town hall on May 27, 1949, and in a Muslim ceremony the next day, the newlyweds lost no time getting down to business. At Longchamp on June 28, the day of the Grand Prix de Paris, Rita fainted into Aly's arms with all of Paris (or at least 100,000 of them) looking on. The press took this to mean that she was pregnant. On December 28 Rita proved the scribes right by giving birth to a daughter, Yasmin. Aly sheepishly explained that seven-month babies were common in his family.

Aly Khan's wealth—and the way he threw it around—had become the stuff of Hollywood legend. Teaming with Bing Crosby in their 1952 picture *Road to Bali,* Bob Hope takes a poke at the heir to the Ismaili Muslim throne when, discovering a decidedly small casket filled with precious jewels, he jokes, "It looks like Aly Khan's garbage can!"

Among the many wedding gifts Aly lavished on his bride were a few of the talented Thoroughbreds he had in training at Chantilly with Richard Carver. One year earlier, a Carver-trained horse—My Love, owned by Aly's father—had won the prestigious Epsom Derby. The best of Aly's gifts to Rita was a promising three-year-old filly named Double Rose. Shortly before their marriage, the dazzling couple had been thrilled by her victory at France's most elegant racecourse, Longchamp, in the Prix Vanteaux. A key prep race for the classic Prix de Diane (better known in American racing circles as the French Oaks), the Vanteaux proved that Double Rose was one of the leading French distaffers of her generation.

Not that Rita noticed. All horses looked the same to her. In fact, she didn't even like horses. "I rode on horseback," she once said, "although I was terrified of them. That was when I was doing Westerns (the eminently forgettable *Hit the Saddle* and *Trouble in Texas*). They were something else again."[4]

In fact, Aly had given Rita the horses in an effort to focus her attention on *his* lifestyle. They were, in a manner of speaking, a bribe. One of the clauses in their marriage contract was that she—Rita Hayworth, one of the most popular actresses in Hollywood—would not make any movies for the duration of their union. But spending afternoons at the track chatting with impossibly boring social aristocrats, plus attending a never-ending round of parties and dinners, was not the sort of lifestyle that appealed to Rita.

And then there was Aly, the playboy of the Western, Eastern, Northern, and Southern worlds. So notorious was his reputation that it was rumored he had cheated on his bride between their wedding ceremony and their wedding night. If there was racing business at Newmarket, Deauville, Saratoga, Keeneland, Santa Anita, or San Isidro, Aly would be there, and like any sailor worth his salt, he had a girl in every port. Rita looked the other way, but all was not well in what the outside world perceived to be a marriage made in heaven.

To the public, it seemed that Aly and Rita were on perpetual honeymoon, but racing was always more important to Aly than romance. On June 5, just nine days after they tied the knot, he had important business in England. It was Derby day at Epsom, and from a breeding standpoint, the Epsom Derby was most important horse race in the world. Aly had to be there because he had a runner named Iran in the big race. His father, the preeminent horseman of the era, was in search of his fifth triumph in the so-called Blue Riband of the Turf with Hindostan, the 100–9 fourth choice. Rita tagged along with her husband and father-in-law but behaved like she would rather be elsewhere. "Miss Hayworth created something of a sensation when she strolled into the paddock among the top-hatted royalty and noblemen," reported the Associated Press. "She was all smiles, but showed little interest in the horses, spending most of her time keeping her big pink and white polka-dot hat stuck on her red hair."[5]

Aly's Iran finished a dull eighteenth in the overflow thirty-two-horse field, while the Aga's Hindostan managed just one place better. A phalanx of 100 bobbies was needed to the escort the royal couple out of the racecourse to the safety of their waiting roadster. Next up, less than two weeks later, came Royal Ascot, another event that Aly and his father couldn't miss. A dutiful Rita put in an appearance, smiling obligingly for the cameras while keeping one eye on Aly and another on her father-in-law's colt, Palestine, who won the Coventry Stakes on his way to becoming European two-year-old champion.

Rita's Compatriots

Rita Hayworth wasn't the first American movie star to make a name for herself in the arena of the French turf. Pearl White, who thrilled audiences with her narrow escapes in the cinematic serial *The Perils of Pauline,* moved to France after bowing out of the American film scene in 1924. Her only French film, *Terreur* (released in America as *The Perils of Paris*), was also her last. She used a portion of the considerable fortune she had amassed as one of the silent screen's most popular attractions to keep a string of ten rather successful Thoroughbreds at France's premier training center in Chantilly.

But the most famous film personality to involve himself in French racing was Jean Gabin, star of the Jean Renoir classics *La Bete humaine* (*The Human Beast*) and *La Grande Illusion,* as well as Marcel Carne's *Le Quai des brumes* (*Port of Shadows*), *Le Jour se leve* (*Daybreak*), and *Pepe le Moko.* Gabin was a lifelong *turfiste* (French for "racegoer"). His taste lay primarily with trotters, which he bred at his own at his farm, La Pichonniere, in Normandy. In the early 1970s he had as many as seventy horses and even owned a trotting track, Moulins-la-Marche, but he was also a regular attendee at the big flat tracks such as Longchamp, Chantilly, Deauville, and Saint-Cloud. He read the French racing daily *Paris-Turf* every day from its inception in 1948 until his death in 1976. In 1962 he even made a racing film, *Le Gentleman d'Epsom,* about a former army officer reduced to touting horses at Parisian tracks.

The extent to which Gabin immersed himself in racing was revealed by Simone Signoret. In 1971 they costarred in *Le Chat* (*The Cat*), a film based on a novel by Georges Simenon in which an aging couple are so estranged that they communicate solely through handwritten notes. Each morning before shooting began, Gabin and Signoret would meet for breakfast. A committed political activist, Signoret would usually bring five or six newspapers to the table, most notably *L'Humanite,* the official organ of the French Communist Party. Gabin, however, satisfied himself with a single paper: *Paris-Turf.* "Suddenly, one morning," Signoret recalled, "Jean became greatly excited. 'Look!' he exclaimed. 'My name is in *Paris-Turf!*' Here was one of the most famous people in the world and he was behaving like a little child because his name was in the fine print in a racing paper."[6]

But while Gabin sometimes let his enthusiasm for racing run away with him, Rita Hayworth was far more phlegmatic about her involvement in the sport of kings.

Double Rose

Although Rita Hayworth, officially known as La Princesse Aly Khan, was listed as the owner of Double Rose, Aly Khan and Richard Carver made all the training and racing decisions. They decreed that Double Rose's next outing would be in the Prix de Diane, the elegant fillies' classic at Chantilly, thirty miles north of Paris. But Double Rose's previous form failed her, and she came home eighth behind Prix Vanteaux runner-up Bagheera. There followed the almost de rigueur summer vacation for leading French three-year-olds. Rita and Aly spent much of August cavorting on the beach at Deauville when they weren't at the nearby racetrack. There, Carver warmed up for the autumn racing season with a victory in the Prix Jacques le Marois, one of the most important 1-mile races in the world, with Amour Drake. That made him the hottest trainer in France, and he had a plan for Double Rose.

Her grandsire, Chateau Bouscaut, had won the 1½-mile Prix du Jockey Club (French Derby) and had come in an unlucky second in the 1⅞-mile Grand Prix de Paris, at the time the centerpiece of the French racing season. Chateau Bouscaut had made a name for himself as a source of stamina, and Carver believed that Double Rose would improve over distances longer than the Vanteaux's 1¼ miles and the Diane's 1⁵⁄₁₆ miles. She lived up to expectations by winning Deauville's Prix de la Municipalite at 1⁹⁄₁₆ miles, so she was entered in the Prix Vermeille, Longchamp's 1½-mile Arc prep for three-year-old fillies, run over the same course and distance as the Arc. Hopes were dashed, however, when Double Rose finished fifth in that race behind Bagheera, beaten by less than three lengths. Still, that effort was good enough to earn her a place in the lineup for the Prix de l'Arc de Triomphe three weeks later.

Double Rose and twenty-seven others made the 1949 running of the Arc the largest up to that point. The reason was money. A Societe d'Encouragement (French Jockey Club) deal with the Loterie Nationale established a sweepstakes on the Arc, raising its value from $21,000 to $110,000. That kind of money could open the eyes of even someone as jaded as Aly Khan. The overflow field included two of Double Rose's Carver-trained stablemates: Jacques le Marois winner Amour Drake and Val Drake. Those two started as the 7–2 cofavored entry, the same price as Double Rose's nemesis Bagheera, who, between her Diane and Vermeille triumphs, had landed the Grand Prix de Paris. The Marcel Boussac–owned entry of Coronation, runner-up in both the English and Irish Oaks; Eclipse Stakes winner Djeddah; and their pacemaker Norval went off at 3.70–1. Double Rose attracted a lot less attention from the betting public than her owner did. All afternoon, eyes were riveted on Rita Hayworth, as Double Rose drifted to odds of 60–1.

Even so, all the favorites had their weaknesses, save Bagheera. Amour Drake was a miler, Val Drake had finished only third in the 1⅞-mile Prix Royal Oak, Djeddah was suspect beyond 1¼ miles, and Coronation, a classic winner going a mile, had failed twice at the Arc distance of 1½ miles against members of her own age and sex. Could there be a *National Velvet*–like upset in the making? If so, Double Rose had Bagheera to beat.

Carver brought Bill Rickaby over from England to ride Double Rose, who received a prerace kiss from Rita in the paddock. The sun was shining brilliantly that Sunday afternoon in October as the Boussac rabbit Norval sped to the lead, with his entrymate Djeddah close up in fifth. Coronation, ridden by French ace Roger Poincelet, was in eleventh, while Double Rose, breaking from the middle of the starting gate, was a few places farther back. Halfway down the hill, on the long, sloping turn with five furlongs to go, Amour Drake was eating up ground on the rail as Norval gave up the lead to the 30–1 Coast Guard. Amour Drake was fifth, and Double Rose and Coronation were together in tenth. Bagheera had been swung wide and was making progress with three furlongs to run.

At the head of the stretch, Amour Drake assumed command, with British hope Beau Sabreur alongside. Double Rose and Coronation were running as a team farther out. Djeddah was fading, and Bagheera's wide run had petered out. Inside the quarter pole, Double Rose and Amour Drake engaged in a duel for the lead. Could Rose get the job done against a rival whose stamina was suspect? For a few seconds, it seemed possible, but Coronation was right behind and traveling best of all. When Poincelet pushed the button, the response was immediate and devastating. Coronation, daughter of 1942 Arc winner Djebel, swept to the lead and drew off to a four-length victory. Double Rose ran on for second, a length ahead of Amour Drake. At least Double Rose had the satisfaction of finishing ahead of Bagheera, who weakened and came in sixteenth. Rita took the loss in stride, as did Aly. "I can't help it if she didn't win," Rita said, "I wasn't running."[7]

Confoundingly, Double Rose had been beaten by a filly who, by any rational criteria, should never have been foaled or conceived. Coronation was the product of incestuous inbreeding: the stallion Tourbillon was both her paternal grandfather and her maternal grandfather. Such creatures sometimes have difficulty walking a straight line, but Coronation was the exception that proved the rule.

Double Rose wasn't the only horse Rita owned. Her filly named Skylarking was good enough to win one of France's most important sprint races, the 6½-furlong Prix Maurice de Gheest, the following August at Deauville. Aly and Rita were on hand to cheer their 4–5 favorite home, and they were present later in the month when Skylarking won again on the same day that Double Rose finished a narrow second in the Grand Prix de Deauville.

Five weeks later, in October 1950, Double Rose would try the Arc again. But the now four-year-old filly, a 32–1 longshot in the big race, never threatened, finishing eleventh of twelve behind the redoubtable Tantieme. Rita and Aly took no consolation in the fact that Double Rose finished just a half-length behind Coronation.

The End of the Affair

During all this excitement at the races, the Khan-Hayworth alliance—one could hardly call it a marriage—was rapidly unraveling. Always attracted by Hollywood glitz, Aly reportedly had affairs with Yvonne de Carlo and Zsa Zsa Gabor. When Rita caught him in a public clinch with Joan Fontaine, she threw a tantrum, filed for divorce on September 2, 1951, and returned to Hollywood with baby Yasmin.

There was a brief reconciliation, followed by another separation. At Del Mar on August 17, 1952, Aly was present as Moonrush (formerly owned by Louis Mayer) won the San Diego Handicap, inspired, no doubt, by a prerace kiss from actress and stuntwoman Anita King. Rita was nowhere in sight. Aly had flown in from the Saratoga yearling sales to spend a day at the track with Rex Ellsworth, to whom he had sold the stallion Khaled, who would later sire Swaps, Ellsworth's outstanding Kentucky Derby winner and Horse of the Year. In the paddock before Moonrush's race, a man ran up to Aly with a hot-off-the-press edition that contained a banner headline about Rita and her husband. "Excuse me," a bemused Aly said. "I've got to read this to see if I'm reconciled with Rita."[8]

Aly never changed his ways. Their divorce was finalized on January 26, 1953, and the ink on the papers was hardly dry when he announced his engagement to Gene Tierney, the sultry star of *Laura* and *Leave Her to*

Heaven. But this time, the Aga Khan put his fatherly foot down and said "No!" Aly tried again shortly thereafter with Kim Novak. Later, the Aga would lament, rather ungraciously, "Ah, if Aly would only choose his women as well as he does his horses!"[9]

The Aga Khan was clearly fed up with his son's behavior, but Aly would not realize *how* fed up until his father's death on July 11, 1957. When his will was read the next day, Aly was horrified to learn that his father had passed him over, awarding the title of ruler of the Ismaili Muslims to Aly's son, Karim, who has held the title Aga Khan IV since that date. Aly continued to carouse with the jet set, and in February 1958 he was named Pakistan's ambassador to the United Nations. After five more unsuccessful tries, Prince Aly Khan finally won the coveted Prix de l'Arc de Triomphe with Saint Crespin in 1959. Seven months later, his life would end tragically when he was killed in an automobile accident while driving to a dinner party after a day of racing at Longchamp. Two decades later, he would be memorialized by his close friends, Calumet Farm owners Gene and Lucille Markey, who named their outstanding colt Alydar, short for "Aly darling," the prince's pet name.

Having freed herself from the velvet clutches of the world's most eligible husband, Rita Hayworth returned to Hollywood and moviemaking. The tropical noir *Affair in Trinidad* grossed $1 million more than the vastly superior *Gilda,* so hungry were moviegoers to see their favorite glamour girl onscreen again. This was followed by *Salome, Miss Sadie Thompson, Pal Joey,* and *Separate Tables,* interspersed with disastrous marriages to actor-crooner Dick Haymes and producer James Hill. Diagnosed with Alzheimer's disease in the late 1970s, Rita Hayworth slowly faded from view, spending her last years with daughter Yasmin in an apartment on Manhattan's Central Park West.

Rita Hayworth would return to Deauville one last time, in a sense. The occasion was the American Film Festival, a celebration of American cinema held every September after the racing crowd has abandoned the seaside resort. In 1987, a few months after her death, she was feted on the same beach where she had once frolicked with Aly and his friends. Hollywood's brief but glittering affair with the elegant world of French horse racing had come full circle.

11

Gene Markey

From Joan Bennett to Hedy Lamarr to Myrna Loy to Calumet Farm

He was the kindest of men with a great wit and a philosophical view of life, beloved by everyone who knew him.

Wife #1 Joan Bennett

Gene and I will be happy forever.

Wife #2 Hedy Lamarr

He could make a scrubwoman feel like a queen.

Wife #3 Myrna Loy

I never knew what love was until I married [Gene].

Wife #4 Lucille Parker Wright

You are the most wonderful and gorgeous woman I've ever known, and that includes those other three women whose names I can't remember.

Gene Markey to Lucille Wright

Uglier than Frankenstein's Monster, Sexier than Valentino

Wit, charm, and more charm: that described Gene Markey in a nutshell. A decidedly nondescript, rather unattractive fellow, his blithe spirit inhabited the body of a perpetually middle-aged man—jowly faced, heavyset, and paunchy. Yet he wooed three of the most beautiful stars in the Hollywood firmament and convinced them to walk down the aisle into conjugal bliss—at least for a few years, until the charm wore off and his roving eye cast about for a new conquest.

At the peak of his powers during the 1930s and 1940s, Gene Markey must have been the most envied man in America. Joan Bennett, a dark-eyed, twenty-two-year-old starlet—and still a blonde at the time—succumbed to his charms on March 12, 1932, between appearances in *She Wanted a Millionaire* and *Careless Lady.* In Markey, she got herself a future screen-writing millionaire. Hedy Lamarr, widely acclaimed as the "most beautiful woman in the world," fell into his loving arms on December 18, 1937, shortly before she started work on her first American picture, *Algiers,* in which she lures elusive criminal Charles Boyer out of his Kasbah hideout. Myrna Loy, having established herself as the "perfect Hollywood wife" playing opposite *Thin Man* husband William Powell, was captured by Markey on January 3, 1946. He must have brought her luck. A few months later, she would perfect her role as the "perfect wife" opposite Fredric March in *The Best Years of Our Lives,* the winner of seven Academy Awards, a total previously topped only by *Gone with the Wind.* In between, Gene wooed Lucille Ball and was engaged for a time to Ina Claire.

With neither looks nor money, Markey's success with women is mystifying because he was, by and large, a member of Hollywood's B team. Born into a military family in 1895 in Jackson, Michigan, he arrived in Hollywood in 1929 with the express intent of becoming a screenwriter. He was already a published author. His second novel, *Stepping High,* was published in 1929; it tells the story of a husband-and-wife dance team living the high life during the Roaring Twenties.

Markey put his considerable social skills to work for him in Hollywood, and MGM was the first major company to take notice. Working under the high expectations of Louis Mayer, Markey turned out a string of modest screenplays, one of the better ones being *The Floradora Girl* (1930), in which former silent-screen comedienne Marion Davies plays an 1890s version of a 1920s Ziegfeld Girl—a job she actually held at the start of her career. Markey followed this with *The Great Lover* (1931), starring Adolphe Menjou. Based on a creaky 1915 play, this updated version of Don Juan fit Markey's persona to a tee. Meanwhile, he was on a first-name basis with the likes of Douglas Fairbanks Jr., John Wayne, Irving Berlin, and Jock Whitney, who was introducing him to the pleasures of the turf.

By this time, Markey was courting Joan Bennett. She had already appeared in a dozen films, most of them forgettable. Although she had made impressions in *Bulldog Drummond* (1929) with Ronald Colman, *Disraeli* (1929) with George Arliss, and *Moby Dick* (1930) with John Barrymore, Joan hadn't broken through to the top like her older sister Constance. In November 1931, while making *She Wanted a Millionaire* with Spencer Tracy, Joan suffered a broken hip and three broken vertebrae when she ran a mare named Gilda Grey into a tree. It was a keen embarrassment to someone who had been riding horses since she was a little girl. Production on *Millionaire* was suspended for six months as Joan lay in the hospital in a plaster cast that stretched from her hip down past her knee.

Gene and Joan had socialized at any number of Hollywood affairs, and he was smitten. He inundated her with love letters. "His funny, dear messages arrived in increasing number," she recalled, and so did his visits. These included spending afternoons at home with Ditty, Joan's daughter with first husband John Marion Fox. "He visited Ditty (then four) almost daily. They loved each other, at tea parties addressing each other as Mr. and Mrs. Grasshopper—he was the father she had never known." There was something oddly Carrollian in this relationship, but Markey knew what he was doing: he was cutting a path to the heart of the mother through that of the lonesome daughter.[1]

Once she was released from the hospital, Joan hopped across the country to visit family in New York, during which time "Gene bombarded me with wires to remind me of his concern and affection." Upon her return to Hollywood, he popped the question, and Joan was delighted to accept. Sister Constance was her matron of honor. Their marriage coincided with a rise in fortunes for both husband and wife. Gene wrote the screenplay for Greta Garbo's *As You Desire Me*. Based on a play by Luigi Pirandello, this was a far cry from the high society and backstage romances that had become his stock-in-trade. Joan starred in *The Trial of Vivienne Ware* and then made *Little Women*, matching wits with Katharine Hepburn line for line, even as the costume designers scrambled to create dresses that would conceal her pregnancy and her increasingly prominent midsection. *Little Women* proved to be the breakthrough Joan was looking for. At the same time, Gene triumphed with the screenplay for the Barbara Stanwyck hit *Baby Face*, the cutting-edge story of a working-class woman who works her way up the corporate ladder by means both fair and foul, trampling a young office clerk played by John Wayne along the way.[2]

Daughter Melinda was born on February 27, 1934, by which time the passion had cooled—perhaps the victim of two successful careers that rarely coincided, either artistically or personally. Gene and Joan were seen together occasionally at Santa Anita or Hollywood Park—like so many other Hollywood couples—but their home life had fallen into a dissatisfying routine. "Gene was a devoted husband but I was feeling something else.

I couldn't account for my discontent," Joan said. "Erosion set in and steadily and quietly wore away our relationship." Gene referred to her as "the most baffling of the baffling Bennetts." Joan attributed this to her domesticity, whereas Gene was an inveterate partygoer. Joan sent out a lifeline to the marriage in June 1936, when she had Ditty's surname changed from Fox to Markey, but in the long run, it didn't help. On May 12, 1937, Joan filed for divorce, claiming mental cruelty, which in those days was a euphemism for adultery. On June 4 their marriage was dissolved. The proceedings were amicable, and there was no custody battle. Gene could visit Mims, as they called daughter Melinda, whenever he wished. "He was a gentleman to the core," Joan said. "Divorce presented no problems for either of us"—a statement that, if true, borders on the miraculous.[3]

Gene Markey proceeded to take a two-year hiatus from wedded bliss. Once he had caught his breath, he trained his sights on Hollywood newcomer Hedy Lamarr, but not before having flings with on-the-skids silent stars Gloria Swanson and Ina Claire. Gene met Hedy at the wedding of Virginia Bruce and screenwriter J. Walter Ruben on December 18, 1937, six months after his divorce from Joan. There followed the type of whirlwind courtship at which Markey excelled: parties, dinners, love letters, days at the track. Hedy, who had shocked the world by appearing bone naked in the 1933 Czech film *Ecstasy,* was still an official secret in Hollywood. *Ecstasy* would not be released in America until 1940, but Markey knew all about Lamarr and her potential for stardom.

"We decided to get married, Mr. Markey and I, while we were having dinner last night," Hedy told *Photoplay.* "Mr. Markey has to start work on a picture at the studio (at 20th Century Fox, *The Adventures of Sherlock Holmes*) where he is a producer. I go into a picture on Monday (*Lady of the Tropics,* her 1939 follow-up to *Algiers*). We thought we had better get married right away, for if we waited it might be weeks before we again had time."[4]

They tied the knot in a Mexicali quickie on March 5, 1939. They would make their home at Hedy's place on Benedict Canyon Drive in Beverly Hills, where she predicted that they would be happy forever. Not quite. Unable to conceive, Hedy interjected herself into the life of Gene and Joan's daughter Melinda, much to the chagrin of the former couple. To ease the situation, Gene and Hedy adopted a seven-month-old boy whom they named James Lamarr Markey, but Gene much preferred his own little Mims, who was now the cutest five-year-old imaginable.

Markey's involvement with Hedy coincided with a new stage in his career. In June 1937 he had signed on with Darryl Zanuck's 20th Century Fox as a producer. They would work closely in making a string of modestly successful films with certain historic value. Two of the earliest were John Ford's sentimental Shirley Temple vehicle *Wee Willie Winkie* (1937) and Allan Dwan's *Suez* (1938) with Tyrone Power and Loretta Young. *Wee Willie Winkie* finished fifth in the 1937 box office race and was number one for Fox. *Suez* was nineteenth at the box office in 1938 and number three for Fox, indications that Markey was as good at producing as he was at screenwriting.

Suez finished one spot ahead of another Markey project that was dear to his heart. *Kentucky,* based on the novel *The Look of Eagles* by John Taintor Foote, was a big-budget production and one of the first pictures to incorporate the three-strip Technicolor technique. Zanuck and Markey employed David Butler as director. A keen racing fan, Butler owned a string of eight horses stabled at Santa Anita, so he was the perfect choice to direct a film about the Bluegrass State's deep involvement in Thoroughbred racing and breeding. Butler also received expert information on the subject from the president of Churchill Downs, Colonel Matt Winn, the man credited with making the Kentucky Derby the first-class race it is today. Hal Price Headley, cofounder and president of Keeneland Racecourse in Lexington and a major owner-breeder himself, also had Butler's ear, as did Warren Wright, who made his Calumet Farm available for filming.

Markey had always been attracted to racing on a social level. The tracks in Southern California were good places to meet people as well as to be seen with Hollywood beauties like Joan and Hedy, neither of whom minded the exposure. But *Kentucky* provided him with the opportunity to meet the movers and shakers of the Thoroughbred world, and he liked what he saw.

The film delves into how Kentucky became the center of the Thoroughbred breeding industry in America. It begins on the eve of the Civil War as Kentuckians debate whether to side with the Union or the Confederacy. During an interlude between the war and the 1930's, Butler shot scenes of mares and foals at Castleton Farm in Lexington including footage of Man o' War and War Admiral romping in their paddocks. The plot thickens with a Romeo and Juliet–like romance between Loretta Young and Richard Greene, whose families take different sides in the War between the States. It all ends happily in the Kentucky Derby winner's circle. Walter Brennan, his usual scene-stealing self, won the second of his three Oscars for best supporting actor, helping to put Markey in the catbird's seat at Fox.

Five days after Gene and Hedy were married, Fox released the newest Markey production: *The Little Princess,* with Shirley Temple in yet another saccharine story of a plucky little girl at odds with the adult world. At the same time, Markey began production on perhaps his most important film, at least from a historic perspective: *The Adventures of Sherlock Holmes.* Although it took a few liberties with its source material, the William Gillett play *Sherlock Holmes,* the film is famous for introducing Basil Rathbone as the world's best and most renowned detective. While many of the later Holmes productions at Fox were rather fanciful (Holmes fighting Nazi spies, for example), Rathbone's portrayal of the great sleuth remains firmly imprinted on the public consciousness to this day.

But had Gene implanted himself firmly into Hedy's consciousness? He had certainly caught the attention of Hollywood society, as Hedda Hopper wrote in her January 31, 1939, column. "Some of our glamour boys could take lessons from Gene Markey. One night he gives a birthday dinner to our beautiful chatterbox Barbara Trippet. The next two he's hand-holding with Hedy Lamarr and in between acts as escort for ex-wife Joan Bennett. . . . But he's still a swell guy, and they're all lucky."[5]

When shooting on Hedy's next film, *I Take This Woman* at MGM, was completed in December 1939, she and Gene accompanied Fox chiefs Darryl Zanuck and Joe Schenck on a cross-country train ride to New York for the premieres of *The Grapes of Wrath* and *The Blue Bird,* yet another Markey-produced Shirley Temple film. The latter flopped, as did *I Take This Woman.* Things were not looking rosy for the Markey-Lamarr entry.

Despite a denial by Louella Parsons in her syndicated column, Markey's second marriage was on the rocks. On July 7, 1940, it exploded with news of their separation. "For many months we have been incompatible," moaned the most beautiful woman in the world.[6] Gossip columnist Sidney Solsky pounced, writing in the *New York Post,* "She (Hedy) imagines she is a much better actress than she really is, and if you tell her otherwise you're in for a family quarrel," a veiled hint that Gene was no longer enamored of his stunning wife. Solsky even intimated that Gene was making secret visits to friends Arthur Hornblow Jr., a fellow Dartmouth graduate and producer of the Oscar-nominated *Ruggles of Red Gap,* and his wife Myrna Loy, whose own four-year marriage was foundering.[7]

Hedy admitted that Gene was charming, witty, and intelligent and that she was crazy about him. But she complained that he was a workaholic who admired her only for her beauty and fame—not unusual in Hollywood, where beautiful and famous women can be found in abundance. She filed for divorce, citing extreme mental cruelty (Joan Bennett had claimed only run-of-the-mill mental cruelty), and testified in court that during sixteen months of marriage, they had spent only four nights alone together (perhaps explaining her inability to get pregnant). The divorce was granted.

With America's entry into World War II, Gene Markey left movie stars and motion pictures behind and joined the navy (he had served as an army lieutenant during the First World War and later joined the Naval Reserve). Before leaving for military duty, Markey had one last fling in Hollywood, writing and producing a picture called *You're the One* for Paramount. It was an unmitigated disaster. Bosley Crowther wrote in the *New York Times*, "Gene Markey . . . is either badly confused or just downright careless," labeling the film "haphazard, pointless, dull, a miserable excuse for a musical farce." It would be the last film Markey made for more than six years.[8]

Markey, however, distinguished himself in the Pacific, serving as an intelligence officer under Admiral William "Bull" Halsey at Guadalcanal and winning a Bronze Star for leading a reconnaissance mission on the Solomon Islands. At war's end, he was promoted to the rank of rear admiral, and from 1945 on, he insisted on being called "Admiral," even by his friends. Those who didn't were ostracized from his circle.

Uniforms were all the rage in those postwar days, and Markey milked his status for every cent it was worth. One night at an Embassy Club charity dinner in Washington, DC, he was seated at table with Jimmy Durante and Harry Warner, horseplayer and horse owner, respectively. The conversation inevitably turned to racing, but Admiral Markey had his eye on the attractive woman seated across from him. Myrna Loy was in town doing good deeds at Walter Reed and Bethesda Naval Hospitals. Gene had been single for five years, and Myrna had been divorced twice—from Arthur Hornblow and from John Hertz Jr., son of the Hertz Rent-a-Car founder. Gene saw his chance and took it. The new couple was spotted by gossip columnists at the Mayflower Club and the Army and Navy Club. One night at a dinner party, Gene was present when Sam Goldwyn offered Myrna the plum role of Milly Stephenson, Fredric March's wife in *The Best Years of Our Lives*.

Gene and Myrna were married on January 3, 1946, in the chapel of Washington's Roosevelt Navy Base, Gene all gilded up in his navy blue and gold, Bronze Star prominently displayed on his chest. Bull Halsey was his best man, and Douglas Fairbanks Jr. and Robert Montgomery were among the small party of twenty guests. Myrna created a little drama of her own by arriving twenty minutes late. She would later describe the affair as "a typical Markey extravaganza, but not a wedding celebration."[9]

Markey's film career was winding down. He had been away from Hollywood for five years, and when he returned with his new bride, he discovered that the town bore little resemblance to the one he had left. There was the usual social whirl, with parties at the homes of Darryl Zanuck and Cole Porter, but Gene seemed to be at sea. Myrna had reached the top of the Hollywood heap with *Best Years,* but he was at sixes and sevens. Gene wrote and produced one more film, and Darryl Zanuck spared no expense. *Moss Rose* (1947), a London-based film noir directed by Gregory Ratoff, lost Fox a bundle. Zanuck himself called it a catastrophe.

Markey was in a generally foul mood. Although he still played the bon vivant socially, he seemed to miss the discipline of navy life. And he took a decided dislike to the new liberal political tone that was becoming fashionable in Hollywood. He was distressed when Myrna read the preamble of the United Nations Charter at a meeting of the American Slav Congress, an outfit the Department of Justice considered subversive and communist. At a Hollywood party one night, Markey revealed an ugly side to his character when he spotted Myrna in deep conversation with Louise Beavers, a black actress famous for playing maids in well-to-do white households. Gene took his wife aside and upbraided her for speaking to someone like that. Myrna brushed it off, but Louise didn't. She subsequently referred to Markey as a skunk.

In late 1949 Gene took Myrna on a London holiday, where he introduced her to Queen Elizabeth, the wife of King George VI. During their time hobnobbing with the royals, Myrna began to suspect that Gene was using his charm and his naval connections to bed a number of local aristocrats. When she returned to Hollywood to make *Cheaper by the Dozen* for Fox, Gene stayed behind. They grew further and further apart, and when Myrna got word that Gene was having an affair with an Irish countess, she filed for divorce. It turned out that she wasn't so liberal after all. She made the standard accusation of mental cruelty in a quickie proceeding in Cuernavaca, Mexico, and on August 11, 1950, Gene Markey and

Myrna Loy were officially kaput. Gene had tried to put on a brave face. "Myrna and I are still very good friends and I am very fond of her but we must separate," he told a newspaper back in January. "Our work keeps us apart most of the time and we see very little of each other." Markey would soon be seeing very little of Hollywood as well.[10]

With his cinematic prospects looking dim, Gene "retired" to a small house in the Bel Air hills, north of the UCLA campus. It was all he could afford on his meager stipend as a postwar rear admiral. Markey was marking time, working on forgettable novels like *The Kingdom of the Spur*, a Tex-Mex western. At the same time, Lucille Parker Wright of Lexington, Saratoga Springs, and Miami Beach was making the social and sporting rounds as the nation's most eligible widow. Her husband, Warren Wright Sr., had died on December 28, 1950, leaving her the most valuable racing empire in the world: Calumet Farm. Restless, Mrs. Wright exchanged her mansion in Miami Beach for one in Bel Air, allowing her to be closer to her California racing operation. It was only a matter of time before the most charming man in Hollywood and the empress of American racing crossed paths.

Hollywood Marries the Races—Part 2

Lucille Parker Wright was a devout Catholic, so her arrival in the neighborhood caught the attention of Los Angeles archbishop James Francis Cardinal McIntyre. His Eminence invited her over for dinner one night, but being a single woman, she needed an escort. Friends suggested the equally eligible and very charming Gene Markey, who lived just around the corner, so to speak. Gene and Lucille hit it off right from the start, their budding relationship seemingly blessed by the Church itself. The deal was sealed when they married on September 27, 1952, completing Markey's transformation from Hollywood playboy into Kentucky colonel, a title he would officially receive six years later from Bluegrass State governor Happy Chandler.

Markey turned his back on Hollywood and moved into Lucille's Calumet Farm mansion in Lexington. By marrying into the Wright family, he attained a position of no little power in the Thoroughbred world, although his wife retained control of the purse strings—at which she was an expert—and continued to make most of the decisions concerning the horses.

And what horses they were! At the time of the Markey-Wright union, Calumet Farm had already won the Kentucky Derby five times with

Whirlaway (1941), Pensive (1944), Citation (1948), Ponder (1949), and Hill Gail, who added luster to the couple's courtship by winning the 1952 Run for the Roses a few months before their wedding. Whirlaway and Citation would add victories in the Preakness and Belmont Stakes, making Calumet the only owner in history with two Triple Crowns to its credit.

Calumet Farm was founded by William Monroe Wright in 1924 as a Standardbred operation and enjoyed some success. Calumet Butler won the Hambletonian, American harness racing's most important race, in 1931. Shortly thereafter, Wright died and left Calumet to his son William, who almost immediately began to transform the farm into a Thoroughbred operation. Following the formula prescribed by Sam Riddle and the Whitney and Vanderbilt families, William looked to European bloodlines to improve the Kentucky breed. He started with the $14,000 purchase at Saratoga of a modest-looking son of the French-bred stallion Bull Dog. This horse turned out to be Bull Lea, the Calumet foundation sire whose sons included Citation, Hill Gail, 1944 Preakness winner Faultless, 1947 Horse of the Year Armed, 1949 champion older horse Coaltown, and 1957 Kentucky Derby winner Iron Liege, as well as champion fillies Twilight Tear, Two Lea, Bewitch, and Next Move.

Calumet also imported Epsom Derby winner Blenheim as part of a syndicate with Bull Hancock's Claiborne Farm and the Whitney family's Greentree Stables. Blenheim would make his mark on the Kentucky Thoroughbred by siring Whirlaway for Calumet and 1947 Kentucky Derby winner Jet Pilot for Claiborne.

Calumet might be called the Thoroughbred equivalent to MGM or Cadillac. Its reputation in 1952 was unmatched by any sporting endeavor in the world, with the possible exception of the New York Yankees. Words like "hallowed" have always been used to describe the ground where the likes of Whirlaway and Citation were bred, foaled, and broken, and there was nothing hyperbolic about its use where Calumet was concerned. However, the realm of the Kentucky breeder-owner was a closed shop, and Gene Markey was an outsider among Lexington society and the Bluegrass elite.

Success in Hollywood depended on talent and charm, and Markey possessed the latter in spades. He would need to pull out all the stops in that regard to ingratiate himself with the locals. He had long been friends with Hollywood and Greentree colleague Jock Whitney, but as the "husband" of Calumet Farm, he would have to win over the others. In the end, he had no problem doing so. Gene quickly became friends with Leslie

Combs, the owner of Spendthrift Farm. They shared a taste for the high life, and together they would revitalize the Bluegrass social scene. Gene was especially helpful, inviting many of his movie star friends such as John Wayne and Douglas Fairbanks over to the house for Kentucky Derby week. Ultimately, Gene Markey fit into Calumet Farm like a hand in a glove.

Derby Doings

Calumet didn't miss a beat after Gene Markey's arrival in Lexington. The Markeys would win the Preakness with Fabius in 1956, the same year their prize two-year-old Gen. Duke, a son of Bull Lea, beat the likes of Bold Ruler, Round Table, and Gallant Man for the juvenile championship. Gen. Duke beat Bold Ruler again in the Florida Derby, setting a Gulfstream Park record of 1:46.80 for 1⅛ miles that still stands today. Given Gen. Duke's performance, the Markeys would have been justified in thinking that Calumet had itself another Citation. In those days, the Florida Derby was run seven weeks before the Kentucky Derby, so Calumet trainer Jimmy Jones wanted to enter Gen. Duke in a prep race closer to the first Saturday in May. He decided on the Derby Trial a week before the big race, but he was concerned because the horse had suffered a foot bruise in the Florida Derby and had missed some training time. His worst fears were confirmed when Duke finished a dull second, resulting in his withdrawal from the Derby. But the talent at Calumet ran so deep that Jones merely reached back into his stable and came up with Iron Liege. Yet another son of Bull Lea, Iron Liege would win the Derby, albeit because of a fluke when one of the greatest jockeys made one of the most notorious riding errors in the history of the sport.

It can be said that the 1957 Kentucky Derby was the best in its history. The field contained three future champions: Bold Ruler, Round Table, and Gallant Man. Bad-boy jockey Bill Hartack, well known for his irascible attitude, especially toward the press, was aboard Iron Liege, whose lone victory of any value had come in the Forerunner Stakes. The great Eddie Arcaro, five-time Kentucky Derby winner, was on Bold Ruler, winner of the Flamingo and Wood Memorial; Ralph Neves was riding Blue Grass Stakes winner Round Table; and Bill Shoemaker was aboard Gallant Man, Hibiscus winner and Wood Memorial runner-up.

Federal Hill, who had defeated Gen. Duke in the Derby Trial, went to the front, tracked by the 6–5 favorite Bold Ruler. On the turn for home, those two faded as Iron Liege took a short lead into the stretch, but Shoemaker and Gallant Man were eating up ground. They had drawn alongside Iron Liege approaching the sixteenth pole, and it looked like they would swoop past when Shoemaker blundered. Mistaking the sixteenth pole (110 yards from the finish) for the finish line itself, he briefly stood up in the irons, allowing Iron Liege to take a half-length lead. Realizing his mistake, "Shoe" got back down to riding and was closing with every stride, but the line came too quickly for him. Iron Liege lasted to win by a nose in the most memorable Kentucky Derby of all. Round Table was third, and Bold Ruler was fourth.

Gene Markey's first Derby triumph during his tenure at Calumet came gift-wrapped in gold. What possessed Shoemaker to stand up in the irons? After the race, he told the stewards that Gallant Man had taken a bad step, but that simply wasn't true. The judges gave him a fifteen-day suspension, but that didn't answer the burning question: why? Here, I offer one possible explanation of a controversy that has perplexed race watchers and historians for more than sixty years.

Since making his debut at Golden Gate Fields in 1949 at age seventeen, Bill Shoemaker had been riding almost exclusively on the West Coast, primarily in Southern California, where all the tracks had short stretches. At Santa Anita and Hollywood Park, they measured slightly longer than a furlong and a half, or about 340 yards. At Del Mar, the stretch in the 1950s was well short of a furlong and a half, less than 300 yards. The stretch at Churchill Downs, however, is just short of two furlongs, or about 430 yards. Jockeys have the ability to judge the pace of a race in their heads, without reference to a stopwatch, and Shoemaker's head contained the finest timepiece of all. He was used to a seventeen- or eighteen-second interval from the top of the stretch to the finish line in California, so from habit, he may have clocked those eighteen seconds in his head, which at Churchill Downs, is the time it takes to travel from the top of the stretch to the sixteenth pole. By the time he realized his mistake, the race was lost.

The Markeys' good fortune was reversed a year later when Tim Tam was denied the Triple Crown due to a heartbreaking loss in the Belmont Stakes. Sired by Jock Whitney's champion older horse Tom Fool and out of Calumet's own champion mare Two Lea, Tim Tam had reeled off six straight stakes wins as a three-year-old, including the Flamingo Stakes and the Florida Derby, before winning the Kentucky Derby and the Preakness. He started as the 3–20 favorite in the Belmont and was ranging up alongside longtime leader Cavan as they entered the stretch. Tim Tam looked like he would run right past Cavan. Instead, he veered to the left and then to the right, fading from contention. Cavan crossed the finish line a six-length winner, with Tim Tam a brave second. It was clear something had happened at the top of the stretch. It turned out that Tim Tam had broken a sesamoid (ankle bone) in his right foreleg. It was a miracle he even crossed the finish line, much less in second place.

It would be ten years before Calumet won another Kentucky Derby, but that one came with an asterisk attached. Forward Pass was Calumet's 2–1 favorite in the 1968 Derby, and he crossed the finish line second, one and a half lengths behind the 7–2 second choice Dancer's Image. Subsequently, a routine urinalysis detected the painkiller butazolidin, which was illegal in Kentucky at the time, resulting in the disqualification of Dancer's Image. The drug had been legally administered six days earlier to relieve pain in the horse's joints, and his handlers thought all traces of it would have dissipated by race day. Owner Peter Fuller contested the decision in a case that lasted four years, but he was ultimately unsuccessful. Beating Calumet Farm in Kentucky was never an easy thing to do.

When Forward Pass beat Dancer's Image by six lengths in the Preakness Stakes, the Markeys had reason to feel vindicated, but there was a growing fear nationwide that a possible Triple Crown for the Calumet color-bearer would be tainted by the Derby drug affair. Leave it to Jock Whitney to come to the rescue in the Belmont Stakes. Having sat out both the Kentucky Derby and the Preakness, Stage Door Johnny came from far back to defeat the front-running Forward Pass by a length. Jock then turned to his Greentree co-owner, sister Joan, who also owned the New York Mets, and quipped, "Well, your team lost today so we had to win something!"[11]

Calumet in Decline

Throughout the 1950s Gene Markey kept in touch with the Hollywood scene but was never really a part of it. He was a horseman now and devoted almost all his energies to assisting Lucille in the running of Calumet Farm. He built a nineteenth-century-style log cabin on the Calumet estate, where he and Lucille treated their dear friend Aly Khan to a taste of rustic charm reminiscent of the pre–Civil War South. Gene also wrote several historical novels set in his beloved adopted home state.

Kentucky Pride (1956), *Until the Morning* (1957), and *That Far Paradise* (1960) were hardly best sellers, but they made him feel connected to his new surroundings. "I cannot restrain my ardor for the place and its people," he said. "No duck ever took to water as I have taken to Kentucky."[12]

Gene had two more brief tilts at Hollywood. In 1951 Douglas Sirk adapted one of his earlier novels, *The Great Companions,* into the film *Meet Me at the Fair* for Universal. In 1955 he reunited with director David Butler, with whom he had collaborated sixteen years earlier on *Kentucky,* to make *Glory.* Decidedly not glorious, the screenplay for this racing film was penned by Markey, who invited RKO's production team to Calumet Farm to film background shots. *Glory* was an unsuccessful effort to turn nineteen-year-old Margaret O'Brien into an adult star, and its cast included three-time Oscar winner Walter Brennan and the inimitable Charlotte Greenwood. The sentimental story of an unpromising filly that wins the Kentucky Derby was old-fashioned even by mid-1950s standards. The film was so weak that the *New York Times* didn't even bother to review it.

With that effort, Markey and Hollywood parted ways professionally, although there remained a social connection. In particular, Gene kept in touch with notorious gossip columnist Hedda Hopper. They had met on the set of one of his most successful screenwriting efforts, the 1932 Greta Garbo film *As You Desire Me,* in which Hedda was cast as a flapper (a role at which she excelled in her acting days). Gene and Hedda remained friendly, even after his departure from Hollywood, and maintained a regular correspondence. In early May 1958 Gene sent her a print of an Arabian stallion, to which she replied on May 14:

My dear Gene:
What a doll you are! Loved the picture; so will Bill [her husband]. Sorry not to have seen Lucille on TV, but happy her horse [Tim Tam] won at the Kentucky Derby. I am sorry to hear that she is selling her Bel Air home. What a pity! Now we will never see you people. Hope she is in the pink again; we can't afford to have her feeling under the weather. I may catch you at the Ritz in Paris. They want me to come over and cover some pictures that are shooting in Europe. Thank you again for the picture and love to you both.
Yours,

Hedda[13]

On December 8 Hedda sent the Markeys this Christmas missive:

My dear Lucille and Gene:
I hear, Lucille, that you haven't been well, which disturbs me no
end. Maybe, your French chef is too good or maybe it is because
of the fact you have chosen to live in Kentucky instead of in
smog-filled Bel Air. I was horrified to learn that you had sold
your Bel Air home. Although we didn't see too much of you two
people here, yet we had the knowledge you were handy, and we
could run around the corner to visit with you, when we felt
we couldn't bear the burden of life any longer. It is mighty dull
here; there is no news except that the picture business is going to
Hell on a broomstick. I will be taking off on the 17th of the month
with Bob Hope; this will be my fourth Christmas tour with him
to entertain our Armed Forces. Hope you will have a glorious
Christmas—we shall miss you. My devotion always—
Yours,

Hedda Hopper[14]

Clearly, Hedda was still enthralled by the Markey charm, enhanced by
two Kentucky Derby victories. Just as clearly, Hedda was no longer
enthralled by Hollywood. The studio system was crumbling before her
eyes, and television had cut deeply into the picture business.

On June 28, 1960, Gene shared his sorrow over the death of their
friend Aly Khan six weeks earlier:

Dear Hedda,
Thank you for sending us the wonderful piece you wrote about Aly
Khan. What a fine tribute that was. Naturally we were shocked and
saddened by his death, which occurred while we were in mid
ocean—and on our way to the English Derby and afterwards to
stay with him at Ascot. The effect on his many friends here—and
on the whole racing world—has been incredible. Yesterday, at
Longchamp, watching his great horse Charlottesville win the Grand
Prix [de Paris] so easily gave us a thrill which was immediately followed by sadness. Lucille had tears in her eyes and so did several of
the ladies around us. Are you coming over this Summer? The Ritz
is a sort of permanent address for us; they will forward mail after

we leave this week. But we will be back here again in September.
Love from us both,

Gene Markey[15]

The death of Aly Khan in an automobile accident had sent shock waves through the racing world, the film world, and the jet-setting world, not to mention the Islamic world. Although wearing the colors of the new Aga Khan, Charlottesville was widely regarded as Aly's horse. In winning the 1⅞-mile Grand Prix de Paris, the premiere event on the French racing calendar, Charlottesville was following up on a victory in the Prix du Jockey Club (aka the French Derby). The emotion the Markeys felt that day makes it plain why they named their last great horse Alydar (short for "Aly darling").

By June 1964, the Markeys had still not recovered from the death of Aly Khan. As Lucille described in a letter to Hedda: "We will not be going to Ascot—the roses in London have lost their charm for us since Aly has gone—we always went with him and had such fun!"[16] This was a late response to Hedda's letter to Lucille dated January 28, 1964:

My darling Lucille:
I loved your Christmas card. I always save yours because it reminds me of other and better years, when we had so much fun. Now so much has gone out of our lives. I suppose you feel the same wherever you are, but then you have Gene. I am invited to attend the Ascot races in England. I wonder if you and Gene will be among those present. I know you won't be racing your horses, nor be at Santa Anita, but I remember with such joy the time you so kindly dragged me along with you as your country cousin. I never had such fun in my life. I miss you two people terribly and if you are going to be at the Ascot races, I want to tell you I am getting a ticket to the Royal Enclosure. I would (love) to see you.
Love to you both always—
Yours,

Hedda Hopper[17]

Throughout the late 1950s and 1960s, the Markeys were full-fledged members of racing's international jet set. Every important race meeting was on their annual agenda: Churchill Downs for the Kentucky Derby,

Epsom for the English Derby, Chantilly for the French Derby, Royal Ascot, the Grand Prix de Paris, and Saratoga. In fact, the Markeys were spending less and less time in Lexington, and their absence—some might call it neglect—began to affect the bottom line. Between the Derby victories of Tim Tam in 1958 and Forward Pass in 1968, the pickings were slim. After 1968, they began to disappear. The proprietors' age and absence were having an adverse effect on the quality of Calumet's Thoroughbreds. In 1976 Calumet horses earned just $87,725 at the track, against expenses of nearly $2 million. Reliance on charm and social connections can take one only so far, and it was leading the Markeys to ruin.

That year, Lucille Markey hired a young man named John Veitch as Calumet's trainer, a move that turned out to be something of a miracle. Veitch hailed from a racing family; his father, Syl Veitch, had trained five American champions, including 1951 Horse of the Year Counterpoint. Although his first year at Calumet was a disaster, Veitch soon had Calumet clicking on all cylinders. In his second year he turned Our Mims from a winless juvenile into the champion three-year-old filly who won the Coaching Club American Oaks and the Alabama Stakes, the distaff equivalent of winning the Belmont and the Travers Stakes. Our Mims's revitalization must have been especially pleasing to Gene, as the filly was named after his daughter Melinda (affectionately known as Mims) with Joan Bennett. And make no mistake, the "Our" in the filly's name was a direct reference to Gene and Joan, or at least his fond memories of being married to her.

Calumet Farm had continued to breed and race its own horses, taking little interest in the booming bloodstock market as either seller or buyer. The breeding of first-class racehorses requires patience and expertise, and it was becoming a lost art in America, but the Markeys continued the tradition. In the late 1970s they were rewarded twice with a pair of homebreds of the highest quality: champion three-year-old filly Davona Dale and the ill-fated Alydar, who would take center stage in the sorry saga of the long, slow decline of Thoroughbred racing in America.

Out of a mare by Calumet's 1958 Kentucky Derby winner Tim Tam, Davona Dale went on a springtime tear, winning four major Grade 1 stakes races in 1979: the Kentucky Oaks at 1⅛ miles, the Acorn Stakes at 1 mile, the Mother Goose Stakes at 1⅛ miles, and the Coaching Club American Oaks at 1½ miles. Tough and versatile, she was a testament to the type of horse being bred in the United States in the 1970s, a decade that marked the last great flowering of the American Thoroughbred. But as good as she was—and she was very, very good—Davona Dale wasn't in the same league as Alydar.

Affirmed versus Alydar

Alydar—by Raise a Native out of a mare by On and On, the stallion that had sired Calumet's 1968 Kentucky Derby winner Forward Pass—had the misfortune of being born the same year as Affirmed, his nemesis, his chastener, and the West Coast rival that barred his path to championship glory. As two-year-olds, they met six times. Affirmed won four of the six races, but Alydar took the most important of them, the 1-mile Champagne Stakes at Belmont Park. Still, Affirmed walked off with juvenile championship honors in 1977.

Affirmed and Alydar would not meet again until the Kentucky Derby, in which Alydar was sent off as the 6–5 favorite, with Affirmed the 9–5 second choice. But the betting public got it wrong, and Affirmed won by a length and a half. Two weeks later in the Preakness, Alydar got to within a half length of Affirmed at the quarter pole but was still a neck behind at the finish. Three weeks after that, Affirmed went for the Triple Crown, and Alydar was the only horse in the field at Belmont that had a chance of stopping him. Only five horses lined up for the 1½-mile contest. Affirmed was the 3–5 favorite, and Alydar was the second choice at 6–5. As usual, Steve Cauthen was aboard Affirmed, and Jorge Velasquez was on Alydar.

Affirmed took the lead almost immediately, but Velasquez boldly moved Alydar from third place to within a length after three furlongs. At the halfway mark, Alydar threw down the gauntlet and moved up alongside his rival. From there to the finish, they raced as a team, with Affirmed's narrow lead ranging back and forth from a nose to a neck and back to a nose. Through the stretch, with the crowd in a frenzy, Affirmed simply would not allow Alydar to pass him, and Affirmed prevailed by that same little nostril.

In the final analysis, Alydar had proved himself to be a great horse, but Affirmed was both indomitable and great. In the Travers Stakes at Saratoga that August, Alydar would gain a measure of revenge, but it came with a Forward Pass–like asterisk attached. Affirmed once again crossed the line in front, one and three-quarters lengths ahead of Alydar, but the order of finish was subsequently reversed. On the far turn, with

Affirmed in the lead, his replacement rider Laffit Pincay had angled him over to the rail just as Velasquez was bringing Alydar to challenge on the inside. Alydar had been sawed off, forcing Velasquez to stand up in the irons and check his mount. The judges had no choice but to disqualify Affirmed.

The Travers was the last meeting between Affirmed and Alydar. The, final score: Affirmed 7, Alydar 3. At stud, Alydar would sire champion Easy Goer and Kentucky Derby winners Alysheba and Strike the Gold, his stud fee rising to $250,000 in 1990. And therein lies a tale of a different color.

The End of Calumet Farm

At the time Alydar was establishing himself as the greatest horse never to win a Triple Crown race, Gene was eighty-three and Lucille was eighty-two. For a long time they had left the day-to-day running of Calumet Farm to the farm managers and trainers and their staffs. They had, in effect, become figureheads, symbols of a once gracious and glorious past that was fading fast, along with the rest of the Kentucky breeding empire. They could be self-effacing about their situation. In 1976, Calumet's nadir year, they sent a Christmas card showing themselves seated at their main gate selling lemonade for 5 cents a glass behind a stand draped with a sign reading "CALUMET MUST SURVIVE." Behind them in the photo (which was headlined "Merry Christmas, Lucille and Gene") was Charles Rankin, their black butler, holding an umbrella over their heads so the "master" and his missus wouldn't catch sunstroke.

The Markeys' plantation mentality of the antebellum South was also evident one day at Keeneland, when they came to see Alydar run in his Kentucky Derby prep, the Blue Grass Stakes. Gene and Lucille were both in wheelchairs by then, Lucille permanently. Gene had been diagnosed with colon cancer, and Lucille was constantly in and out of the hospital. They had received permission for their chauffeur to drive onto the track apron in front of the grandstand, giving them a close, unimpeded view of the race. On his way to the start, jockey Jorge Velasquez saw their car, removed Alydar from the post parade, and walked him over to where Gene had managed to hobble to the rail. The old man smiled beatifically as Velasquez paraded Alydar back and forth for the Markeys. "Bless you, boy, bless you boy, thank you very much, Jorge!" called Gene to the thirty-two-year-old Panamanian who had been one of America's leading jockeys for the past ten years.[18]

After their deaths—Gene's on May 1, 1980, and Lucille's on July 24, 1982—Calumet passed into the hands of Lucille's son-in-law John T. Lundy, husband of her daughter Cindy. Cindy cared nothing for the family business, and Lundy systematically drove Calumet into the ground, using fouler and fouler means with each passing year. The failure of the farm that had been the most important and successful breeding ground in the world for nearly forty years, an exemplar of how to run a Thoroughbred stable, was the first visible evidence that something was rotten in the state of Kentucky. Other examples would soon emerge.

The decline of American racing and the simultaneous decline of the American film industry were unconnected. However, the reasons behind their decline sprang from the same tainted font. Since 1980, racing and cinema, once inseparable, have grown farther apart as new modes of entertainment, new art forms, new technologies, and new social mores have eroded their once seemingly impregnable foundations.

12

The Post Golden Age
In Search of Seabiscuit

You can go out and make book on this: as the movie crowd learns that
owning race horses is an expensive luxury, you will find more and
more of the movie celebs withdrawing from active interest in the turf.
Ed Sullivan

The Decline and Fall of Horse Racing in America

Ed Sullivan's prediction came true during the 1950s, by which time people like Bing Crosby, Louis B. Mayer, and Barbara Stanwyck had largely
divested themselves of their racing stock. On the whole, however,
Hollywood's love affair with the horses continued, followed by a long,
slow decline in interest over the next four decades.

Some Hollywood stars continued to have sporadic success at the races.
Greer Garson and her husband, Texas oilman Buddy Fogelson, formed
Forked Lightning Ranch in New Mexico. In 1971 they purchased the out-
standing five-year-old Ack Ack from the estate of Harry F. Guggenheim of
Cain Hoy Stable and oversaw his championship season as Horse of the
Year. That year, Ack Ack won six stakes races, including California's two
most prestigious events—the Santa Anita Handicap and the Hollywood
Gold Cup. The luminous star of *Mrs. Miniver* (Louis B. Mayer once com-
pared her to his champion horse Busher—a classy filly who takes orders
and comes home with blue ribbons), knew a good thing when she saw one.
"Ack Ack has changed our life and our marriage," she said at the Waldorf-
Astoria Winner's Circle Dinner in January 1972. "I stand in awe of him.
He's a miracle of strength and determination. He's proud and tempera-
mental and awesome. I think this horse would die to win a race."[1]

The Fogelson-Garson purchase of Ack Ack spotlighted one of the key
reasons for the decline of horse racing in America. The death of
Guggenheim had put an end to Cain Hoy Stable, which had produced the

great horses Bald Eagle and Never Bend. And therein lies the tale, for it was during the 1970s that many of America's leading families—the Guggenheims, the Whitneys, the Vanderbilts, and the Markeys—saw their Thoroughbred empires unravel.

Ironically, that happened during the same decade of horse racing's artistic peak. After twenty-five years without a Triple Crown winner, Secretariat reinvigorated the sport in 1973, landing the Crown with his astonishing thirty-one-length victory in the Belmont Stakes. Five years later, Seattle Slew followed suit, and a year after that, Affirmed made it three Triple Crown winners in one memorable decade. But the seeds of decline were already being sown in the American Thoroughbred soil.

Meanwhile, Hollywood's involvement in the sport, especially at the top end, was growing thinner and thinner. One stalwart who never abandoned the game was Mervyn LeRoy—producer of *The Wizard of Oz;* director of *Little Caesar, I Am a Fugitive from a Chain Gang,* and *Gold Diggers of 1933;* and both producer and director of *The Bad Seed* and *Gypsy,* LeRoy was a devoted horseman and racetrack administrator to the end of his days. He teamed with his father-in-law, Harry Warner, to form W-L Ranch, and he was on Hollywood Park's board of directors from 1941 until his death in 1987. He served as president of the track from 1955 to 1985. In 1962, during his tenure, Hollywood Park became the first track to open its doors for morning training sessions, where the public was invited to watch and have breakfast. LeRoy always maintained that "horsemanship is showmanship. The track is a stage, the horses are the star performers."[2]

LeRoy certainly knew his stuff. He is credited with discovering Clark Gable, turning Edward G. Robinson into a star in *Little Caesar,* and having the perspicacity to select Judy Garland over Shirley Temple for the lead in *The Wizard of Oz.* As early as 1970, he could see the rot setting in in Hollywood. "Our business today—this is going to give you a shock when you hear it—has too many people with bad taste. I don't mean the studio heads, I mean filmmakers."[3]

Jack Klugman, who played Oscar Madison on the long-running ABC television series *The Odd Couple* (a character he resembled in a number of ways), parlayed his love of horse racing into a near Kentucky Derby triumph when his horse Jaklin Klugman (a colt, despite the feminine name) finished third to filly Genuine Risk in 1980. Burt Bacharach, who perfected the art of the pop song as Muzak with treacly hits such as "Raindrops Keep Falling on My Head," owned multiple 1995 stakes winner Afternoon

219

Deelites, sire of Popcorn Deelites, a sprinter whose main claim to fame was that he was one of six horses to portray Seabiscuit in the 2003 film of the same name. More recently, television talk-show host Merv Griffin achieved some success on the track. His two-year-old colt Steviewonderboy won the Del Mar Futurity and the Breeders' Cup Juvenile in 2005, raising hopes that he would be a Triple Crown contender the following year. Unfortunately, a hairline fracture early in his three-year-old season forced his retirement.

The rise and rather quick fall of Jaklin Klugman in 1980 represented a turning point in the twin declines of racing and cinema in America. Although the Golden Age of American cinema was nearly twenty years past by then, the racing world was still turning out Thoroughbreds of the highest quality, both in America and in Europe. Ironically, it was European and Arab interest in the Kentucky Thoroughbred that laid the groundwork for the decline of American racing.

The European and Arab Invasion

The Kentucky Thoroughbred industry—indeed, the entire American nation—seemed to be unaware that western Europe had fully recovered from World War II by 1980. Britain, France, West Germany, and even tiny Ireland were all back on their feet economically, thanks largely to the Marshall Plan and the American economic powerhouse on which much of the rest of the world depended. For decades before 1980, American horsemen had plucked from some of the better British and French bloodlines, and by the mid-1950s, the United States was the world's most prominent racing nation. In the late 1970s, however, European horsemen, backed by prosperous businessmen, and horse-loving, oil-rich Arab potentates turned their sights on the select yearling sales at Keeneland and Saratoga.

Irishman Vincent O'Brien, arguably the greatest Thoroughbred trainer in the history of the sport, had determined that Northern Dancer, the Canadian-bred winner of the Kentucky Derby and Belmont Stakes in 1964, would become the most influential stallion of his era. Indeed, Northern Dancer, a son of Nearctic out of the Native Dancer mare Natalma, was one of the toughest horses of the second half of the twentieth century. O'Brien liked to point out that the Dancer had raced nine times as a two-year-old before his championship three-year-old season.

He was a combination of toughness and class that could replenish the European Thoroughbred industry, which had suffered at the hands of wealthy American horsemen since the end of the First World War.

O'Brien teamed with Englishman Robert Sangster, who had made a fortune running the Vernon football pools but was now completely devoted to horse racing. They traveled to Keeneland and engaged in a monumental bidding war with the three Maktoum brothers of Dubai: eldest brother Maktoum, the ruler of Dubai; second brother Hamdan, the emirate's finance minister, and defense minister Mohammed, the most charismatic of the three and the one keenest about racing. They were formidable opponents for the O'Brien-Sangster team. The Maktoums never bid against one another, but they were happy to bid against Sangster, Saudi prince Khalid Abdullah, and any Americans whose pockets were as bottomless as theirs. Sangster and the Maktoums, however, usually got the horses they wanted.

Rich as they were, American breeders had never seen such prices being offered for their yearlings. In 1982 Sangster paid $4.25 million for a colt by Northern Dancer's son Nijinsky. Three years later, Sheikh Mohammed dished out $7.1 million for a Northern Dancer colt. In the early 1980s dozens of yearlings sold for more than $1 million at Keeneland and Saratoga, most of them winding up at O'Brien's Ballymany Farm in Ireland or with British trainers employed by the brothers Maktoum. Many others were dispersed around England, Ireland, and France, bought by other enterprising Europeans who had latched on to the American good thing.

For a few years, the Maktoum versus Sangster bidding war was conducted at lunatic proportions. The winning bidder often paid millions more than any horse, especially a yearling, could ever be worth, so in 1983 they got wise. The Maktoums called Sangster and O'Brien to Dubai for a meeting, where they all agreed that the brothers would not bid against Sangster for prize American yearlings. Whether this was ethical is not the point. This scheme led to a precipitous drop in yearling prices that, combined with a decline in the market in general, caused the American yearling market to collapse. That collapse, coupled with over-spending by American breeders (who had never seen money like the Arabs were throwing around), led to the bankruptcy of many Kentucky breeding establishments. They were forced to vacate their long-held family properties and turn them over to the very people who had been buying their best yearlings by the hundreds and sending them back to Europe: Darley Stud, owned by Sheikh Mohammed; Shadwell Farm, owned by Sheikh Hamdan; Gainsborough Stud, owned by Sheikh Maktoum; and Juddmonte Farms, owned by Khalid Abdullah. For a century, these great swaths of prime Kentucky real estate had been producing racehorses exclusively for American racing. They were now controlled by Arabs, who sent most of their horses to Europe to race.

The effect on American racing was quietly devastating. The Arabs (and their British agents) and Europeans like Sangster were knowledge-able horsemen who were picking clean some of the best American blood-lines, not merely the Northern Dancer–Nijinsky line but the Mr. Prospector and Raise a Native lines as well. The Maktoums and the Europeans contin-ued to raid Keeneland and Saratoga through the 1990s, collecting what remained of what had once been the preeminent bloodstock market in the world.

The proof is in the pudding. From 1980 through 1986 American-bred horses won the prestigious Epsom Derby five times: Henbit (1980), Golden Fleece (1982), Teenoso (1983), Secreto (1984), and Shahrastani (1986). That period coincided with the beginning of a dry spell that would see no American Triple Crown winners from 1980 through 2014. Many factors can be cited for that lapse, but the simple fact is that Europeans and Arabs had taken control of the international bloodstock market.

In the meantime, American owners showed no interest in participat-ing in the leading European yearling sales at Tattersalls in Newmarket, England; Goffs in County Kildare, Ireland; and Agence Francaise in Deauville, France. So, for the last fifty years, the traffic in high-class Thoroughbred yearlings has been strictly one way: America to Europe. And more recently, Japanese owners have entered the market. In 2017 they spent more than $20 million to buy sixty-seven American-bred yearlings at the prestigious Keeneland September sale.

Racing Says No to Television

There was a corresponding decline in interest in American horse racing that can be traced back to 1960. That was when the three American televi-sion networks—ABC, NBC, and CBS—made a pitch to all the major sports to put more of their events on TV. Baseball, which was already prominent on the airwaves, agreed wholeheartedly, as did football and basketball. At the time, professional football and basketball couldn't hold a candle to either baseball or horse racing. The NFL and the NBA were minor league operations compared to major league baseball, and their commissioners, particularly Pete Rozelle of the NFL, jumped at the opportunity to enter the wide-open TV market for professional sports.

Golf, tennis, and automobile racing also took advantage of television's interest. Programs like ABC's *Wide World of Sports* became overnight sensations featuring track and field, figure skating, skiing, swimming, and gymnastics. On the horse racing front, however, there was little interest. Major races such as the Kentucky Derby, Preakness Stakes, and Belmont Stakes were already televised nationally, while key media markets like New York usually had a Saturday afternoon program televising the feature race at a local track. But the lords of racing disdained TV's offer of regularly televised horse races nationwide. They were afraid that putting the races on TV would cut into attendance at the tracks, but in that judgment, they were decidedly wrong. Television would have whet fans' appetite for racing, and they might have flocked to their local tracks to see what the real thing was all about. Instead, football and basketball won throngs of new fans, at horse racing's expense. The people who have been running racetracks since 1980 failed to understand that racegoers are sports fans first and bettors second, that horse racing competes with baseball, football, and basketball just as much as it competes with casinos, lotteries, and sports betting. As a result, they succeeded in alienating the typical American sports fan.

Yet racing was still very popular during the 1960s, and there was little, if any, decline in racetrack attendance through the 1970s. Midsummer crowds at Belmont Park routinely reached 30,000 on weekends and 12,000 on weekdays through 1980. But by then, the racing crowd was aging, and younger fans gravitated to other sports. Declines in track attendance and handle continue to this day, claiming the lives of a number of once-profitable racetracks, including Rockingham Park; Garden State Park, which hosted the greatest three-runner race in history when Bold Ruler defeated Gallant Man and Round Table in the 1958 Trenton Handicap; Hialeah Park, arguably the most beautiful racetrack in America; Washington Park, site of the great match between Swaps and Nashua; and, most distressing of all, Hollywood Park, the racetrack most closely connected to the filmmaking community. Hollywood Park's demise serves as a signpost of the health, or lack thereof, of both the racing and the film industries in this country.

Table 3. American Racetrack Closures since 1972

Track	State	Year Closed
Tropical Park	Florida	1972
Washington Park	Illinois	1977
Narragansett Park	Rhode Island	1978
Commodore Downs	Pennsylvania	1983
Bowie	Maryland	1985
Longacres	Washington	1992
Ak-Sar-Ben	Nebraska	1995
Atokad	South Dakota	1997
Detroit Race Course	Michigan	1998
Yakima Meadows	Washington	1998
Playfair	Washington	2000
Garden State Park	New Jersey	2001
Hialeah Park	Florida	2001
Sportsman's Park	Illinois	2003
Bay Meadows	California	2008
Hollywood Park	California	2013
Beulah Park	Ohio	2014
Colonial Downs	Virginia	2014
Suffolk Downs	Massachusetts	2014
Atlantic City	New Jersey	2015
Rockingham Park	New Hampshire	2016
Portland Meadows	Oregon	2019

Many tracks are hanging on by a thread. For instance, the Meadowlands in New Jersey has just six days of turf racing per year in September. Others, like all the tracks run by the once mighty New York Racing Association (Aqueduct, Belmont, and Saratoga), keep their heads above water only through the revenue derived from casinos attached to their grandstands.

Calumet Tanks

And then there was the collapse of Calumet Farm. The long, slow decline of America's most prestigious Thoroughbred establishment was accelerated by the deaths of Gene and Lucille Markey in 1980 and 1982, respectively. Upon Mrs. Markey's death, the farm passed into the oily hands of her son-in-law John T. Lundy, an ambitious Kentucky hardboot who had married Mrs. Markey's eldest child, Lucinda. Cindy, as she was called, had never shown any interest in horse racing, while her younger brother, Warren Jr., had fallen out with his mother and distanced himself from the family's racing interests altogether. Thus Calumet Farm became the plaything of a man who knew how to play the racing game only one way: crooked.

Calumet was already facing the misfortunes of a changing international age, and Lundy was all at sea from the start. To keep the farm's head above water, he tried every trick in the book, many of them illegal. The one bright light in Calumet's long, dark night was Alydar, whose stud fee reached $250,000 after he sired Kentucky Derby winners Alysheba and Strike the Gold, Belmont Stakes winner Easy Goer, and champion filly Althea and had become the broodmare sire of Prix de l'Arc de Triomphe winner Peintre Celebre and two-time Breeders' Cup Mile winner Lure. He was also the sire of Calumet's last notable horse, the aptly named Criminal Type. A son of the No Robbery mare Klepto, Criminal Type would be named champion American racehorse in the fateful year of 1990.

On November 13 of that year, stable hands at Calumet discovered Alydar's right hind leg smashed to bits, his life hanging by a thread. Lundy claimed that the horse had kicked the wall of his stable and broken his leg in the process, but no one who had ever worked for Calumet, from trainer John Veitch down to the most inexperienced groom, had ever seen Alydar kick in his stall. Lundy's explanation of Alydar's injury stank to high heaven. Dr. Robert Bramlage performed surgery on the injured leg, but it broke again, and Alydar was put down on November 15.

After Alydar's death, Calumet collected $50 million in insurance from Lloyd's of London. The farm had been bleeding money for nearly a decade, thanks in large part to Lundy's profligate spending. The new infusion of cash did him little good. He continued to spend unwisely, falling into murkier and murkier schemes. He finally sold Calumet to Polish-Canadian horseman Henryk de Kwiatkowski in 1992, but Calumet never recovered. In 2000 Lundy was sentenced to four and a half years in prison for fraud, conspiracy, and bribery, having bilked the First City National Bank of Houston out of $65 million. Did Lundy order the killing of Alydar to collect the insurance money? No one will ever know for sure.

Calumet's demise was only the most visible failure among America's great racing families. The Whitney, Vanderbilt, and Guggenheim empires had already disappeared, victims of their failure to find heirs willing to carry on their breeding and racing operations in the new, more commercial age dominated by Arab and European interests. Most new American Thoroughbred owners over the last twenty-five years, members of the nation's burgeoning nouveau riche, play the Thoroughbred game the way they play the stock market. Expecting a quick return on investment, and lacking the patience required to breed horses for racing, they have produced an overwhelmingly high percentage of horses that are bred for speed, precocity, or both. These horses can hardly stay a mile, and because of their inbred precocity, they are often useless after the springtime of their three-year-old seasons, sometimes even earlier.

Kentucky farms like Calumet and Greentree have been replaced by Darley, Shadwell, Juddmonte, and John Magnier's Coolmore Stud. Most of the horses bred by these new foreign owners in Kentucky are being sent to Europe; the same foreign interests have pillaged the best American bloodlines and decimated the American breed. American horse racing has been mismanaged, failing to attract new blood into the grandstands. To all this must be added the pernicious influence of race-day medication.

The American Thoroughbred as Junkie

In the mid-1970s American racing jurisdictions from coast to coast decided that the use of Lasix (trade name for the diuretic furosemide) would be an aid to racing, in that it helped prevent internal bleeding during races. Maryland was the first to legalize use of the drug in 1973. By 1975, thirteen states allowed its use on race day. More states followed during the next decade, and in 1986 New York finally caved and became the last racing state to allow its use.

Although Lasix does prevent internal bleeding, it also acts as a performance enhancer, giving horses a boost and allowing them to run beyond their natural ability. At first, proof of internal bleeding during a race was required before Lasix could be administered on race day, but as time passed, that requirement no longer applied; it could be obtained simply by asking for it. After administration of the drug, horses excrete ten to fifteen liters of urine, dehydrating them and thus preventing internal bleeding. However, sensible horsemen believe that the long-term effects of Lasix are deleterious; horses take longer to recover after each dose of Lasix, putting their health at risk and necessitating longer intervals between races. The stated intention of using Lasix was to enable horses to run *more* frequently, but since 1985, the average number of races run by horses in America has dropped from thirteen a year to seven. Lasix is one of the primary reasons for the decrease. Moreover, Lasix can serve as a mask for other illegal drugs. The most notorious of these is the "milk-shake," a concoction of illicit medications meant to soup up a horse well beyond its natural ability.

American trainers who use Lasix claim that it is necessary, given the nature of American racing, but this is simply not true. Administering Lasix on race day is illegal throughout Europe, Asia, Africa, Australia, and New Zealand. Interestingly, there has been no decline in the quality of the sport in any of those places, while American trainers hide behind a haze of drugs that are systematically destroying the American Thoroughbred.

Lasix is not the only drug allowed in the United States but banned in most of the rest of the world. Painkillers like butazolidin are legal in California, as are other similar drugs in various states. Their administration before a race allows horses with leg injuries to run through their pain, without doing anything to treat the cause of that pain. Sometimes the strain on an injured leg—to which a horse treated with a painkiller is oblivious—becomes so great that the horse breaks down midrace. The number of such breakdowns in America far exceeds those in the rest of the world.

Back in the 1970s, a veterinarian was called in to examine a horse only when the animal was sick or injured. For more than thirty years now, vets have been examining horses every time they are entered in a race, and that number is enormous. At least 95 percent of all American Thoroughbreds race on Lasix, a drug on which horse racing in America has become dependent. The use of this and other drugs has led many American racing fans to abandon horse racing, as they question the integrity of the sport. Given this widespread drug use, questionable breeding practices, lack of foreign imports, and poor marketing of the sport, it is not surprising that horse racing has fallen off this country's sporting agenda. The people in charge of the game in America—the Jockey Club, the Thoroughbred Owners and Breeders Association, Breeders' Cup Ltd., the New York Racing Association, Churchill Downs Inc., and the Stronach Group, among others—are not merely oblivious to the problems facing horse racing; they are the perpetrators and enablers of the sport's steep decline.

English trainer John Gosden put American racing in perspective when he explained why he declined to attend Keeneland's September yearling sale in 2017. During the first ten years of his career (1979–1988), Gosden trained Bates Motel to win the Santa Anita Handicap and Royal Heroine to take the first Breeders' Cup Mile. After returning to his home-land in 1989, he won numerous stakes races in Britain, France, Ireland, Germany, Italy, and the United Arab Emirates, among them two Epsom Derbies and three Prix de l'Arc de Triomphes. Surveying the American racing scene in June 2018, Gosden said: "American horses used to be a lot tougher 30 or 40 years ago than they are now. The influence of medication has covered up a lot of the weaknesses in horses. Most of them go to stud and you're never quite sure what they were racing on."[4]

Many American horsemen, inured to the decades-long practice of race-day medication, argue that the practice is acceptable, but outside of North America, that is decidedly a minority opinion. The Water, Hay, and Oats Alliance (WHOA), a Lexington, Kentucky–based group, is devoted to the elimination of race-day medication in the United States. Its mem-bership includes some of the leading horsemen and women from around the world. In announcing her membership in WHOA in October 2018, Amanda Elliott, chair of the prestigious Victoria Racing Club in Australia, captured the foreign attitude toward drugs in horse racing. "There is no world-class sport anywhere that allows doping or performance enhanc-ing drugs—it is absolutely fundamental," she said. "What is the U.S. miss-ing that the rest of the world has fully understood for quite some time? This world stage of racing, with uniform international standards, should have America at the forefront, not isolated at a time when global rele-vance is so important."[5] Her words, unfortunately, remain unheeded in the highest echelons of the American racing industry.

Outside of big events like the Triple Crown races and the Breeders' Cup, attending the races has become an almost antisocial occasion, exactly the opposite of what a day at the races should be. Most racetrack attendees nowadays are hard-core gamblers—aging men with their heads stuck in racing work stations in darkened rooms where they can bet on almost any race in the country without ever seeing a live horse or engag-ing a fellow racegoer in conversation. And with the advent of the World Wide Web has come website wagering, allowing people to bet using their laptops without ever leaving their homes. Americans have little interest in the game beyond gambling, and very few of these gamblers show any inclination to become owners, trainers, racetrack administrators, or racing writers. Is it any wonder that Hollywood, like the rest of the nation, has abandoned the sport?

The Decline and Fall of American Film

The number of racing films produced in Hollywood declined in the 1950s, and the genre dried up entirely shortly thereafter. Television had been cutting into film attendance, and by 1960, when TV was seeking to broadcast more sports events, Hollywood was tightening its belt. Racing films were one of the first genres to go. During the turbulent 1960s there were only a handful of them, and ironically, the two best were made for television: "The Horseplayer" on *Alfred Hitchcock Presents,* directed by Hitchcock himself; and "The Last Night of a Jockey," an installment of *The Twilight Zone* written by Rod Serling as a one-man show for Mickey Rooney. By contrast, at least sixty racing-themed films had been produced during the 1930s, when the openings of Santa Anita, Del Mar, and Hollywood Park sparked Tinseltown's interest in all things Thoroughbred. The war-ravaged 1940s saw that number drop to barely forty, while the 1950s—the first television decade—yielded no more than twenty racing films. The approximately 120 racing-themed pictures made over that thirty-year Golden Age represent an average of four per year—or about as many made in each decade since the 1950s.

Laura Hillenbrand's 2001 best-selling book *Seabiscuit: An American Legend* spurred a PBS production of *The American Experience* two years later. It was also made into a successful 2003 film by Gary Ross. Although completely up-to-date technically, the film is otherwise a typical 1930s racing movie in which the hopeless underdog overcomes all obstacles to save the day. Whereas movies like *Broadway Bill* and *A Day at the Races* restricted the salvage job to the local farm or the Broadway show, *Seabiscuit* laid claim to redeeming America's depression-laden spirit. It did well at the box office, grossing $148 million, and was nominated for seven Academy Awards but went home empty-handed. Ultimately, the film is an exercise in high-gloss nostalgia, presenting a misty-eyed view of racing as a sport that could capture the imagination of an entire nation.

Seabiscuit's Oscar nominations may have prompted the Disney Studio to try its hand with a biopic about the great Secretariat seven years later. *Secretariat*, which tells the story of the 1973 exploits of the first Triple

Crown winner in twenty-five years, turned a handsome profit but is loaded with factual errors. In attempting to add contemporary dramatic impact, the film portrays Secretariat's owner Penny Chenery as a feminist icon, which she was not, and it depicts Secretariat himself as a hippie idol, which was untrue. Young people with long hair were present at his races, but the horse was hardly the darling of the Grateful Dead set. Even worse, the film paints Frank "Pancho" Martin, the trainer of Secretariat's archrival Sham, as an arrogant boor who was continually disparaging the equine champion. In reality, Martin was a perfect gentleman who fully appreciated Secretariat's greatness. The movie unravels with its depiction of Secretariat's thirty-one-length Belmont Stakes triumph incongruously filmed at Keeneland with all the dramatic impact of a midweek morning workout.

Hollywood's general disinterest in the racing genre since 1960 hasn't done the sport any favors. In fact, it signaled that racing was losing its cachet with the American public. Meanwhile, as the studio system crumbled, Hollywood seemed to change its spots with each succeeding decade, searching for a new identity. In this, it was ultimately unsuccessful, at least from moviegoers' point of view. In 2017 film attendance dropped to a twenty-five-year low, with 1.24 billion tickets sold; in contrast, film attendance in the 1930s averaged 4.25 billion a year, at a time when the population was about half of what it is today. Tellingly, it is estimated that since 1970, just 10 percent of Americans go to the movies at least once a week, compared with 65 percent in the 1930s.

The cinematic 1960s were dominated by blockbusters such as *Spartacus, Lawrence of Arabia, Cleopatra,* and *Doctor Zhivago* and by musicals like *West Side Story, My Fair Lady,* and *The Sound of Music.* These were big productions intended to lure Americans out of their living rooms, where the small screen (dubbed the "idiot box" by its severest critics) was ill equipped to showcase such large-scale fare. But the Golden Age of cinema was drawing to a close. Largely the product of a single generation that had come of age in the 1930s, both it and its practitioners were on their last legs by the 1960s. The 1970s provided a mini-revolution of sorts, with a new generation of filmmakers that included Francis Ford Coppola, Steven Spielberg, and Robert Altman. These directors offered a more personal style of American film based in no small part on the European auteur concept popularized by the Italian neorealists Roberto Rossellini and Vittorio de Sica and the French New Wave directors Francois Truffaut and Jean-Luc Godard. The results were Coppola's *The Godfather* and *The Godfather: Part 2*; Spielberg's *Duel, Jaws,* and *Close Encounters of the Third Kind*; and Altman's *M*A*S*H* and *Nashville.* Hollywood appeared to be taking a new path, offering the world a form of entertainment enriched by a personal and political overview but still couched in the classic concepts of the Golden Age.

Visions of a new Golden Age, however, proved to be a chimera. Say what you will about the all-powerful movie moguls of the past: Louis B. Mayer, Jack and Harry Warner, Darryl F. Zanuck, Joe Schenck, Adolph Zukor, Harry Cohn, Sam Goldwyn, and David Selznick meddled in the creative process, sometimes sabotaging the efforts of directors and screenwriters. But these men ate, drank, slept, and breathed film. The movies were their lifeblood, and producing quality films was uppermost in their minds.

But just as horse racing became more of a business and less of a sport in the 1980s—fulfilling Jock Whitney's predictions in his 1963 speech to the Thoroughbred Club of America—Hollywood began to develop business and marketing models that took the nation by storm. Control of the studios fell away from filmmakers and into the hands of corporate marketeers at Sony, ABC, Viacom, and Comcast. Seeking to generate the highest possible number on the bottom line, they introduced the era of the franchise film. *Star Wars, Batman, Raiders of the Lost Ark,* and their numerous spawn took control of a Hollywood that seemed to turn its back on adult entertainment. For the last thirty years, American moviegoers have been fed a steady diet of superhero pablum. *Spider-Man, Wonder Woman, The Avengers,* and *Black Panther* are only the latest entries in a long list of cartoonish exercises in catharsis guaranteed to bring teen and twenty-something audiences to peaks of psychosexual excitement previously restricted to inmates of the local laughing academy.

The excesses of contemporary Hollywood have led to a reactionary brand of filmmaking that markets itself under the broadest terms as "independent." Its practitioners want to distant themselves from the capitalist concerns of corporate Hollywood, but not so far as to discourage the studios from distributing their product. These filmmakers are men and women of the so-called slacker generation, which philosopher Allan Bloom pegged so perfectly in his book *The Closing of the American Mind.* They have chosen to delve into the deepest recesses of the American soul—almost always their own—and in so doing, they have turned their backs on the world at large. Their films explore in minute detail the day-to-day mechanisms of family life, the tremendous difficulties of growing up in the confines of a restrictive middle class, the crushing effects of parental and societal expectations, and the impossibility of finding true and lasting love in contemporary racist, sexist, and homophobic America. Most of these pedantic exercises are based on the directors' very dull lives, with virtually no cinematic extrapolation. Their leading exponent is Richard Linklater, who has devoted his career to making films that explore his own nondescript upbringing in middle-class America in a style that is painstakingly devoted to an investigation and admiration of personal minutiae.

This type of "small" filmmaking has probably been aided and abetted by the advent of the digital age, which enables people to watch films on their tiny cell phone screens, rather than sitting in a darkened theater and experiencing films communally, as they were intended to be seen. In the same way, attendance at racetracks has declined, as many fans prefer to watch and bet on races at home on their computers. And so contemporary America has become a less and less sociable place.

In between these two contemporary styles of filmmaking—Hollywood and the independents—there lies the black hole once occupied by Frank Capra, George Cukor, Michael Curtiz, Cecil B. DeMille, John Ford, D. W. Griffith, Howard Hawks, Alfred Hitchcock, John Huston, Elia Kazan, Ernst Lubitsch, Raoul Walsh, William Wellman, Billy Wilder, William Wyler, and all the other great American directors who, with their broad and varied visions, turned the Hollywood product into the greatest artistic achievement in the history of this nation. These films captured American culture and society more definitively and with greater brilliance than any other art form before or since.

The farsighted Mervyn LeRoy saw the decline sooner than most, writing in his 1974 autobiography: "Nowadays, movies aren't made by great creative minds, but by a cartel of businessmen on the one hand and a haphazard group of young and undisciplined rookies on the other."[6] His prescient statement perfectly describes the looming split in American filmmaking between the corporate marketeers and the film-school graduates obsessed with relationship dramas and coming-of-age stories.

John Huston observed that, for many young directors, their cinematic education occurred almost exclusively in the secluded aeries of film schools, resulting in filmmakers who know a lot about the history of film but very little about the art of filmmaking. He expressed concern that contemporary American cinema was "in terrible danger of cannibalism. If you make movies about movies and about characters instead of people, the echoes get thinner and thinner until they're reduced to mechanical sounds."[7]

Incisive observations by two of France's greatest filmmakers, Jean Renoir and Francois Truffaut, pinpoint the problems inherent in contemporary American cinema. Though they made these observations decades ago, they are still valid today. Renoir, son of Impressionist master Auguste Renoir and director of the timeless classics *Rules of the Game* and *The Grand Illusion,* once reminded his fellow filmmakers that art is supposed to look artificial. Taken a step further, one can say that when art resembles real life, as it tends to do in independent American cinema, it loses its artistic value. Simply stated, the more art resembles real life, the more boring it becomes.

Truffaut, France's most popular postwar filmmaker and a great admirer of classic American cinema, said that for a film to be successful, it must possess two characteristics. First, it must tell the truth. Second, it must be *une spectacle,* that is, it must be a show or, in other words, it must entertain.

For the last three decades, American filmmakers have been making two different kinds of movies. Corporate Hollywood's apocalyptic Marvel Comics machine makes movies that are all spectacle but contain little, if any, truth. In contrast, the independents—with their eyes fixed firmly on their navels as they minutely explore their childhoods, their sexual awakenings, and their failed adult relationships—make films that tell a certain brand of the truth but lack any sense of spectacle. Both kinds of films, according to Truffaut, are failures.

All of this leads to the conclusion that Hollywood is not merely not at the races anymore. It isn't anywhere at all.

Acknowledgments

Thanks to David Ashforth, Rachel Bernstein, Cinematic Arts Library (USC Libraries), Neil Cook, Alastair Donald, Alexis Garske, Kip Hannan, Louise Hilton, Lincoln Center Library for the Performing Arts, Margaret Herrick Library (Academy of Motion Picture Arts and Sciences), Mac McBride, UCLA Special Library Collections, and most especially copy-editor Linda Lotz.

These are some of the people and institutions who provided me with professional support that ultimately made *Hollywood at the Races* possible. However, these acknowledgments would be incomplete if I did not include a curious, quite coincidental incident that occurred on March 2, 1957, through which the magical world of Hollywood introduced me to the equally entrancing world of horse racing.

Born in Newark, New Jersey, and raised in nearby Hillside and Linden, I was lucky to live in the suburbs of New York City where we had access to New York City's seven television stations at a time when most of the nation's homes had no more than three or four stations at their disposal. We had CBS (Channel 2), NBC (Channel 4), Dumont (Channel 5), ABC (Channel 7), WOR (Channel 9), WPIX (Channel 11), and WNTA (Channel 13).

This cornucopia of televised product gave New Yorkers and suburbanites a distinct advantage in the early days of mass media. It gave us a leg up on the rest of the nation, especially in movies, which all networks used to flesh out their schedules in the 1950s and 1960s. Programs like the *Late Show* and the *Late Late Show* on CBS, and more to the point, WOR's Million Dollar Movie, which introduced me to the exotic pleasures of *King Kong, The Hunchback of Notre Dame,* and *Gunga Din,* provided a crash course in Hollywood 101.

The non-national networks like Dumont, WOR, and WPIX frequently aired silent comedies as part of their midweek afternoon children's programs. Dumont was especially adept at this tactic. Throughout the late 1950s, the station made a habit of showing a Laurel and Hardy feature every Saturday afternoon at four o'clock. It only took one viewing in 1956 to make of me a lifelong Stan and Ollie fan.

Then, on Saturday, March 2, 1957, Dumont followed its Laurel and Hardy film with a telecast of a horse race from Hialeah Park in Florida. The occasion was the Flamingo Stakes, then a key early prep race for the Kentucky Derby, and Win Elliot, erstwhile hockey and basketball announcer, was the host. As he ran down the entries in the race my nine-year-old self was caught by the name of Bold Ruler. Never having seen a horse race before, I thought, "That sounds like a good, strong name for a racehorse. I'll pick him to win." And win Bold Ruler did. And then he won the Preakness Stakes, and was eventually named champion sprinter, champion three-year-old, and Horse of the Year. At stud he would be champion sire eight times. In his last crop he sired the great Secretariat, who in 1973 became the first Triple Crown winner in twenty-five years.

It's called beginner's luck. Without it, I might never have taken the slightest interest in horse racing. And so here are special acknowledgments for Stan Laurel, Oliver Hardy, Win Elliot, and Bold Ruler.

Appendix
Selected Racing Films

Black Gold (1947), USA
Studio: Allied Artists
Director: Carroll Ballard
Cast: Anthony Quinn, Katherine DeMille

The Black Stallion (1979), USA
Studio: Omni Zoetrope
Director: Phil Karlson
Cast: Kelly Reno, Mickey Rooney

Bob Le Flambeur (1956), France
Studio: Organisation Generale Cinematographique
Director: Jean-Pierre Melville
Cast: Roger Duchesne, Daniel Cauchy, Guy Decomble

Boots Malone (1952), USA
Studio: Columbia
Director: William Dieterle
Cast: William Holden, Johnny Stewart

The Bride Wore Boots (1946), USA
Studio: Paramount
Director: Irving Pichel
Cast: Barbara Stanwyck, Robert Cummings

Brighton Rock (1947), Great Britain
Studio: Charter Films
Director: John Boulting
Cast: Richard Attenborough, Carol Marsh

Appendix

Broadway Bill (1934), USA
Studio: Columbia
Director: Frank Capra
Cast: Warner Baxter, Myrna Loy

Broadway Melody of 1938 (1937), USA
Studio: MGM
Director: Roy del Ruth
Cast: Robert Taylor, Eleanor Powell

Champions (1983), Great Britain
Studio: Archerwest/Ladbroke/United British Artists
Director: John Irvin
Cast: John Hurt, Edward Woodward, Ben Johnson

Charlie Chan at the Race Track (1936), USA
Studio: 20th Century Fox
Director: H. Bruce Humberstone
Cast: Warner Oland, Keye Luke, Frankie Darro

A Day at the Races (1937), USA
Studio: MGM
Director: Sam Wood
Cast: Groucho Marx, Harpo Marx, Chico Marx

Dead Cert (1974), Great Britain
Studio: Woodfall Film
Director: Tony Richardson
Cast: Scott Anthony, Judi Dench

The Derby (1896), Great Britain
Studio: Paul Cinematograph
Director: Robert W. Paul
Cast: Persimmon, St. Frusquin

The Derby (1913), Great Britain
Studio: British Pathe
Cast: Emily Davison, Herbert Jones

Derby Day (1952), Great Britain
Studio: Herbert Wilcox Productions
Director: Herbert Wilcox
Cast: Anna Neagle, Michael Wilding

The Derby 1913: The Race from Start to Finish and Incidents of the Day
(1913), Great Britain
Studio: Williamson Kinematograph Company
Cast: Emily Davison, Herbert Jones

Don't Bet on Love (1933), USA
Studio: Universal
Director: Murray Roth
Cast: Lew Ayres, Ginger Rogers

Down Argentine Way (1940), USA
Studio: 20th Century Fox
Director: Irving Cummings
Cast: Don Ameche, Betty Grable

Down the Stretch (1936), USA
Studio: Warner Bros.
Director: William Clemens
Cast: Mickey Rooney, Patricia Ellis

Dreamer (2005), USA
Studio: DreamWorks
Director: John Gatins
Cast: Kurt Russell, Dakota Fanning

Even as I.O.U. (1942), USA
Studio: Columbia
Director: Del Lord
Cast: Moe Howard, Larry Fine, Curly Howard

The Ex–Mrs. Bradford (1936), USA
Studio: RKO Radio
Director: Stephen Roberts
Cast: William Powell, Jean Arthur

Fast Companions (1932), USA
Studio: Universal
Director: Kurt Neumann
Cast: Tom Brown, Maureen O'Sullivan

The First Saturday in May (2007), USA
Studio: Hennegan Bros.
Directors: Brad Hennegan, John Hennegan
Cast: Barbaro, Michael Matz

Francis Goes to the Races (1951), USA
Studio: Universal
Director: Arthur Lubin
Cast: Donald O'Connor, Piper Laurie, Cecil Kellaway

From Hell to Heaven (1933), USA
Studio: Paramount
Director: Erle C. Kenton
Cast: Carole Lombard, Jack Oakie

Gallopin' Gals (1940), USA
Studio: MGM
Director: Hanna/Barbera
Cast (voices): Bea Benaderet, Harlow Wilcox

The Galloping Major (1951), Great Britain
Studio: British Lion
Director: Henry Cornelius
Cast: Basil Radford, Jimmy Hanley, Hugh Griffith

Garrison's Finish (1923), USA
Studio: Pickford Productions
Director: Arthur Rosson
Cast: Jack Pickford, Madge Bellamy

Le Gentleman d'Epsom (1962), France/Italy
Studio: Compagnie International de Production Cinematographique/ Compagnia Cinematografica Mondiale

Director: Gilles Grangier
Cast: Jean Gabin, Madeleine Robinson, Louis de Funes

The Gentleman from Louisiana (1936), USA
Studio: Republic
Director: Irving Pichel
Cast: Eddie Quillan, Chic Sale, Charlotte Henry

Going Places (1938), USA
Studio: Warner Bros.
Director: Ray Enright
Cast: Dick Powell, Anita Louise, Louis Armstrong

The Great Dan Patch (1949), USA
Studio: W. R. Frank Productions
Director: Joseph M. Newman
Cast: Dennis O'Keefe, Gail Russell, Clarence Muse

The Heart of a Race Tout (1909), USA
Studio: Selig Polyscope
Director: Francis Boggs
Cast: Tom Santschi, Charles Dean

Hollywood Handicap (1938), USA
Studio: Lewis Lewyn Productions
Director: Buster Keaton
Cast: The Original Sing Band, Mickey Rooney

The Homestretch (1947), USA
Studio: 20th Century Fox
Director: H. Bruce Humberstone
Cast: Cornel Wilde, Maureen O'Hara

The Horseplayer (1961), USA
Studio: Shamley Productions
Director: Alfred Hitchcock
Cast: Claude Rains, Ed Gardner, Alfred Hitchcock

Hot Tip (1935), USA
Studio: RKO Radio
Director: Ray McCarey
Cast: Zasu Pitts, James Gleason

In Old Kentucky (1935), USA
Studio: Fox Films
Director: George Marshall
Cast: Will Rogers, Dorothy Wilson

It Ain't Hay (1943), USA
Studio: Universal
Director: Erle C. Kenton
Cast: Bud Abbott, Lou Costello

Kentucky (1938), USA
Studio: 20th Century Fox
Director: David Butler
Cast: Loretta Young, Richard Greene, Walter Brennan

Kentucky Pride (1925), USA
Studio: Fox Films
Director: John Ford
Cast: Henry B. Walthall, J. Farrell MacDonald

The Killing (1956), USA
Studio: Harris-Kubrick Productions
Director: Stanley Kubrick
Cast: Sterling Hayden, Marie Windsor, Elisha Cook Jr.

The Last Night of a Jockey (1963), USA
Studio: Cayuga Productions
Director: Joseph Newman
Cast: Mickey Rooney, Rod Serling

The Lemon Drop Kid (1934), USA
Studio: Universal
Director: Marshall Neilan
Cast: Lee Tracy, Helen Mack, William Frawley

The Lemon Drop Kid (1951), USA
Studio: Hope Enterprises/Paramount
Director: Sidney Lanfield
Cast: Bob Hope, Marilyn Maxwell

Let It Ride (1989), USA
Studio: Paramount
Director: Joe Pytka
Cast: Richard Dreyfuss, Terri Garr, Robbie Coltrane

Little Miss Thoroughbred (1938), USA
Studio: Warner Bros.
Director: John Farrow
Cast: John Litel, Ann Sheridan, Frank McHugh

Long Shot (1939), USA
Studio: Fine Arts Pictures
Director: Charles Lamont
Cast: Gordon Jones, Marsha Hunt, Harry Davenport

Maryland (1940), USA
Studio: 20th Century Fox
Director: Henry King
Cast: Walter Brennan, Faye Bainter, John Payne

Men of Chance (1931), USA
Studio: RKO Radio
Director: George Archainbaud
Cast: Ricardo Cortez, Mary Astor

Million Dollar Legs (1939), USA
Studio: Paramount
Director: Nick Grinde
Cast: Betty Grable, Peter Lind Hayes

Money from Home (1953), USA
Studio: Hal Wallis/Paramount
Director: George Marshall
Cast: Dean Martin, Jerry Lewis, Marjie Millar

My Brother Talks to Horses (1946), USA
Studio: MGM
Director: Fred Zinnemann
Cast: Peter Lawford, Butch Jenkins

Nana (1926), France
Studio: Films Renoir
Director: Jean Renoir
Cast: Catherine Hessling, Werner Krauss, Jean Angelo

National Velvet (1944), USA
Studio: MGM
Director: Clarence Brown
Cast: Elizabeth Taylor, Mickey Rooney

Palio (2015), Great Britain/Italy
Studio: Palio Pictures
Director: Cosima Spender
Cast: Giovanni Atzeni, Gigi Bruschelli

Phar Lap (1983), Australia
Studio: Edgely International
Director: Simon Wincer
Cast: Tom Burlinson, Martin Vaughn

Premieres armes (1949), France
Studio: Films de France
Director: Rene Wheeler
Cast: Jean Cordier, Guy Decomble, Paul Frankeur

Pride of the Bluegrass (1939), USA
Studio: Warner Bros.
Director: William McGann
Cast: Edith Fellows, James McCallion

Racetrack (1933), USA
Studio: James Cruze Productions
Director: James Cruze
Cast: Leo Carrillo, Frank Coughlan Jr.

Racetrack (1985), USA
Studio: Zipporah Films
Director: Frederick Wiseman
Cast: Pleasant Colony, Jorge Velasquez

Racing Lady (1937), USA
Studio: RKO Radio
Director: Wallace Fox
Cast: Ann Dvorak, Smith Ballew, Harry Carey

The Rainbow Jacket (1954), Great Britain
Studio: J. Arthur Rank Organization
Director: Basil Dearden
Cast: Robert Morley, Kay Walsh

The Return of October (1948), USA
Studio: Columbia
Director: Joseph H. Lewis
Cast: Glenn Ford, Terry Moore, James Gleason

Riding High (1950), USA
Studio: Paramount
Director: Frank Capra
Cast: Bing Crosby, Coleen Gray, Charles Bickford

Ruffian (2007), USA
Studio: ESPN
Director: Yves Simoneau
Cast: Sam Shepard, Frank Whaley

Salty O'Rourke (1945), USA
Studio: Paramount
Director: Raoul Walsh
Cast: Alan Ladd, Gail Russell, Stanley Clements

Saratoga (1937), USA
Studio: MGM
Director: Jack Conway
Cast: Clark Gable, Jean Harlow, Lionel Barrymore

Seabiscuit (2003), USA
Studio: Universal/DreamWorks
Director: Gary Ross
Cast: Jeff Bridges, Tobey Maguire, Gary Stevens

Secretariat (2010), USA
Studio: Walt Disney
Director: Randall Wallace
Cast: Diane Lane, John Malkovich, Dylan Walsh

Shadow of the Thin Man (1941), USA
Studio: MGM
Director: W. S. Van Dyke
Cast: William Powell, Myrna Loy

Shergar (1998), Great Britain/USA
Studio: Blue Rider Pictures
Director: Dennis C. Lewiston
Cast: Tom Walsh, Laura Murphy, Ian Holm

She Went to the Races (1945), USA
Studio: MGM
Director: Willis Goldbeck
Cast: James Craig, Frances Gifford, Ava Gardner

Silver Blaze (1937), Great Britain
Studio: Julius Hagen Productions
Director: Thomas Bentley
Cast: Arthur Wontner, Ian Fleming, Lyn Harding

Sing You Sinners (1938), USA
Studio: Paramount
Director: Wesley Ruggles
Cast: Bing Crosby, Fred MacMurray, Donald O'Connor

Sporting Blood (1931), USA
Studio: MGM
Director: Charles Brabin
Cast: Clark Gable, Ernest Torrance

Stablemates (1938), USA
Studio: MGM
Director: Sam Wood
Cast: Wallace Beery, Mickey Rooney

The Story of Seabiscuit (1949), USA
Studio: Warner Bros.
Director: David Butler
Cast: Shirley Temple, Barry Fitzgerald

Stretch (2011), France/Thailand
Studio: MK2
Director: Charles de Meaux
Cast: Nicolas Cazale, David Carradine

Sweepstakes (1931), USA
Studio: RKO Pathé
Director: Albert S. Rogell
Cast: Eddie Quillan, James Gleason

That Gang of Mine (1940), USA
Studio: Monogram/Banner
Director: Joseph H. Lewis
Cast: East Side Kids

They're Off (1947), USA
Studio: Walt Disney
Director: Jack Hannah
Cast: Goofy and company

Thoroughbreds Don't Cry (1937), USA
Studio: MGM
Director: Alfred E. Green
Cast: Mickey Rooney, Judy Garland

Three Men on a Horse (1936), USA
Studio: Warner Bros.
Director: Mervyn LeRoy
Cast: Frank McHugh, Joan Blondell, Allen Jenkins

Two Dollar Bettor (1951), USA
Studio: Jack Broder Productions
Director: Edward L. Cahn
Cast: John Litel, Marie Windsor

Under My Skin (1950), USA
Studio: 20th Century Fox
Director: Jean Negulesco
Cast: John Garfield, Micheline Presle, Luther Adler

Unwelcome Stranger (1935), USA
Studio: Columbia
Director: Phil Rosen
Cast: Jack Holt, Mona Barrie

The Winner's Circle (1948), USA
Studio: Richard Polimer Productions
Director: Felix E. Feist
Cast: Jean Willes, Morgan Farley, Johnny Longden

Wygrany (The Winner) (2010), Poland/USA
Studio: Saco Films
Director: Wieslaw Saniewicki
Cast: Pawel Szajda, Janusz Gajos

You Can't Buy Luck (1937), USA
Studio: RKO Radio
Director: Lew Landers
Cast: Onslow Stevens, Helen Mack, Hedda Hopper

You Were Never Lovelier (1942), USA
Studio: Columbia
Director: William A. Seiter
Cast: Fred Astaire, Rita Hayworth

Notes

Epigraph

Ed Sullivan, "The Hollywood Race Track Crowd," *Silver Screen*, September 1939, 38.

1. Hollywood before Santa Anita

Epigraph: Raoul Walsh, *Each Man in His Time: The Life Story of a Director* (New York: Farrar, Straus & Giroux, 1974), 214.

1. Francisco Manuel Acuna Borbolla, *Tijuana: Identidades y Nostalgia: La Colecion de Andre Williams* (Tijuana: XVIII Ayuntamiento de Tijuana, 2007), 25.
2. David Jimenez Beltran, *The Agua Caliente Story: Remembering Mexico's Legendary Racetrack* (Lexington, KY: Eclipse Press, 2004), 182.
3. Jimenez Beltran, *Agua Caliente Story,* 185, 191.
4. Acuna Borbolla, *Tijuana,* 251.
5. Marilyn Anne Moss, *Raoul Walsh: The True Adventures of Hollywood's Legendary Director* (Lexington: University Press of Kentucky, 2011), 139.
6. Harry Haller, "What's Become of Caliente," *Los Angeles Times,* December 13, 1936.
7. James Hill, *Rita Hayworth: A Memoir* (New York: Simon & Schuster, 1982, 15.
8. E. J. Fleming, *The Fixers: Eddie Mannix, Howard Stricking, and the MGM Publicity Machine* (Jefferson, NC: McFarland, 2004), 174–77.
9. Walsh, *Each Man in His Time,* 135.
10. Moss, *Raoul Walsh,* 151.
11. Jimenez Beltran, *Agua Caliente Story,* 192.
12. Jimenez Beltran, *Agua Caliente Story,* 65–74.
13. Paul J. Vanderwood, *Satan's Playground: Mobsters and Movie Stars at America's Greatest Gaming Resort* (Durham, NC: Duke University Press, 2010), 233.
14. Doreen Podelty, "Where the Stars Lose Their Salaries," *Film Weekly,* April 22, 1932.
15. Jimenez Beltran, *Agua Caliente Story,* 90.
16. Acuna Borbolla, *Tijuana,* 168.

2. Santa Anita

Epigraph: "Roach Back of Ambitious Southern California Track Venture," *Los Angeles Examiner,* September 13, 1933.

1. Doreen Podelty, "Where the Stars Lose Their Salaries," *Film Weekly,* April 22, 1932.

2. *Pari-mutuel* is a French term best translated as "betting amongst ourselves." It is pool betting in which a bet on any given horse lowers the odds on that horse while raising the odds on all the other horses in a race. It was offered as an alternative to "man-to-man" wagering, in which the bettor accepts the odds on a horse offered by the bookmaker at the time the wager is placed. When betting with a bookie, all the money taken in goes to either the winning bettors or the winning bookie. In pari-mutuel wagering, a certain percentage of each bet is returned to the winning bettors, a certain percentage goes to the racetrack, and a certain percentage is turned over to the state government. Introduced in France in 1867 by Joseph Oller, pari-mutuel wagering is the only legal form of wagering at American racetracks.

3. Tracy Gantz, *Santa Anita Park: 75th Anniversary 1934–2009* (Los Angeles: Los Angeles Turf Club, 2009), 24.

4. William Grimes, "Hal Roach Recalls His First Century," *New York Times,* January 23, 1992.

5. *Los Angeles Examiner*, September 13, 1933.

6. "Roach Back of Ambitious Southern California Track Venture."

7. Gantz, *Santa Anita Park,* 28.

8. Gantz, *Santa Anita Park,* 27.

9. Bob Herbert, "Opening of Santa Anita Proved Off-the-Cuff Affair," *Los Angeles Times,* January 31, 1991.

10. Gantz, *Santa Anita Park,* 31.

11. Gantz, *Santa Anita Park,* 31–32.

12. Grimes, "Hal Roach Recalls His First Century."

13. Gantz, *Santa Anita Park,* 50.

3. Del Mar

Epigraph: Bing Crosby and Pete Martin, *Call Me Lucky: Bing Crosby's Own Story* (New York: Simon & Schuster, 1953), 125.

1. Crosby and Martin, *Call Me Lucky,* 127.

2. Crosby and Martin, *Call Me Lucky,* 128.

3. Crosby & Martin, *Call Me Lucky,* 130.

4. Crosby and Martin, *Call Me Lucky,* 131.

5. Eddie Read, "Bing's Baby: The Del Mar Story," *San Diego Magazine,* July 1967, 56–57.

6. Read, "Bing's Baby," 55

7. Read, "Bing's Baby," 56.

8. Julia Polloreno, "The Frontrunner: Del Mar Racetrack Celebrates 70 Seasons," *San Diego Magazine,* July 2009.

9. Read, "Bing's Baby," 60.

10. William Murray, *Del Mar: Its Life and Good Times* (Del Mar, CA: Del Mar Thoroughbred Cub, 2003), 21–23.

11. Crosby and Martin, *Call Me Lucky,* 132.

12. Mickey Rooney, *I.e. an Autobiography* (New York: G. P. Putnam's Sons, 1965), 92.

13. Crosby and Martin, *Call Me Lucky*, 134.

14. Gary Giddins, *Bing Crosby: A Pocketful of Dreams; the Early Years 1903–1940* (New York: Little, Brown, 2001), 372.

15. Crosby and Martin, *Call Me Lucky,* 158.

16. Pat O'Brien, *The Wind at My Back: The Life and Times of Pat O'Brien* (Garden City, NY: Doubleday, 1964), 208.

17. Crosby and Martin, *Call Me Lucky,* 167.

4. Hollywood Park

Epigraph: Colonel Walter Moriarity, "America's Newest Racetrack," *Turf and Sport Digest,* June 1938.

1. Biff Lowry, *Hollywood Park: From Seabiscuit to Pincay* (Los Angeles: Hollywood Park, 2003), 9–11.

2. Sheilah Graham, "Hal Roach Defends Mussolini Deal," *Milwaukee Journal*, October 5, 1937.

3. Graham, "Hal Roach Defends Mussolini Deal."

4. Lowry, *Hollywood Park,* 11.

5. *Past Daily* website: pastdaily.com2016/06/11/hollywoodpark-june-9-1938 -pop-chronicles (posted June 6, 2011).

6. John Branch, "A Last Hurrah for Hollywood Park," *New York Times,* December 14, 2013.

7. Branch, "Last Hurrah for Hollywood Park."

8. Lowry, *Hollywood Park,* 35.

9. Lowry, *Hollywood Park,* 63–64.

5. The Stars Come Out

Epigraph: Ed Sullivan, "The Hollywood Race Track Crowd," *Silver Screen,* September 1939, 38–39.

1. Sullivan, "Hollywood Race Track Crowd," 40.

2. Mervyn LeRoy as told to Dick Kleiner, *Mervyn LeRoy: Take One* (New York: Hawthorn Books, 1974), 111–12.

3. "Racing in Hollywood," *Times of Oman,* December 13, 2012.

4. *Deranged LA Crimes* website: derangedlacrimes.com/?p=273 (posted on December 26, 2012).

5. Jennings Parrott, "Fred Astaire's Days at the Races," *Los Angeles Times,* May 9, 1979.

6. Fred Astaire, *Steps in Time: An Autobiography* (New York: Harper & Brothers, 1959), 113–14.

7. Bill Halligan, column in *Variety,* September 28, 1938.

8. Pat O'Brien, *The Wind at My Back: The Life and Times of Pat O'Brien* (Garden City, NY: Doubleday, 1964), 166.

9. O'Brien, *Wind at My Back,* 213.

10. O'Brien, *Wind at My Back,* 213.

11. Lupton A. Wilkinson, "Racing Daze at Santa Anita," *Movie Mirror,* April 1938, 45.

12. "We're Not the Least Bit in Love," *Los Angeles Times,* June 8, 1942.

13. Louella Parsons, *Los Angeles Herald-Examiner,* October 9, 1949.

14. Maxine Arnold, "Betty Takes a Bow," *Photoplay,* July 1952.

15. Victoria Wilson, *A Life of Barbara Stanwyck* (New York: Simon & Schuster, 2013), 649–55.

16. For example, Swanson's photo and caption appeared in *Wilmington, California, Press,* June 10, 1941.

17. For example, Hayward's photo and caption appeared in *Los Angeles Herald-Examiner,* May 29, 1941.

18. John Huston, *An Open Book* (New York: Alfred A. Knopf, 1980), 155.

19. "The Untold Story of Lucy and Desi," *People*, February 15, 1991, 16.

20. "Untold Story of Lucy and Desi," 18.

21. "Untold Story of Lucy and Desi," 20.

22. "Untold Story of Lucy and Desi," 21.

23. "Santa Anita Fake Bomb Stirs Turmoil," *Los Angeles Times,* May 4, 1951.

6. The Gamblers

Epigraph: Mickey Rooney, *Life Is Too Short* (New York: Villard Books, 1991), 47.

1. Bill Christine, "Mickey's Other Life at the Track," *Los Angeles Times,* February 20, 1982.

2. Rooney, *I.e. an Autobiography,* 89.

3. Christine, "Mickey's Other Life at the Track."

4. Christine, "Mickey's Other Life at the Track."

5. "Morning Briefing," *Los Angeles Times,* June 8, 1981.

6. Christine, "Mickey's Other Life at the Track."

7. Rooney, *I.e. an Autobiography*, 98.

8. Rooney, *I.e. an Autobiography,* 114.

9. Maxine Marx, *Growing up with Chico* (New York: Limelight Editions, 1980), 89.

10. Joe Schoenfeld, "Time and Place," *Variety,* September 15, 1954.

11. Schoenfeld, "Time and Place."

12. Robert S. Bader, *Four of the Three Musketeers: The Marx Brothers on Stage* (Evanston, IL: Northwestern University Press, 2016), 258.

13. Marx, *Growing up with Chico,* 165.

14. "Jolson's Favorite Role," *Los Angeles Times,* June 5, 1927.

15. Michael Freedland, *Jolie: The Story of Al Jolson* (New York: Virgin Books, 1972), 99.

16. Jimmy Durante, "I Ups to London," *Los Angeles Times This Week Magazine,* July 27, 1952.

17. Durante, "I Ups to London."

18. Melvin Durslag, "How the 'Schnozz' Lost His Shirt," *Los Angeles Times,* September 8, 1964.

19. Durslag, "How the 'Schnozz' Lost His Shirt."

20. Sid Ziff, "Durante Picks," *Los Angeles Times,* September 3, 1965.

21. Gordon Jones, "The Mayor of Del Mar," *Los Angeles Herald-Examiner,* August 29, 1969

22. "Director John Huston Dies," *Guardian,* August 30, 1987.

23. Huston, *Open Book,* 5.

24. Huston, *Open Book,* 152.

25. Huston, *Open Book,* 157–59.

26. Telegram from Jean Thiroux to John Huston, November 19, 1947, John Huston Papers, Margaret Herrick Library, Academy of Motion Picture Arts and Sciences, Beverly Hills, CA.

27. John Huston to Joseph Russo, April 14, 1948, Huston Papers, Herrick Library.

28. Cablegram from Jean Thiroux to John Huston, April 30, 1948, Huston Papers, Herrick Library.

29. Cablegrams from Jean Thiroux to John Huston, May 1 and 10, 1948, Huston Papers, Herrick Library.

30. Cablegram from Jeanne to John Huston, May 20, 1950, Huston Papers, Herrick Library.

31. Cablegram from Jeanne to John Huston, May 27, 1950, Huston Papers, Herrick Library.

32. Ben Goetz to John Huston, October 4, 1954, Huston Papers, Herrick Library.

33. The 2000 Guineas Stakes and the 1000 Guineas Stakes are two classic one-mile races run at Newmarket.

34. Harold Mirisch was the head of Allied Artists. He would later cofound an independent film company, the Mirisch Corporation, with his brothers Walter and Marvin.

35. Jack Gerber to John Huston, May 30, 1955, Huston Papers, Herrick Library.

36. Jack Gerber to John Huston, June 6, 1955, Huston Papers, Herrick Library.

37. Jack Gerber to John Huston, September 2, 1955, Huston Papers, Herrick Library.

38. Huston, *Open Book,* 251.

39. John Huston to Jack Gerber, November 9, 1955, Huston Papers, Herrick Library.

40. Jack Gerber to Lorry (Huston's secretary), November 24, 1955, Huston Papers, Herrick Library.

41. John Huston to Jack Gerber, June 11, 1956, Huston Papers, Herrick Library.

42. Tim Durant to John Huston, May 7, 1954, Huston Papers, Herrick Library.

43. Jim Murray, *Los Angeles Times,* April 10, 1964.

44. Tim Durant to John Huston, March 11, 1964, Huston Papers, Herrick Library.

45. Aljean Harmetz, "John Huston Honored by American Film Institute," *New York Times,* March 1, 1983.

7. Louis B. Mayer

Epigraph: Quoted in Vincent X. Flaherty, "Horses and Stars Interest Mr. Mayer," *Los Angeles Examiner,* February 12, 1946.

1. Bosley Crowther, *Hollywood Rajah: The Life and Times of Louis B. Mayer* (New York: Henry Holt, 1960), 69.

2. Irene Mayer Selznick, *A Private View* (New York: Alfred A. Knopf, 1983), 357.

3. Crowther, *Hollywood Rajah,* 249.

4. Crowther, *Hollywood Rajah,* 249.

5. Maurice Bernard, "42,159 See Mayer Filly Score Easily at 3–5," *Los Angeles Examiner,* October 7, 1945.

6. William H. P. Robertson, *The History of Thoroughbred Racing in America* (New York: Bonanza Books, 1964), 366–67.

7. Gantz, *Santa Anita Park,* 58.

8. Crowther, *Hollywood Rajah,* 264.

9. Crowther, *Hollywood Rajah,* 269.

10. "Mayer Divests Himself of Racing Stock," *Time,* March 10, 1947.

11. Crowther, *Hollywood Rajah,* 270.

12. Pinterest website: ar.pinterest.com/pin/77898268527818532/?lp=true.

13. Brainy Quotes website: Brainyquotes.com/quotes/luise_rainer_690260.

8. Hollywood Horsemen and Horsewomen

Epigraph: Quoted in David Zeitlin, "I Train Just Like a Race Horse," *Life,* October 29, 1965.

1. Astaire, *Steps in Time,* 42.

2. *Variety,* August 11, 1926.

3. Astaire, *Steps in Time,* 114.

4. Astaire, *Steps in Time,* 263.

5. Astaire, *Steps in Time,* 284.

6. Astaire, *Steps in Time,* 286.

7. *New York Herald-Examiner,* October 26, 1968.

8. Astaire, *Steps in Time,* 288.

9. "Astaire's New Partner a Jockey?" *Los Angeles Herald-Examiner,* March 5, 1980.

10. Deborah Moss, "Robyn Smith, Trailblazing Jockey," *Sports Illustrated*, July 31, 1972.

11. David Griffen, "Astaire Misstep?" *People,* April 27, 1981.

12. Irene Lacher, "From Ace Jockey to Fred's 'Baby,'" *Los Angeles Times,* August 17, 1997.

13. Claudia Wallis, "Fred and Robyn Settle Down," *Time,* August 11, 1980.

14. Griffen, "Astaire Misstep?"

15. Sarah Giles, *Fred Astaire: His Friends Talk* (New York: Doubleday, 1988), 179; Lacher, "From Ace Jockey to Fred's 'Baby.'"

16. Spero Pastos, *Pin-Up: The Tragedy of Betty Grable* (New York: Penguin Publishing Group, 1986), 48.

17. Ann Marsters, "Not the Least Bit in Love," *Chicago Herald-American,* October 9, 1940.

18. Louella Parsons, "Betty Backstage and at the Track," *Los Angeles Herald-Examiner,* October 9, 1949.

19. *Look,* August 16, 1949.

20. Duncan Blair, "Betty Grable 9 to 6," *Picturegoer,* June 17, 1950.

21. Jeane Hoffman, "Big Noise Really Is Big Noise around Gable Stable These Days," *Los Angeles Times,* June 19, 1952.

22. Staff Correspondent, "Betty Grable Insures Her Horse's Legs Too," *Sydney (Australia) Sun-Herald,* February 21, 1954.

23. Parsons, "Betty Backstage and at the Track."

24. Staff Correspondent, "Betty Grable Insures Her Horse's Legs Too."

25. Jim Bolus, *Kentucky Derby Stories* (Gretna, LA: Pelican Publishing, 1993), 67.

26. Yvette Grant, ed., *The Little Red Book of Horse Wisdom* (New York: Skyhorse Publishing, 2012), 40.

27. Charles Champlin, "Don Ameche Finally out of His Cocoon," *Los Angeles Times*, March 6, 1986.

28. Ben Ohmart, *Don Ameche: The Kenosha Comeback Kid* (Albany, GA: BearManor Media, 2007), 191.

29. Susan Braudy, *This Crazy Thing Called Love: The Golden World and Fatal Marriage of Ann and Bill Woodward* (New York: Alfred A. Knopf, 1992), 250.

30. Robertson, *History of Thoroughbred Racing in America,* 356.

31. Bosley Crowther, "Capra and Crosby Inspired in 'Riding High,'" *New York Times*, April 11, 1950.

32. James Agee, "'Riding High' Scores High," *Time*, April 20, 1950.

33. Kathryn Grant, *My Life with Bing* (Los Angeles: Collage Books, 1983), 182.

9. Jock Whitney

Epigraph: Selznick, *Private View,* 207.

1. E. J. Kahn Jr., *Jock: The Life and Times of John Hay Whitney* (New York: Doubleday, 1981), 76.
2. It is believed that the term "stage-door Johnny" originated around 1912. Perhaps its literary debut came in P. G. Wodehouse's 1915 short story "*Extricating Young Gussie.*"
3. Kahn, *Jock,* 80.
4. Graham Greene, "Becky Sharp/Public Hero No. 1/Barcarole," *Spectator,* July 19, 1935.
5. Kahn, *Jock,* 110.
6. Stephen Bach, *Marlene Dietrich: Life and Legend* (New York: HarperCollins, 1992), 130.
7. Kahn, *Jock,* 113.
8. Kahn, *Jock,* 117.
9. Kahn, *Jock,* 113.
10. Bob Thomas, *Selznick* (Garden City, NY: Doubleday, 1970), 148.
11. Thomas, *Selznick,* 149.
12. Robertson, *History of Thoroughbred Racing in America,* 575, 577.

10. La Princesse Aly Khan

Epigraph: Quoted in Anne Edwards, "The Goddess and the Playboy," *Vanity Fair,* June 1993.

1. "Rita Reveals," *Picturegoer,* November 17, 1941.
2. Neil Grant and Rita Hayworth, *Rita Hayworth in Her Own Words* (London: Hamlyn, 1992), 94.
3. Edwards, "The Goddess and the Playboy."
4. Barbara Leaming, *If This Was Happiness: A Biography of Rita Hayworth* (New York: Viking, 1989), 142.
5. Associated Press, "Nimbus Wins by a Head in Epsom Derby," *Chicago Tribune,* June 5, 1949.
6. Francois-Charles Truffe, "Le Gentleman de Vincennes," *Paris-Turf,* January 30, 2016.
7. *New York Times,* October 9, 1949.
8. Paul Lowry, "Moonrush Responds to Kiss with San Diego ''Cap Victory," *Los Angeles Times,* August 17, 1952.
9. Edwards, "The Goddess and the Playboy."

11. Gene Markey

Epigraphs: Joan Bennett and Lois Kibbee, *The Bennett Playbill* (New York: Holt, Rinehart & Winston, 1970), 89; Stephen Michael Shearer, *Beautiful: The Life of Hedy La-*

marr (New York: Thomas Dunne Books/St. Martin's Press, 2010), 76; Emily W. Leider, *Myrna Loy: The Only Good Girl in Hollywood* (Berkeley: University of California Press, 2011), 172; Linda Carroll and David Rosner, *Duel for the Crown: Affirmed, Alydar and Racing's Greatest Rivalry* (New York: Gallery Books, 2014), 59; "Gene Markey, Author, Screenwriter, Producer and Breeder of Horses: Decorated in World War II," *New York Times*, May 2, 1980.

1. Bennett and Kibbee, *Bennett Playbill*, 93.
2. Bennett and Kibbee, *Bennett Playbill*, 94.
3. Bennett and Kibbee, *Bennett Playbill*, 98, 101.
4. Adele Whitley Fletcher, "The Dilemma of Lamarr," *Photoplay*, June 1939.
5. Hedda Hopper, "Hedda Hopper's Hollywood," *Los Angeles Times*, January 1, 1939.
6. *Los Angeles Times*, July 7, 1940.
7. "Sidney Solsky," *New York Post*, July 12, 1940.
8. Bosley Crowther, "Movie Review—You're the One—The Screen," *New York Times*, February 10, 1941.
9. Shearer, *Beautiful*, 196.
10. *Madera (CA) Tribune*, January 9, 1950.
11. Kahn, *Jock*, 190.
12. Ann Hagedorn Auerbach, *Wild Ride: The Rise and Tragic Fall of Calumet Farm, Inc., America's Premier Racing Dynasty* (New York: Henry Holt, 1994), 69.
13. Hedda Hopper to Gene Markey, May 14, 1958, Margaret Herrick Library, Academy of Motion Picture Arts and Sciences, Beverly Hills, CA.
14. Hedda Hopper to Lucille and Gene Markey, December 8, 1958, Herrick Library.
15. Gene Markey to Hedda Hopper, June 28, 1960, Herrick Library.
16. Lucille Markey to Hedda Hopper, June 1964, Herrick Library.
17. Hedda Hopper to Lucille Markey, June 28, 1964, Herrick Library.
18. ABC News, youtube.com/watch?v=tXBr4sQk81.

12. The Post Golden Age

Epigraph: Ed Sullivan, "The Hollywood Race Track Crowd," *Silver Screen*, September 1939.

1. Steve Cady, "Mrs. Miniver Yields to Ack Ack," *New York Times*, January 27, 1972.
2. Mary Blume, "LeRoy Knows His Stars," *Los Angeles Times*, November 28, 1970.
3. Blume, "LeRoy Knows His Stars."
4. Lee Mottershead, "Gosden to Miss Keeneland Sale," *Racing Post*, June 18, 2018.
5. Water, Hay, and Oats Alliance (WHOA) press release, January 18, 2019.
6. LeRoy, *Mervyn LeRoy*, 201.
7. Peter B. Flint, "John Huston, Film Director, Writer and Actor, Dies at 81," *New York Times*, August 29, 1987.

Selected Bibliography

Astaire, Fred. *Steps in Time: An Autobiography.* New York: Harper & Brothers, 1959.

Auerbach, Anne Hagedorn. *Wild Ride: The Rise and Tragic Fall of Calumet Farm, Inc., America's Premier Racing Dynasty.* New York: Henry Holt, 1994.

Bader, Robert S. *Four of the Three Musketeers: The Marx Brothers on Stage.* Evanston, IL: Northwestern University Press, 2016.

Behlmer, Rudy, ed. *Memo from David O. Selznick.* New York: Modern Library, 2000.

Bennett, Joan, and Lois Kibbee. *The Bennett Playbill.* New York: Holt, Rinehart & Winston, 1970.

Crosby, Bing, and Pete Martin. *Call Me Lucky: Bing Crosby's Own Story.* New York: Simon & Schuster, 1953.

Crowther, Bosley. *Hollywood Rajah: The Life and Times of Louis B. Mayer.* New York: Henry Holt, 1960.

Durante, Jimmy. "I Ups to London." *Los Angeles Times This Week Magazine,* July 27, 1952.

Eyman, Scott. *Lion of Hollywood: The Life and Legend of Louis B. Mayer.* New York: Simon & Schuster, 2005.

Fowler, Gene. "Schnozzola: Jimmy D's Life Story." *Colliers,* June 30, 1951.

Freedland, Michael. *Jolson: The Story of Al Jolson.* New York: Virgin Books, 1972.

Gantz, Tracy. *Santa Anita Park: 75th Anniversary 1934–2009.* Los Angeles: Los Angeles Turf Cub, 2009.

Giddins, Gary. *Bing Crosby: A Pocketful of Dreams; the Early Years 1903–1940.* New York: Little, Brown, 2001.

Giles, Sarah. *Fred Astaire: His Friends Talk.* New York: Doubleday, 1988.

Grant, Kathryn. *My Life with Bing.* Los Angeles: Collage Books, 1983.

Grant, Neil, and Rita Hayworth. *Rita Hayworth in Her Own Words.* London: Hamlyn, 1992.

Hill, James. *Rita Hayworth: A Memoir.* New York: Simon & Schuster, 1982.

Huston, John. *An Open Book.* New York: Alfred A. Knopf, 1980.

Jimenez Beltran, David. *The Agua Caliente Story: Remembering Mexico's Legendary Racetrack.* Lexington, KY: Eclipse Press, 2004.

Kahn, E. J., Jr. *Jock: The Life and Times of John Hay Whitney.* New York: Doubleday, 1981.

Leaming, Barbara. *If This Was Happiness: A Biography of Rita Hayworth.* New York: Viking, 1989.

Leider, Emily W. *Myrna Loy: The Only Good Girl in Hollywood.* Berkeley: University of California Press, 2011.

Selected Bibliography

LeRoy, Mervyn, as told to Dick Kleiner. *Mervyn LeRoy: Take One.* New York: Hawthorn Books, 1974.

Lowry, Biff. *Hollywood Park: From Seabiscuit to Pincay.* Los Angeles: Hollywood Park, 2003.

Marx, Arthur. *The Nine Lives of Mickey Rooney.* New York: Stein & Day, 1986.

Marx, Maxine. *Growing up with Chico.* New York: Limelight Editions, 1980.

Murray, William. *Del Mar: Its Life and Good Times.* Del Mar, CA: Del Mar Thoroughbred Club, 2003.

O'Brien, Pat. *The Wind at My Back: The Life and Times of Pat O'Brien.* Garden City, NY: Doubleday, 1964.

Ohmart, Ben. *Don Ameche: The Kenosha Comeback Kid.* Albany, GA: BearManor Media, 2007.

Read, Eddie. "Bing's Baby: The Del Mar Story." *San Diego Magazine,* July 1967.

Robertson, William H. P. *The History of Thoroughbred Racing in America.* New York: Bonanza Books, 1964.

Rooney, Mickey. *I.e. an Autobiography.* New York: G. P. Putnam's Sons, 1965.

———. *Life Is Too Short.* New York: Villard Books, 1991.

Selznick, Irene Mayer. *A Private View.* New York: Alfred A. Knopf, 1983.

Shearer, Stephen Michael. *Beautiful: The Life of Hedy Lamarr.* New York: Thomas Dunne Books/St. Martin's Press, 2010.

Thomas, Bob. *Selznick.* Garden City, NY: Doubleday, 1970.

Vanderwood, Paul J. *Satan's Playground: Mobsters and Movie Stars at America's Greatest Gaming Resort.* Durham, NC: Duke University Press, 2010.

Index

Index

Index

Index

Index

Index

Index

Index

Index